WHAT MATTERS MOST

A JOURNEY THROUGH CANCER, FAITH, AND LESSONS OF GRATITUDE WITH WISDOM FOR TODAY

RYAN HAGEN

For Mary

TABLE OF CONTENTS

INTRODUCTION

Why I Wrote this Book

I have taught and coached young adults now for over 17 years in the public-school system. During my career, I've come to realize that kids today are growing up in uncertain and confusing times, and I for one wouldn't want to trade places with them. In today's world, there is a great need of positive influences and role-models in the lives of children, especially in the lives of young adults who are searching for answers to life's biggest questions. In search of those answers, far too many kids today are looking in the wrong places. They are looking to numerous social media outlets, to celebrities, to athletes, and to pop culture. Often kids today aren't even asking themselves the right questions, the questions that lead to truth, real love, real meaning, and peace and fulfillment in life.

In our ever-increasing secular world, many young adults are not looking to God and Faith for life's meaning and purpose. Many do not grow up in any kind of religious household and sadly are never really exposed to the truth, love, and meaning that only a relationship with God so generously provides. Polls among teens today show that they are increasingly unhappy, and this is occurring today while kids are growing up with more wealth and amenities than generations before. Most children today are educated in public schools where any mention of God, specifically Christ, is outlawed. For the students that do attend weekly religious education classes during the school year, the vast majority are hardly interested, and see it only as something they must put up with until they are freed from their parents' reigns.

Although that is true, in essence, young adults today are not any different from young adults during any other time. They still want to love and be loved. They still want to find their place in the world. They still look to their surroundings for affirmation and for meaning in life. Too often, they end up uncertain about their future and purpose while a relationship with God is frequently absent. I wrote this book in an attempt to share my story of going through cancer and re-evaluating my life and relationship with God. Through this process, I decided to become a teacher in part to share my faith and pass on lessons of gratitude and wisdom. I hope that the book can help young adults and anyone of any age to find in their lives a greater meaning and purpose, which of course cannot be thoroughly found without God.

Going through cancer at a young age has made me realize how fragile life can be. I've realized how dependent upon God we are for everything, whether we realize it or not. As a cancer survivor I've realized the importance of gratitude. I learned to love and cherish my Catholic faith and my experience surviving illness has strengthened my faith and trust in the mercy and love of God. After going through cancer, I began to realize more fully God's presence in my life and began to live my life in a more deliberate way. In doing so, I have gained gratitude and wisdom that I feel would help today's generation. In more fully embracing my Catholic faith, a love for our Blessed Mother has granted me a peace like no other especially in my visit to Lourdes and Fatima, but also in my encounter with Saint Bernadette. I've always felt that in reading a book, if I could take one insight from reading it, that it would be well worth my time. In that respect, I hope that readers will find a few lessons of gratitude, wisdom, or even a story that may stay with them long after they have put the book down.

PREFACE

Writing this book has been on my heart for many years. As a teacher of now over seventeen, I've always felt that the most important lessons taught are not of academics, but of the heart and of the soul. Good teachers everywhere continuously think about what they can do to make successful students. Questions like, "what can I do to help a child improve in reading or math," run through the minds of good teachers. These are noble goals no doubt, but my greatest concern, the one that keeps my mind occupied, even more so than finding ways to aid the academic success of students, is what can I do to help create good people? How can I instill character values and encourage young people to pursue meaningful lives and goals? I have thought over this question as a middle school math teacher in a public school. As a catechist at my local Catholic parish, I also spend time asking myself another question, what can I do to help my 8th grade confirmation students treasure and love their Faith?

With any book that I have read, I've found that a worthwhile read is one in which I get just one insight that helps me grow. In the pages that lie ahead, I hope that anyone that chooses to read it will find at least just that, one good insight that will help you grow and become better in some small way. Part of this book reads like an autobiography as it includes the details of my journey through cancer, and also my journey through faith, both of which can't be separated. Other pages are written with the specific intention of sharing some of the lessons, experiences, and thoughts I have had in my life that may help others, especially the young adult generation today.

While much of the book gives references to my faith, whether you are Christian, Catholic, or not religious at all, I feel there are lessons of gratitude and wisdom that all can take from these pages. Similarly, while the book in some way is geared towards our younger generation, I feel in the same way that in reading these pages, there is something relevant to everyone regardless of age.

The picture above is a photo I took while climbing Croagh Patrick, the mountain in County Mayo, Ireland that St. Patrick is said to have climbed and fasted on for 40 days. Many Catholics today, especially Irish Catholics, consider climbing Croagh Patrick as a pilgrimage. During the summer of 2010, I visited Ireland, and made the accent up to the top of the mountain. It's a tough climb, especially as you get closer and closer to the peak where there are many loose rocks which make it difficult to maneuver and keep your footing. As I think back to that day as I was making my way to the summit, I can't help but think of C.S. Lewis' book, *The Great Divorce*. In the book, a man is making his way up to the top of a large mountain, Lewis' analogy for Heaven, with the help of an angel guide. As he makes his way higher and higher, he realizes that each step forward that he takes is more difficult than the previous one, yet with the angel's encouragement and guidance he continues on. This was similar to what I witnessed of many pilgrims climbing the mountain. Due to the rocky terrain and the steep incline, many lost their balance and some fell, yet they had the courage and the desire to continue the journey. Like the character in the *The Great Divorce*, with each step, no matter how difficult, he continues on and puts his own desires aside and puts God in front. The premise of C.S. Lewis' book is really that if you believe Heaven exists, it does.[1] Likewise, if you believe you can become a better person and live a meaningful life, you can, but you have to take the right steps.

We are all on a journey, and all us are not meant to live our lives at the bottom of a mountain. We are all meant to make the journey, and like all journeys, there will be difficulty. It won't be easy, and if we are to take steps towards the top, we have to know what in life is most important so we know how to spend our short time on this Earth. I hope this book will give you wisdom that every meaningful life needs, and I hope that in your own journey, you will find the courage and perseverance to continue forward even when you fall.

1

The Waiting Room

Deep in my heart I knew, but I didn't let on that I knew, at least that's the impression I tried to give. It was the middle of August 2002 and my sister Jenny and I left our little family weekend getaway in the Wisconsin Dells early to make this doctor appointment. The trip was one final family gathering before my younger brother John would leave for college in downstate Illinois.

Two weeks prior I had visited a local podiatrist in the Southwest Chicago suburbs to see about a "mole" on the bottom of my right foot, but if I had the choice, I wouldn't have made the initial visit.

This was the summer after I had graduated from the University of Illinois with a degree in Accounting, and as I wasn't terribly excited about beginning what seemed like an eternal corporate career, I decided to spend my summer working at a Chicago summer program for inner-city boys at the Midtown Center. I had been a volunteer in a university mentoring program for local youth in Champaign and had enjoyed it, so I figured I would enjoy one more "college summer" before entering the "real world." Midtown is a center that is geared towards helping young boys develop character and study habits to succeed in high school and go on to college

(Metro is its partner program for young girls). As of this writing, Midtown and Metro boast some impressive results. For the past twenty years, 100% students enrolled at Midtown and Metro graduate from high school and earn enrollment in college.[2] I was a Midtown advisor during that summer 2002 and I often would play basketball with some of the kids during and after the program. Toward the end of the program, however, I started feeling a pain in my right foot, a pain severe enough that I became unable to run up and down the court without a limp.

In early August, I decided to show my bruised right foot to my mother, a former nurse. After taking one look she knew a doctor appointment was inevitable. There was a blackish mole the size of a quarter on my foot and I had noticed it while I was still a college senior just four months earlier in April. This wasn't your average little mark on the skin that you would have known about for years. This was a raised, dry-like mole with irregular borders that felt like sandpaper to touch. It has been said that the Irish are stubborn, and if there is any example of my life that shows my at times stubborn nature, this episode does much justice.

A trip to podiatrist Dr. Michael Byrnes ensued shorty after. He studied my foot with its black mark and was immediately concerned. He showed me pictures of what melanomas looked like in a book and I had to admit that what he was showing me could be what was on the bottom of my foot. He mentioned that melanoma was cancerous and dangerous, but still I was only 22 years old. These types of things just don't happen to young adults my age. Dr. Byrnes was concerned enough that he decided to surgically remove the mole right then and there in his small surgical room in the back of his office. He told me that he just wanted to use precaution and he put me at ease with the whole process, so much that I really didn't think much of the ordeal. I would later find out that Dr. Byrnes was nerve-wracked with concern over everything…from telling me the possibilities of a cancerous tumor, the surgery itself, and just worried about what the future or lack thereof that would hold for me.

Even after the minor surgery to take the mole off with a decent line of stitching now on my foot, I was really not too worried about it. For a young man in his early 20's, I really can't blame myself. Dr. Byrnes told me he would have to send the biopsy to pathology, and he'd get back to me as soon as he knew the results.

When I came home from the doctor's office, now with crutches and a medical boot, my mom was a little surprised and although she tried not to show it, there was concern in her face. I just explained to my mom matter-of-factly that Dr. Byrnes was sending the tissue to pathology and we would just see what the results were.

In the meantime, summer was drawing to a close and my family had made plans to travel to the Wisconsin Dells, a popular vacation destination in the Midwest. The initial pathology report was inconclusive, as doctors from our local hospital couldn't quite agree on whether the tissue was melanoma or not, so the specimen was shipped to special group of pathologists in Texas. While we were waiting, my family decided to keep their mini-vacation plans in Wisconsin in the next 3-4 days.

On the night before we were supposed to head home, Dr. Byrnes called to say the results were in. He spoke with my mom and told her that I should come to his office tomorrow. Unbeknownst to me, he did let my parents know that the pathology report was indeed melanoma, and he wanted to start testing and refer me to an oncologist to develop a treatment plan as soon as possible.

I can only imagine how hard that phone call was for my mom. In front of me at least, she held it together and informed me that I had to see Dr. Byrnes tomorrow as his appointment schedule was filling fast. My sister Jenny and I would leave in the morning to make it back to the Chicago suburbs in time for the appointment. My mom didn't tell me the pathology results, I guess she just didn't want me worrying and dwelling on the situation during the three-and-a-half-hour ride home.

Jenny and I arrived in the late afternoon. We must have been in the waiting room for nearly 3 hours, at least that's what it seemed like. Patient after patient arrived and were called to see the doctor, but still I waited, wondering why all these people were jumping ahead of line. I could tell my sister was restless and trying her best not to let on that she knew something that I didn't. She was doing a great job, but I knew my sister well enough to know that she was holding in her emotions. What was going on? Something is different. If there was any doubt in my mind, this whole situation gave me the feeling that what I was about to hear from Dr. Byrnes was not good news. The fact that Jenny and I left the Dells early before the rest of our family, the long wait in the waiting room, and my sister's nerves all made it clear that something wasn't right.

I remember late afternoon started to turn into evening and the sun was starting to set. My parents then arrived around this time, and by now there was no one else in the waiting room. I was finally called in to see the doctor and my parents accompanied me, while my sister left to go home as she had to get up early for work the next morning.

Dr. Byrnes is a wonderful doctor, and as I have gotten to know him much better throughout the years, he has become a wonderful friend. I could tell he was concerned and although he was doing his best to be professional with a matter-of-fact attitude, I could tell that he was nervous for me. He told us that indeed the tumor was cancerous, a specific type of melanoma. What was brilliant of Dr. Byrnes, was that once he explained what melanoma was and what I was up against, he immediately talked about what his plans were for the next steps I had to take. This is the kind of approach I wanted. I didn't have time to feel sorry for myself or ask why this is happening to me, or why this is happening now just after my college graduation. I was diagnosed with cancer and if this was the hand I was dealt, I didn't have time for pity. I was determined to do everything I could to give myself the best possible chance to survive.

2

Faith During Uncertainty

After my diagnosis of melanoma, the biggest concern we dealt with was trying to determine if the cancer had spread anywhere in my body. Melanoma is a fast-growing cancer, and the most dangerous type of skin cancer. When detected in the early stages, the survival rate is very high, however according to recent studies, if the cancer reaches the lymph nodes, the survival rate falls to 65%, and if the cancer metastasizes in internal organs, the survival rate plummets to 25%.[3] I found out later that at about six months, melanoma is very difficult to fight and half of the time the melanoma has metastasized after that period of time.

In my case, to the best of my knowledge, I figured that I had the tumor for approximately four and half months, if not longer. Dr. Byrnes was a doctor I immediately trusted as did my family. I will go into depth later about Dr. Byrnes, but not only is he an excellent doctor at the top of his profession, but because of this and his friendly and jovial nature, he seems to know everyone, including all the best doctors in every specification in the Chicagoland area.

Dr. Byrnes immediately recommended an oncologist, Dr. Suby Rao, and a surgeon, Dr. James Schenker (more on these two men later as well). My oncologist initially recommended a PET scan to be done at Northwestern Memorial Hospital. At the time the PET scans were relatively new, and Northwestern had apparently had the most up-to-date PET scan machines in the area. According to the Mayo Clinic, a Positron Emission Tomography scan (PET), "is an imaging test that helps reveal how your tissues and organs are functioning. The scan sometimes detects disease before it shows up on other imaging tests."[4]

Dr. Rao ordered the PET scan because it would include the slightest sign that the cancer had spread to other tissues and organs. I remember being injected with a radioactive dye and found out later that the scan detects areas of activity in the body and more radioactive material collects in cancer cells than normal cells.[5]

The results weren't good. The PET scan showed increased activity in areas of my abdomen, which I knew wasn't a good thing. The question we still couldn't answer for sure, and this included my doctors, was whether those spots in my abdomen that the radioactive dye centered on were cancerous cells?

More tests were ordered shortly after that. An MRI, a CT scan, and x-rays. The MRI and CT scan were inconclusive for the most part, but the CT scan did reveal something in the bone structure on the side of my left knee. Dr. Rao then ordered a bone biopsy from my knee. I still remember going to the hospital to have the biopsy done. I was under a local anesthetic and could hear what sounded like a drill go in into my knee. The doctor told me that it took some effort to drill into the bone for the biopsy as my bones were strong. I always had drunk a lot of milk from childhood and even as I went through college, I would even drink a glass of milk on a daily basis. My bone strength must have been due to all that milk!

The results of the bone scan didn't take nearly as long as the initial biopsy from my foot. The results, thank God, were negative. If that wasn't the case, having the cancer metastasize in the bone required a greater concern. I'm not sure what doctors would have recommended if the bone was positive for cancer, but for me if a decision had to be made between my leg and my life, I'd quickly agree to amputate my leg without hesitation.

After the initial surgery, Dr. Byrnes gave me an enlarged open-toed medical shoe and crutches and told me to make sure to use them both. He had just surgically removed a tumor that was maybe slightly smaller than the size of a quarter and maybe two to three millimeters deep. I have to confess that I didn't always listen to Dr. Byrnes' orders. I sometimes would walk short distances without the crutches and even a couple weeks after the initial surgery, I would play catch with a baseball with my younger brother Kevin who was twelve at the time. I had helped coach his little league team earlier that summer, and still had the itch to toss the ball around. I would also occasionally take a mitt and a rubber ball and throw it against a brick wall at one of the local schools in the area. I had watched a men's league game over the summer and wanted to try and pitch in the league at some point. I had played baseball in high school and missed it a lot. By doing this, I obviously wasn't using my crutches, and being right-handed I was pushing off my right foot, the same foot that had the tumor and stitching.

When I got my stitching removed in Dr. Byrnes' office, he could tell that I hadn't always used my crutches. My foot was red and irritated. This was not good, since I still had to have another surgery on that foot, a wide excision with a skin graft, and an inflamed foot would make healing even more challenging.

My surgery was scheduled for September 30th with Dr. Schlenker and his surgical team. Dr. Schlenker is a brilliant surgeon, and he comes from a brilliant background as his father was part of the Manhattan Project in the 1940s in the race to construct the atomic bomb before Nazi Germany. There are many qualities about Dr. Schlenker that I admire, and I will elaborate on these later in another chapter, but one quality he showed me and my family was his honesty and his ability to be as upfront as possible. After reviewing my test results, it was his recommendation that I undergo surgery to remove all the lymph nodes in my right leg, which would cause permanent swelling in that leg. He told my parents and I that he had recently done this procedure on another patient with melanoma in her leg, and even after removing all lymph nodes the patient still lost her life. My mom especially was shaken by this, and I felt for her, but I was glad he told us. I wanted to be given the truth of what I was facing.

I can't imagine how difficult my illness was on my parents. Unfortunately, many parents know too well the pain and helplessness of watching your child suffer through serious illness, and whether or not the child survives, the couple is affected forever. My parents felt helpless, and I know they were suffering knowing that there was nothing more they could do, but to pray, have faith, and trust in God no matter what the outcome.

They were realistic and were prepared for the fact that cancer may indeed take my life. I later asked my Dad about this, and while he was praying tirelessly, he was ready to accept whatever God's will was. It was my parents' faith that gave them this sense of peace in times of pain and uncertainty. My family, as Catholics, believe in an afterlife, that God's faithful servants would not see Hell, and would be eternally happy with God in Heaven (although I think that I may have to take a detour to Purgatory, at least I hope). My parents also placed all their trust in the outcome God had decided, knowing what the Bible tells us, that "my ways are higher than your ways, my thoughts than your thoughts" (Isiah 55:9).

Still with their faith, my parents were human. I know my mom was hurting inside and trying her hardest to be strong for me. It must have been very difficult, since by this time I had to hold off from pursing a job after college to focus on my treatment, which meant that I was living at home and often it was just my mother and me home during the day as my Dad and sister, Jenny, were at work, my brother John, was away at college and my brother Kevin attended grade school. My mom, home with me each day, held all her worries and pain inside in an attempt to be strong for me.

My Dad is a man of few words and he rarely shows his emotion, but even for him, my health had taken its toll on his soul. He also was trying to do his best to remain strong in front of me. Years later I learned from my good friend Gabe, that when my Father was talking to his Mom, Maria, telling her of the latest details of my condition, he broke down in tears.

I don't know what it is about having this idea that we have to be strong all the time for our families. Yes, there is truth to this, and in many ways I am glad that my parents and family members did not show their true worries about my health. It did help me to not think so much about my condition and focus on getting better. However, if someone, whether a family member or not, did break down and show emotion about my condition, I would have been moved by their outward show of love as well. This is what it means to be in a family. To be able to go through life's challenges and difficulties knowing that your family will support you and sometimes that does mean shedding tears.

My oncologist, Dr. Rao, knew that the surgery Dr. Schlenker had mentioned was an option, but he gave me another choice to consider. Instead of removing all the lymph nodes in my right leg, in the second option a dye would be injected into my lymph nodes near the site of the removed tumor. The dye would be monitored during surgery and Dr. Schlenker would remove the lymph nodes where the dye finally rested, which could be on possible cancer cells. Those would be the lymph nodes that would be biopsied. In this option, I would only lose a fraction of the lymph nodes in my leg. If the biopsy was negative, I would have kept the majority of my lymph nodes with little permanent swelling in my leg. With a positive biopsy, obviously the cancer would have then spread, and more treatment would be necessary in the form of another surgery and Interferon radiation (radiation therapy similar to chemotherapy that is used for melanoma patients).

One constant to both surgical options was that both included a wide excision of my right foot (a radius of about 2 centimeters) with a skin graft. Dr. Rao explained that historically melanoma tumors can come back in the same area and to be sure that all of the tumor was gone, tissue from around the tumor site would have to be taken out. To replace the tissue lost, Dr. Schlenker would take tissue from my right thigh and place it on my right foot.

I had to make a decision. As far as how I was physically feeling at the time, I felt pretty "normal." I couldn't really tell if I was more tired than I should be feeling. I can't remember feeling sick or running a temperature, having hot sweats, or in light of the test results having any abdominal pain or discomfort. If the cancer had indeed spread to my abdomen, or other areas of my body, what was I supposed to feel? I didn't know what was "normal" for cancer patients.

Dr. Rao left the decision up to me, and a few days before my surgery, I called him and told him of my decision to use the dye and have the lymph node biopsy of my right leg while holding off, at least for now, from removing all the lymph nodes in that leg. It wasn't that I was afraid of having permanent swelling in my leg, it was just that based on how I was feeling symptomatically, I just didn't think removing all my lymph nodes in my leg was warranted at this time, and besides if it was shown that the dyed lymph nodes were positive, I could always have the additional surgery.

Leading up to the surgery date, September 30th, there were decisions and preparations to be made. From the time of my initial diagnosis, there was maybe a month before the actual surgery date. I wanted to make sure that both my body and soul were prepared. My mother and both of my grandmothers made sure I was eating healthy and getting as many nutrients as possible into my body. My mom would cook healthy meals and when she didn't cook it was because one of my grandmothers had cooked a meal and brought it over. My grandparents on my Dad's side would take me out to lunch about every week or so for nice meal as well. It was great getting out of the house and taking my mind off what was ahead.

This also gave me time to prepare spiritually. I took time to go to Confession and my parents arranged for me to receive the Catholic Sacrament of the Sick administered by Father Dudley Day, a wonderful priest and friend of my family. All this gave me a sense of peace before my surgery, even though at the time I wasn't overly worried or didn't fully realize the gravity of my health situation.

In the end, however, I was at peace. I was at peace with the decision I had made, and I was at peace with God. Whatever happened was up to Him and I had to place my trust in Him. I had prayed, along with so many others, to be healed and to be able live a "normal life," but in the end we can only hope that His will is carried out whether it is what we want or not. I had no choice but to trust in God.

3

Surgery Day

I still remember the night before my surgery. Up into this point I hadn't really reflected too much about the possibility that I may not survive this. The night before my scheduled surgery, that changed. I had to be at the hospital very early and had to wake up at 4 or 4:30 A.M. in the morning. I couldn't sleep. I then started to become anxious, and suddenly I had all these questions? Would I live? What if I only had months left? What if the cancer was found too late? Had I lived a good life? Had I lived the life that God had designed for me?

When the morning came, I rose, took a shower, and got dressed. I couldn't have breakfast since I had to fast before surgery. I still had these thoughts, but I couldn't let these thoughts simmer in my mind. I had to put my faith entirely in God and trust in His mercy.

As I mentioned I had these questions in my mind... had I lived a good life, the life God wanted for me? I was a good guy. I still went to Church, still had my faith, but I was by no means perfect. I still was a work in progress (and still am), and I needed to give all of myself to God, not just the minimum, and not just go through the motions of being a Catholic or Christian. God was asking more of me and deep down I knew it.

When my parents and I drove to the hospital, it was still dark outside, and the sun was just starting to come up. The actual surgery itself was to be done at Dr. Schleker's own surgical center. He wanted his own trusted team to perform a surgery of this magnitude. Dr. Schlenker was well-known in his field and was thought of as one of the best surgeons in Chicago. The surgery I was to have was a challenging one for any plastic surgeon, but I could tell Dr. Schlenker was the right doctor for the job. Like many great doctors, he thrived on challenges. He was confident and his confidence helped put me at ease. The reason, however, that we had to go to the hospital, was so the dye could be injected into my right foot. From there, I would be taken to the surgical center where Dr. Schlenker and his team would perform the surgery.

To this day, getting injected with that dye was probably the greatest physical pain I have ever been in. I was scheduled for surgery in the early afternoon and I could not take any local anesthesia since I would be receiving general anesthesia at the surgical center. A doctor at the hospital had to inject the dye deep into my right foot where the initial tumor had been. As I mentioned before, my foot was already irritated from walking without crutches and from my brilliant idea of throwing a baseball over the past few weeks. The doctor really had to inject the dye deep into the tissue in my foot, and I was in so much pain that the doctor had to apologize several times during the process. He really felt bad for me, but I know nothing was his fault as he was just doing his job. The procedure probably only took 2-3 minutes, but to me it felt like an eternity. I was in enough pain where I even had tears in my eyes.

I read stories about people going through chemotherapy or recovering from a serious accident, and many will say they would rather die than go through it all over again. I think that all depends on the person. I am in no way comparing what I have endured to what others have gone through. I do have some setbacks that I will discuss later, but I have been incredibly fortunate to have the relatively pain-free life that I have today. Many people look at suffering in a different light and are willing to go through any

18

amount of pain to have a chance at life. The one constant in this approach to life, is that those who feel this way believe there is a meaning and value in life, and most often those people believe they have unique purpose in life that has been given to them by God, and they will endure anything for it.

I feel the same way as those people. Recently, I lost my cousin Mike. He passed away at the relatively young age of 70. Mike loved being a grandpa to his grandchildren and he loved his wife and two daughters dearly. When he was diagnosed with a form of lymphoma, which was located in an inoperable area of his body, he remained positive, optimistic, and strong. When things started taking a turn for the worse, he didn't give up. When chemotherapy stopped showing improvement, he tried other treatments, anything that would give him the chance at life. He endured this suffering because he saw value in being there for his grandchildren and imparting his wisdom and his faith to them. He also hung on as long as he could to be there for his wife. He loved her very much and didn't want her to go through life's trials alone. Mike had so many reasons for living. He enjoyed life, but if I had to guess, I would say he wanted to survive so that he could be there for others.

My grandfather, who I have also lost in the resent past, fought for the same reasons too. He was nearly 92 before he died and had been sick for many years prior. But still, like Mike, my grandpa fought hard to stay alive regardless of the pain. He did this for his wife, my grandmother. Like my cousin Mike, he too did that for unselfish reasons.

Not everyone feels like my cousin or my grandfather. The society we live in has shifted more and more to an individualized life outlook and more and more people are living for themselves or for comfort instead of sacrifice. Sadly, more young people today are unhappy and depressed. They feel lonely and isolated. I don't think it is a coincidence that our youth have these feelings while living in a society that puts little regard on God and a belief in living for something bigger than yourself. Statistics among millennials today show that more and more do not practice any religion at all.

This is troubling, but also sad. I was 22 years old when I was going through the uncertainty of cancer, and if I was 22 today, I would be considered a millennial. I can't imagine going through a serious illness and not having any kind of belief or faith in God. I just can't accept that I was put on earth by a series of coincidences, and that all that I am is a bunch of cells banded together based on chance, that life is lived without any real meaning and greater purpose.

For those who are going through storms of some kind, without knowing God's love, I genuinely feel for them, especially our youth. Even at age twenty-two in the year 2002, I was certain I had a purpose and meaning in life and I was willing to go through anything to continue forward. I felt that God wasn't done with me, and I had to fulfill an obligation to Him, and even if I wasn't meant to come through it all, I still had to trust His will. What other choice did I have?

After the dye injection, my parents drove me to Dr. Schleker's surgical center in Oak Lawn, a suburb on the Southwest side of Chicago. The basement of the medical building was where surgeries were performed, and on that day, mine was the last scheduled due the length of time the surgery would require, approximately 4 to 5 hours. My sister had met my parents and I at the surgical center, and I still remember saying goodbye to her before I was wheeled into the recovery room, in which only two people, my parents, were allowed. It was really thoughtful of Jenny to take a day off work and meet us there.

When it was my turn to enter the operating room, I remember saying goodbye to my parents and feeling a bit scared. It all just seemed surreal to me. Was this really happening? Just months ago, I was in Assembly Hall at the University of Illinois walking down an aisle to receive my college diploma. While my other friends were starting their careers, here I was about to have a surgery that could affect me forever, if I was lucky. Years ago, I had been given a medal of St. Anthony while going to confession at St. Peter's Church in downtown Chicago. The priest told me to pray to St.

Anthony to find guidance in life and even to find a wife that I could love and cherish someday. I carried that medal with me, and although the medal wasn't allowed to be on my person during the surgery, Dr. Schlenker made an exception and a nurse taped the medal to my palm using medical tape.

One minute, I remember having a conversation with the anesthesiologist, and then that was it. About 5 hours later, I awoke in the recovery room, wondering what in the world had just happened? And it seemed that as soon as I woke up, a nurse kept trying to get me out of the bed to use the bathroom. I understand why they need to do that, but at the time, I just wanted to be left alone. I had just undergone a long surgery and I was exhausted.

After a few hours of recovery, I was then taken to another hospital, Little Company of Mary Hospital in Evergreen Park (another suburb on the southside of Chicago) for further recovery and observation. I stayed there for two days and although I couldn't wait to get home, looking back I am glad I was at the hospital due to all the pain. My foot was throbbing terribly, and even though I was given morphine, it really didn't make much of a dent. After two days in the hospital, I was released where my family and I had to wait for what we were all anxious to find out, the results of the pathology from the lymph node biopsy.

4

Thanksgiving

After being diagnosed with cancer, the amount of people praying for me was countless. So many were praying for me including all my relatives, family, friends, alumni and teachers at my old high school Northridge, and the parishioners of St. James, the parish in Lemont, IL where my family belonged. Vast amounts of people were praying, and I am forever grateful to them.

After surgery, Dr. Schlenker ordered me to 6 weeks of bed rest. Since I had not quite abided by Dr. Byrnes' order in using crutches after the first surgery, Dr. Schlenker made it clear to me that I absolutely needed to follow his directive this time. My parents live in three-bedroom townhome. Having one sister who had her own room, I grew up sharing a bedroom with my younger brother John, and then later Kevin as well. When I arrived back from Little Company of Mary Hospital, my parents had brought my bed downstairs in the living room. They thought having me downstairs would make it easier for my mom to help care for me while I was laid up.

The surgery was on a Monday, and after two nights in the hospital, we were still waiting for the results of the pathology of the lymph node biopsies. Even though my mom tried not to show her anxiety, I could tell she was on edge. On Friday during that week, late at night after 10 P.M., the phone rang. It was Dr. Schlenker, and my mom answered the phone. I immediately knew the results of the biopsies. Negative!

Well, that Friday night, my grandma was over at the house when we got Dr. Schlenker's call. On the phone, Dr. Schlenker told my mom that he wasn't sure he should call since it was later in the evening past 10 P.M., but obviously, and especially with the great news, she didn't mind one bit. My mom got off the phone and told me I was cancer free. I immediately felt relief, and then gratitude to God for allowing me to live. My grandma, dad, and siblings, who were all home at that moment were overjoyed and thankful.

All in all, this whole process from start to finish lasted about two months. Thinking about how quickly time goes by, two months does not feel long at all. But these were difficult months for my family. The diagnosis as well as the driving back and forth to different hospitals for various tests, scans, and procedures. My parents were drained physically, mentally, and spiritually. It was a trying time for them. They were doing all they could do for their son fully knowing that they were not in control of the end result. There is a helplessness that they felt as only a parent of a seriously ill child could possibly know.

I was elated, relieved, grateful, and now optimistic for my future, but one of the biggest emotions I did have was the relief that now my parents could breathe again. They no longer had to live day by day in a state of uncertainty and fear. I believe God acknowledged their prayers, perseverance, and trust which they placed in Him.

Obviously, my parents were praying very hard. My dad told me later that he would stop by a church near his office on the way home from work every day and pray for my healing. My grandparents were praying hard too. My Irish grandma, whom I lived with in Chicago while going to the University of Illinois at Chicago, would pray her rosary aloud every night before bed. When I lived there, I could see her nightly through her slightly cracked open bedroom door, kneeling at her bed with her rosary beads in hand. Maybe she left that door cracked on purpose in an effort to encourage me to make time for God and to place an importance on prayer. During the time of my illness, she made a promise to the Blessed Mother that if I was healed, she would take me to Lourdes, France out of gratitude.

* * *

The story of Lourdes is a fascinating one. In 1858, the Blessed Mother appeared to a young peasant girl, named Bernadette Soubirous. Bernadette was hardly literate. She was also the oldest child of a very poor family, and with the oldest of nine children, she often stayed home from school to help her Mother with her younger siblings. She also missed much of her schooling due to chronic illness as a child. When the Blessed Mother appeared to her in 1858, Bernadette was fifteen years old, hardly literate, and was years behind the education of her peers. She still hadn't finished the basic catechism needed to receive Holy Communion at the time.

On February 11th, 1858, while out looking for firewood, Bernadette saw a beautiful lady near a dumping ground in Lourdes. The Lady, with a rosary in hand, smiled at Bernadette and made the sign of the cross. Instinctively, Bernadette knelt down and began praying with the Lady.

From February 11th, 1858 to July 16th, 1858, Our Lady appeared to Bernadette 18 times. Bernadette quickly realized that she was the only one that could see Our Lady. The townspeople began to mock her and even members of her own family had serious doubts about these appearances. Bernadette knew the day and times Our Lady would appear to her, and soon the crowds of people began to increase. There were many people that came hoping to see the vision of Our Lady themselves, but still many more were coming to ridicule Bernadette and the religious who believed she did see Mary.

Throughout these apparitions, the message she gave Bernadette was "Penance. penance, penance. Pray for sinners." Our Lady also asked Bernadette to relay to the local priest a message that she wishes for a chapel to be built here, and for people to come here in procession. Also worth noting is that when Bernadette asked what Our Lady's name was, she responded, "I am the Immaculate Conception."[6] This was significant because only four years prior, Pope Pius IX proclaimed the Catholic dogma of the Immaculate Conception. Our Lady was affirming the Catholic teaching that she was without sin.

Today, Lourdes, France, is widely known for the apparition of Our Lady to Bernadette on February 25th, 1858. On that day, in front of a massive crowd of townspeople, Our Lady asked Bernadette to drink from the spring water. Seeing there was no spring nearby, Our Lady pointed to a place in the ground near were Bernadette was kneeling. Bernadette began to dig with her hands, and trusting Our Lady's request, she drank the muddy ground, even going so far as to smear some it on her face.[7]

As you can imagine, the people laughed and mocked Bernadette openly. Her family was embarrassed, and Bernadette left the Grotto of Lourdes in shame. However, shortly after leaving the Grotto ridiculed, water indeed had sprung out of the hole she had dug. Days later a quarry miner named Louis Bouriette, who for 19 years prior had been blind in his right eye from a mining accident, was cured of his blindness after washing his eye in the spring water. Later a two-year old crippled boy named Justin Bouhort, who was labeled a "hopeless case," and had recently contracted tuberculosis, was also cured after his mother, desperate to save her child, bathed him in the spring water. Justin lived long enough to be present for Bernadette's canonization in 1933.[8]

From 1858 until present day, there have been 67 cures that have been approved by the Catholic Church's strict standards. There is a rigorous process for cures to be considered miraculous. The Church has doctors and scientists investigate each case and they all must agree that there is no known medical rationale behind a certain phenomenon. It is so stringent that any case that is reviewed is always dismissed even if the person took any medication or sought any treatment after washing with Lourdes spring water. The process takes years, and through thorough investigations and interviews, many people who know in their heart that God has intervened and given a cure, do not feel the need to go through the demanding process, especially with the intense investigation and aggravation that comes with it.

The story of Bernadette to me is one of humble faith and trust in God. In the history of the Catholic Church, God continues to use the humble, the meek, and the unassuming to relay His message. Bernadette, who was impoverished, sickly, and little educated, was chosen to be a messenger of conversion and penance, but also a message of hope and love. Even when we look to the life of Christ, He came to Earth not in wealth and esteem, but into poverty and humility.

* * *

There are some people who know my history of cancer, and with modern technology they think that my survival was not a miracle at all, but a wonderful outcome of modern medicine. I don't dispute those that think that this offers a very plausible explanation. There were MRI and CT scans that did not show any further spread of cancer, but then there was the PET scan that showed activity in my abdomen. To this day, I am not entirely sure if the melanoma did spread further in my body. I tend to believe that it was contained because of the quick actions of Dr. Byrnes and my Mom's insistence to see a doctor immediately. I have however asked myself many times questions like, what if I hadn't mentioned the legion on my foot to my Mom? What if I wasn't feeling any pain playing basketball, and what if didn't play basketball in the first place? Would I have noticed any significant pain enough to get a medical opinion? What if I just put any notions of seeing a doctor aside? What if I waited just two more weeks? Would I still be here if I did? What if Dr. Byrnes, a podiatrist and not a dermatologist, didn't recognize the seriousness of my case?

What I do feel more than anything else is gratitude. Gratitude to God, to my mom and dad, to my many doctors, especially Dr. Byrnes, and to all those who were praying for me. Whether God used the prayers said on my behalf to take any lingering cancer away from my body, I do not know. But as I think of today, maybe those prayers were used moreover for my soul, that I be given a grateful heart and live out my life for the purpose God has given me.

Either way, I knew I had to travel to Lourdes. I wanted to honor my grandma's promise to Our Lady, and I wanted to say thank you to God. It was 2008 when I decided to visit Lourdes and travel to France. By this time, my grandma was unable to travel with me, so I decided to go alone.

It was my first trip to Europe, and I had booked my flight, hotels, and train passes with a local travel agency. I was 28 years old, and I had just gotten a cell phone, being the last of my friends to get one. Even though I had just gotten a cellular phone, I didn't bring it with me to Europe. People may find this strange, but I enjoy not being connected for periods of time, even in a foreign country like France. I had to rely on help from French people in getting on the right train or finding my hotel or restaurant. As Americans, we hear that the French are rude and unhelpful, but from my experiences, the great majority of people I encountered were nothing but helpful. Lourdes is on the Southwest corner of France in the Pyrenees Mountains, and it is not the easiest of destinations to get to. After changing planes in Frankfort, Germany, I landed in Toulouse, France, and then took a bus to the train station where I boarded my train for Lourdes. Amazingly I found my way easily without a phone!

It was a beautiful crisp and sunny July day when I arrived in Lourdes. After I checked into my hotel, I walked the ½ mile to the Shrine. I immediately went to the Grotto and knelt in prayer. All these emotions and thoughts came running through my head. It just felt surreal that I was actually here, at the very place where Our Lady appeared to little Bernadette. The most overwhelming thought that came into my head and continued throughout my time there was gratitude, but I also had a feeling of obligation to God for all that He had done for me. I also felt an undeniable deep love for Mother Mary and a commitment to her.

One of the constant reminders that I give my students throughout every year is the message of gratitude. Gratitude is essential to happiness, and I challenge anyone to find someone that is ungrateful and yet also happy at the same time. It's an impossibility. We all have things in life to be grateful for and it is better to go through life with an attitude of being thankful then an attitude of envy. I tell my students that there will always be someone who is better than you or who has been given different talents and gifts than you, but on the contrary there will also be someone who is not as fortunate as you. I make the point of going to a hospital and seeing the sick, many of which who are fighting for each breath.

Kneeling in front of the Grotto there on this beautiful day, I felt so grateful that I was alive, and I knew in my heart that there was a reason for it, a purpose in life. The feeling of gratitude overwhelmed me again the next morning while I was at Mass at the basilica as I couldn't help but weep tears of joy and gratitude during the service. With these emotions, I also felt an obligation to God. There is nothing I can do to repay God for what He has done for me, and here I don't just mean for my life after cancer, but especially for Christ giving His life so that we may live with Him in the next life. With that said however, I did feel an obligation to God to live the rest of my life with a greater sense of service. I really felt God was asking me to give more of myself to Him.

I spent four days and three nights in Lourdes. During that time, I saw nurses pushing patients in wheelchairs for the candlelight procession that was held every evening. While some people did indeed look sickly or disabled, I saw many more people with heavy hearts, which is what is known in Lourdes as the "walking wounded." Without a doubt, I believe there are many people who come to Lourdes for a physical cure, and as I have mentioned before, this number is greater than the 67 approved miracles of Lourdes. Everyone that comes to Lourdes, however, comes away with a renewed sense of faith and peace. Many people will come to Lourdes in distress but leave with a sense of peace and trust that no matter what events unfold, they now have the strength to bear it. Lourdes is widely known for physical cures, but I'd say there are more pilgrims that come away with more of a spiritual cure, a renewal of faith, and deep sense of peace.

* * *

I thought of my grandmother especially while I as there. Without the promise she made to Our Lady of Lourdes, I would not have traveled across the ocean to France. I am very close with my Grandma. I lived with her in her Chicago home for two years while attending the University of Illinois at Chicago. Often, we'd have tea and cookies in the evening, and one of her favorite cookies were these European biscuits with Orange filling called Pim's. Each night in Lourdes, I would have tea and a few of the Pim's cookies.

My Grandma also had quite a sense of humor. We would often tease each other. I would tease her about getting older and her insistence of not using her hearing aids. I'd often do impressions of her right in front of her using her mannerisms and talking in her Irish brogue. She'd give it right back to me, calling me "daft" for my silliness. I knew she enjoyed the teasing, otherwise I would not have done it so often, and I never minded her ribbing me either. It was just the bond that we had.

The Grotto at Lourdes can be a very crowded place. During one afternoon, I went to visit the Grotto and it was so crowded that I decided to go over the bridge across the river where I found a bench underneath a tree still in view of the Grotto. Then in the middle of praying my rosary, some bird poop fell on my shoulder. Immediately I started to laugh and think of my grandma. She was with me in spirit and she was laughing at me!

5

Three Wise Men

Every year after going through cancer, I have made a point to give a Christmas gift to each of the three doctors that cared for me during the Fall of 2002. Dropping off a box of chocolates, a book, or some holiday treat cannot nearly repay these gentlemen for what they have done for me and my family, but a small gift and a note of thanks a small gesture that lets them know that I haven't and will never forget their generosity.

With technology ever increasing day by day, I still appreciate hand-written notes. As a teacher, I am grateful for little notes that students write to me during Christmas or at the end of the school year. I sometimes get notes from former students that are in high school, college, and beyond. It's notes like these that add years to the career of teachers, and I imagine a kind message of gratitude has the same effect on any profession, especially doctors.

Dr. Rao, my oncologist, is a wonderful doctor and person. For 6 years after surgery, I got to know Dr. Rao much more during my checkup appointments. For the first three years after I was pronounced in remission, I had to have checkup appointments with Dr. Rao every 3 months, and then the final three years, after making continued progress those visits were lessened to every 6 months.

When I was going through all this, Dr. Rao was in his mid-40s, fairly young in his profession. I could tell he was a devoted husband and father. He knew I taught junior high aged kids and would ask me what to expect in school when his children reached that age. Dr. Rao is an East Indian-American and he told me that he and his wife had an arranged marriage, which is not out of the ordinary in Indian culture. "We get along just fine," he'd say. In our American culture, an arranged marriage sounds frightening and outdated, but studies show that they are successful marriages that have a higher percentage of staying together. I think there is something Americans can learn from them. One lesson is that there is no such thing as a perfect marriage or a fairy tale marriage. From what I gather, marriage requires work and sacrifice, and it thrives when couples understand this, but is doomed to failure when a husband or wife look for and expect perfection. Some men want to find someone with looks like a supermodel (the same guys are often not exactly handsome princes), instead of finding a woman they are physically attracted to with genuine personal character and similar values. Some women, I believe, are guilty of thinking along similar lines. All I know is that in Dr. Rao's case, he and his wife have a successful marriage partly because they didn't look for all the things that the world tells us are important.

Dr. Rao once told me of his decision to become an oncologist. He comes from a family of doctors and when he told his family that he wanted to study Oncology, his family tried to talk him out it. They told him it would be too depressing, and the job would understandably bring added pressure to his work and stress to his family life. I can't imagine how challenging it is for oncologists to have difficult conversations with patients and family members. Could you imagine telling a patient that he or she has only months to live? Could you imagine witnessing the deaths of patients one day and then having office hours the next? Oncologists have one of the most challenging medical professions there is, and I am thankful that Dr.

Rao decided to be true to his conviction to become an oncologist. Dr. Rao, by nature, is a calm, patient, and an understanding man, but also honest and straightforward at the same time.

I remember my first appointment with Dr. Rao after my diagnosis. He spent a good hour or more with my parents and I. He went over the prognosis and answered several questions. As you might imagine, my parents were worried, and my mom had made a lengthy list of questions for Dr. Rao. He answered each of them slowly without any medical jargon. He was also realistic about the surgical options and the possibility that the cancer had spread. He further warned that melanoma can come back at any time even years later and that even if all the cancer had been removed, I'd still have to be diligent about checking for it and avoiding prolonged sun exposure. I left there with a good sense of what was to come, but because of the calm nature he exhibited, I left without additional stress or worry, still hopeful and positive. Regardless of the stage of cancer that his patients are going through, I believe that Dr. Rao makes his patients feel that no one has an immediate death sentence, and there is always a reason for hope. Dr. Rao realizes hope is essential to life.

* * *

Dr. Byrnes, my podiatrist, is a character and he definitely has the gift of gab. Over the years, he has become more to me than just a doctor. He has become a friend. Dr. Byrnes really cares deeply for all his patients, and his jovial, friendly, and compassionate nature gives patients a great sense of trust and comfort. He takes a genuine interest in the lives of his patients and if I am ever in the waiting room, I can even hear him conversing with patients and half of the time they are talking about subjects completely unrelated to the patient's feet. Every Christmas season, without appointment, I stop by his office to deliver a gift for him and his family. In between seeing his patients, he greets me with a big hug and takes time spending a few minutes to talk with me, asking me how everything is going at my school, how my family is doing, or giving good tips for travel destinations. On these little visits, he goes out of his way for a brief visit even with patients still waiting in the waiting room. I always feel a bit guilty thinking I am making his patients wait a little longer, but I'm sure the personal interest he takes with his patients is the very reason he is so well respected and admired, and I'm sure the people waiting a minute or two longer choose him as their doctor because he is personable and he cares for the whole patient, not just their feet.

When you walk into Dr. Byrnes' office, one of the first things you'll notice is a framed newspaper article from the Chicago Tribune. If you take the time to read the article it relates the heroic story of when Dr. Byrnes witnessed a man assaulting a woman near his office. In an instant, Dr. Byrnes in his sneakers ran over to the scene and the man immediately fled. It turned out that the women was married, and after her husband was made aware that it was Dr. Byrnes who had saved his wife from the assault, the man, a handy tradesman, made sure that the grass and landscaping outside Dr. Brynes' office was always done well and without charge.

You'll also see a photo that he has of Pope John Paul II as Dr. Byrnes is a devout Catholic and graduate of Loyola University Medical School. He is so devoted to his Catholic faith, that he refuses to perform surgeries at local hospitals that perform abortions. He is a man of faith, integrity, and generosity. Over the years, Dr. Byrnes has come to know me personally and found out that I am part of a Committee that helps organize and assemble Chicago's Nativity Scene on the public square at Daley Plaza. Once he became aware that, he now always sends a generous donation check to help offset the costs.

Dr. Byrnes isn't just a friendly doctor, he's exceptional in his field and very highly recommended. On few occasions I was in need of an orthopedic doctor, once for my back, another time for my knee, and yet another time for my shoulder. I didn't have the slightest idea of where to find a reputable and trustworthy doctor, but I knew Dr. Byrnes would. He gave me referrals to excellent orthopedic doctors. Regardless of one's profession, individuals who pursue excellence in their work know others who also pursue excellence in their profession. This is especially true of Dr. Byrnes. It was he who recommended my Oncologist Dr. Rao, and he also recommended my surgeon, Dr. Schlenker.

* * *

As mentioned earlier, Dr. Schlenker was the very skilled surgeon on my case. Through Dr. Schlenker's successful medical history, he has created an unmatched reputation as one of the finest plastic surgeons in the Chicagoland area, if not the whole country. He has a very gifted family as his son is also a talented surgeon, and Dr. Schlenker himself comes from pedigree and brilliance as his own father was involved in the Manhattan Project, the secret operation conscripted by the U.S. government to construct the atomic bomb in a race to do so ahead of Germany. In all my appointments with Dr. Schlenker, he never told me about the accomplishments of his father. It was Dr. Byrnes who made me aware of that, while Dr. Byrnes also made me aware of just how skilled a surgeon Dr. Schlenker was as well. During my surgery, knowing that I had such a brilliant doctor on my case gave me great relief.

Dr. Schlenker is an esteemed and distinguished doctor, yet an unbelievably humble and generous man. One thing I found out from one of his staff members was that from time to time, he travels to underdeveloped countries to perform free plastic surgeries for the poor, which often includes restructuring cleft lips in children.

As I've visited his office over the years, I've made comments to his secretaries and nurses that he seems like he is a busy guy and they will tell me he is constantly working, seeing patients in his office and performing surgeries. He has a gift for medicine, and the passion to go along with it. During one of my office visits, after I commented about his work ethic, dedication, and his overall busyness, he who had been divorced, remarked that he wished he had spent less time at work in hindsight. For me and for many of us, this is an important lesson. I still remember the commencement speech from my Illinois Business College Graduation when the Vice President of Kraft Foods at the time said, "nobody on their deathbed wishes they spent more time at work, but instead more time with their families." More on that graduation speech later. Each year, I tell that story to my class and this is true for so many who live in our country where many are to driven by our work and often, though not always intentionally, end up neglecting family. Many on their deathbed will indeed say that they wished they'd spent more time being a better father or mother, a better husband or wife, a better person. They certainly won't say they wish they gave more time to their job.

When Dr. Schlenker isn't working or volunteering his time, he most likely is skiing! Dr. Byrnes who has become a close friend of Dr. Schlenker, once told me that about him. When I heard this, I imagined that Dr. Schenker, who would have been in his mid to late-60s at the time would be skiing on smaller bunny hills, but I would be wrong. He would ski the most difficult inclines available. Dr. Schlenker is not one to shy away from challenges.

As I do with Dr. Byrnes and Dr. Rao, I also stop by his office every Christmas season to give him a gift. When possible, I try and buy a special German Christmas cake called Stollen. My mom bought one for Dr. Schlenker for the Christmas after my surgery and I remember him remarking that his mother would make one every year for Christmas.

When I think of Schlenker, there are two thoughts that come to mind. The first is his generosity. As we know, healthcare costs are very expensive, and surgeries, especially the more involved ones, can cost a great deal even after factoring in insurance. After the insurance took effect, the surgical bill was still enormous. My dad started making payments of one or maybe two hundred dollars. After I was cleared to work and started working, I started helping my dad with payments too in any small way I could. Well, after maybe a year of making these little payments, my mom got a call from Joan, a wonderfully, kind person who was Dr. Schlenker's head nurse. She was asked by Dr. Schlenker to call us and "tell them they have paid enough." And that was that. No more payments to make. It turned out that there was close to about $20,000 still left to pay! What an unselfish, generous man. To this day, I still can't get over the fact that he did that, and his act of generosity has stayed with me.

The second thought I have of Dr. Schlenker is a picture he has in the front of his office. It wasn't until about 10 years or so of stopping by his office to drop off these little Christmas gifts of gratitude, that I noticed it. When you walk into his second story office and check in, there is a picture of a surgeon in the operating room and behind the surgeon is Christ guiding his hands. Dr. Schlenker is a brilliant, unbelievably skilled physician, and it would be easy for a man like him to become conceited or even arrogant or overconfident, but even after all his success and prestige, he remains humble and recognizes that the successes of his surgeries and practice are completely dependent upon God. Knowing him and seeing that picture on his wall is a great reminder to us all that we are not in control, and that we rely on God for absolutely everything. For a man of his stature to live by this humility, it has made a deep impression on me!

As of this writing, Dr. Schlenker recently retired. In fact, when I visited his office in late December of 2019, he had only a few weeks left of follow up appointments after he conducted his last surgeries. This time, my mom and I went to his office and we each had a gift for him. Every year I would include a hand-written card expressing how grateful I am for all he has done for me, but this year knowing this would probably be the last time I would see him, I wanted to make sure he really knew how sincerely grateful I was. The most important part of what I wrote, I also told him that day too, and it was simply this, "There are number a of people who I believe I owe it to to live a good life, and I want you to know that you are one of them." When I told him that, my mom and I saw that he was about to cry.

I could never repay him for what he did for me, but it is the little things in life that can have the most meaningful impact and I hope at least in some small measure, I let him know just what an impact he had made on me.

6

The Light at the End of the Tunnel

After graduating high school, I wasn't exactly sure what I wanted to do or study. I always admired police officers who put their life on the line every day, so I ended up attending the University of Illinois at Chicago as a Criminal Justice major. After a semester, I still wasn't exactly sure about being a police officer, so I switched to Political Science thinking I didn't need a criminal justice degree in order to enter the police force.

After my freshman year in college, I realized law enforcement wasn't for me. I have the utmost respect for police officers, in fact my own brother is currently a police officer, but I just didn't feel this was where I was called in life. After thinking about it some more, I settled on changing my major to Accounting with the thinking that since I was good at math and accountants make a good living, this would allow some financial stability to possibly provide for a family someday. Having had spent time in the criminal justice department, I was lucky enough to be introduced to professor, Joseph Peterson. All freshman had to take an Introduction to University course during their first semester, and since at the time I was a criminal justice major, Professor Peterson, a Criminal Justice professor, taught my section of this introduction course.

I immediately liked Professor Peterson. He was obviously bright and well educated, but I could tell he was humble and genuine. Like me, he was also was a baseball fan, and had even played Division III baseball at Carthage College, a small liberal arts college in Wisconsin. After my first year of college I did well enough to get accepted into UIC's Honors College, and each student is assigned a fellow. To my delight, I was assigned Professor Peterson as my fellow and mentor in the Honors College. Students in the Honors College would meet their assigned fellow a couple times a semester, and our meetings usually revolved around lunch and talking baseball. Besides baseball, he would ask questions like where I wanted to be in 5 or 10 years, and he understood and respected that my answers where not always career based. He had a family of his own and knew the importance of a balance needed between work, family, and life in general. As he got to know me better, he could sense that I wasn't completely sold on Accounting, and I can remember him reminding me to keep my options open, which turned out to be some of the best career advice I had ever received.

I stuck with Accounting my sophomore year and because of that I applied to the University of Illinois at Urbana-Champaign, which is about a two hour drive south of Chicago. I applied to transfer there because of the reputation of their Accounting program, and Professor Peterson was kind enough to write me a great letter of recommendation.

When I arrived at U of I for my Junior year and started taking more advanced Accounting coursework, I started to again have second thoughts about my choice of major and a career in Accounting. I was really just bored with it. Part of me thought that this was just the nature of Accounting and that it would just be a job, and not the only part of my life. Even still, I knew that most accountants for much of the year spent 60 to 70 plus hours a week at work, and I just couldn't see myself doing that for the rest of my life, especially if I lacked the necessary passion or interest.

During my Junior year while at the University of Illinois (U of I), I started volunteering some of my free time working with children in the community. On Saturday mornings I volunteered at a Vietnamese Church and outreach center. I tutored Vietnamese children who were learning English and my time was spent helping them with homework, but also playing different games and sports. There were also a few local field trips that were put together as well.

I also became involved with Volunteer Illini Projects (VIP), which was basically a Big Brother/Big Sister program in which university students were paired up with a local child to act as a mentor. I was assigned to a 5th grade boy, but he had an older junior high aged brother who ended up coming along to events too. Their father lived in another state and unfortunately was not very involved in their lives. We did things like go bowling, see a movie, get pizza, play basketball in the park, or attend other VIP functions. I also took them to an Illini football game and a basketball game. Even though they lived in Champaign most of their lives, they had never been to an Illini football or basketball game. This was 2001-2002 when Illinois won the Big Ten in both Football and Basketball in the same season, and the games were exciting! I still remember taking them to a football game that Illinois played against Penn State. The game was back and forth, and the Illini ended up pulling out a last-minute victory! After the game, I remember the PA system playing a Michael Jackson song, and the boys, excited after seeing a great game, started dancing creating their own section of cheering fans! We had fun together, and both boys enjoyed the time we spent.

During this time, I was having doubts about staying in Accounting. I kept thinking how much fun I had volunteering with kids, and it felt good to help them and try to make an impact. In the back of my mind, I starting to think that teaching was the career that I was really meant to pursue. Towards the end of the fall semester of my junior year, I decided to make an appointment with one of my Accounting Professors and explain my dilemma. I told her that I was thinking of leaving the Accounting program and Business College to pursue becoming a teacher and coach. This was a big leap for me. I really worked hard to get into U of I's highly ranked and well-known Business College, and I wasn't sure if I should give all that up.

I discussed this with my Professor and to my surprise, she encouraged me to explore the teaching career. She told me there would be sacrifices with whatever I choose and that while Accounting would be a lucrative profession, money is not the only reason for choosing a career. She also told me that her sister was a teacher, and that while she felt she was making a difference, my professor told me that not all teachers are in it for the right reasons. Having taught now for over 15 years, I think this to be true for a few individuals. Teaching is indeed a calling, and not just a paycheck, but this really is true for any profession. There are people who work hard and give their best at their job on a daily basis, and there are those who simply don't. This was somewhat surprising to hear about education, as I felt that a noble profession like teaching would have only noble people in it, but character is not something that comes naturally. Character is something we must work at every day.

So, I did listen to her advice and found out more about what I would have to do to become a teacher. My first instinct was to be a high school math teacher and coach baseball, so I made an appointment with an academic advisor at U of I's Math Department. I was told that I had to have a Mathematics major with a Minor in Secondary Education, and since I hadn't taken enough math coursework, I would have to be in school for almost another four years to become a high school math teacher. That wasn't an option. I simply did not have the money to be in school for another four years, nor did I want to be an undergraduate for that long of a time.

I still had this desire to teach and I wasn't giving up hope. This time I made an appointment with Professor Ken Travers, who was both a professor of Education and student advisor. On the day of the appointment in late January of 2001, there was snowstorm, and the university had to cancel classes. The power and phone lines were all down. My appointment with Mr. Travers was in the late morning, and I had no way of getting a hold of him to see whether our appointment was still on.

His office was on the second floor of the Armory. I remember when I entered the building, I had to climb a flight of stairs, which with the power being out all throughout the campus, created a staircase of complete darkness. Here I was taking one step at a time not able to see each step that was in front of me. As I got closer and closer to the top of the flight of stairs, I began to see a light. The Armory is a spacious building used for ROTC training exercises and there are large windows on both the East and West sides of the structure as you can imagine. It was from these windows that illuminated my path at the end of the hallway of stairs. I walked down the balcony on the Armory and when I reached Professor Travers' office, he was there.

I still remember our conversation vividly. Professor Travers was an older man probably in his mid-60s or early 70's at the time, but for years he had been a middle school teacher and when he spoke of his time teaching adolescents, I could tell that he genuinely missed it. When talking of teaching kids that age and making a difference in their lives, there was a joy about him. Middle School he said is a challenging age for kids, but he said these kids need someone to help them through it, to be a role-model, a mentor to guide them. He also mentioned how these were kids that you could have a deep impact on. They weren't high school students who may seem like they have it all figured out. These were adolescents who were more impressionable, looking for guidance and meaning. We talked for a good hour, and I left his office convinced that I wanted to become a middle school math teacher.

The absolute joy he had about him when talking of teaching middle school made a deep impression on me. There was something noble and honorable about a man who devoted his entire life to making a difference in the lives of young people. I wanted what he had. As it turned out, since I was only a year away from graduating with my Accounting degree, I decided to finish it out, but Professor Travers planted a seed and I wouldn't forget it.

Many students after high school today feel similar to how I felt at their age, feeling not exactly sure what they want to do with the rest of their lives. Should you go to college? Should you learn a trade? Take a year off? Looking back, it seems absurd to expect an 18-year old to know exactly what career they want to pursue at such a young age. As a 7th grade teacher today, I never tell my students that they must go to college to be successful. I do tell them that whether they attend a college or not, they must have a strong work ethic and be able to work well with people. I also remind students, even my honors students, that there are great opportunities that don't require a university education. Many of my students, however, will, and do go on to college. One of the projects that I have students complete during the school year is a college loan project, in which students choose a college and career, find their loan amount, interest, repayment, and monthly payment to the bank. With the incredible rise in college tuition, students see how expensive college education has become, and for the first time see the value starting at a community college, or explore other career options such as trade school.

Still most of my students probably end up attending a four-year university after high school. Although I transferred to a school based on rankings and reputation, in my opinion the college or university you attend makes little difference for a lot of professions. The university you attend does make a difference for some careers such as medicine or law, but for most other areas of study, it is of little significance. Besides a job interview, I can't remember another professional setting that I was asked which college I attended. And to keep your job, you need to demonstrate a good work ethic, dependability, trustworthiness, and the ability to work well with others, which if summarized in a word: character.

When I was considering a teaching career, one of my concerns was money. Money isn't everything, however it still is an important factor in deciding a career. I knew that a job in accounting, especially working for a large public accounting firm, paid good money. A teacher on the other hand would make significantly less than a business career, but a teacher can still make a living. Yes, I won't be able to have a large house, glamorous cars, or frequent luxurious vacations or summer homes, but those things never really meant anything to me anyway. My parents were married at a young age and after renting an apartment for a few years, they bought a townhome as a starter home, but as life continued and children arrived their starter home became their home. My parents never had beautiful cars or elaborate vacations, but their cars ran, and going to Wisconsin Dells and local vacation getaways as a kid was wonderful. My siblings and I were happy growing up in that townhome, and we never felt like we were missing anything. Now as adults we definitely appreciate things just a little more.

Finding my way up that darkened stairwell while following the sunlight at the top led me to Professor Travers. There are moments in life where I feel God is more deliberately speaking to us. That power outage in January of 2001 for me was a sign that I was meant to be a teacher, and at the end climbing those stairs in the dark, there was a reason that Professor Travers was there waiting for me. In the many steps we take in life, I am glad I had the inclination to take those steps and I pray I have the courage to continue on my journey forward.

7

Finding Liberty

Once I received the good news that I was now in remission, I still had a long journey ahead. Dr. Schlenker had ordered me to 6 weeks of bedrest. This was tough, and not just on me; it was tough on my whole family. My Mom made the mistake of giving me a bell to ring if I needed anything. Well that lasted all of two days! I loved the idea and started ringing at my leisure. I would ring the bell for no reason at all, especially when my siblings were around. The bell would ring and my sister or brother would come down the stairs, and then I'd say, "I just wanted to see if it worked!" Well as you could imagine, the novelty wore off quickly and the bell was taken away. My mom, who was a nurse before having children, said that because of that bell, I would be her last patient!

I was on bed rest during October, which is one of my favorite months of the year because of the major league baseball playoffs. To this day, I don't really follow the football season until the World Series is over. I just absolutely love baseball. My parents were very generous and bought a month subscription to the MLB network and I got to follow the playoffs from my bed. I wasn't the reader that I am now, so I did watch too much television. After six weeks, how much of Dr. Phil, Judge Judy, or any daytime TV could one watch? My mom and I would watch some episodes together and we got a kick out of a few of them, but after six weeks I had seen enough, although I do admit that Judge Judy is a guilty pleasure of mine and I'll watch her show if I happen to be home during the summer at 4 PM. She just lets people have it!

When the six weeks of bed rest were over, I had six weeks of physical therapy at Palos Community Hospital three times a week. My right leg had been in a cast up to my knee for those six weeks in bed, and my leg had significantly atrophied. I had to work my way back to walking normally. The skin graft on the bottom of my foot was painful to put pressure on. I can still remember when Dr. Schlenker took out the staples from my graft. It was painful enough that I thought the graft would completely come off my foot. However, week to week, I began to get stronger. My physical therapist was a nice guy just starting out in physical therapy in his late twenties. When I was assigned to him, I think he was happy to have a younger patient as most of his patients he saw were older with different goals. His goal for me was to be able to run without a lot of pain before being released. It took time, but soon enough I was making gains from walking without crutches, walking without pain, and then eventually running.

After I was released, it was time to get a job. I was ready and my mom was ready too. For all this time, it was just my Mom and I at home with my brothers in school, and my sister and Dad at their jobs. My Mom needed a break and a return to normalcy, and I am the type of person that has always liked to stay busy. The three months was essential to my healing, and in some ways, it was nice to relax, but I was anxious to move on to the next chapter in my life. In fact, I had even gone on an interview on crutches. I was turned down for an accounting job that I felt I was very qualified for. I thought that maybe walking into an office on crutches had something to do with it.

It was January 2003, and after September 11th, our economy hadn't quite gotten back together so good jobs were scarce. I really didn't want to work in accounting, and although the desire to teach was still in my heart, I needed money and I wanted to at least use the business degree that I had put so much time and effort into earning. I decided not to pursue an accounting job, so I sent out a dozen or so resumes to insurance companies in the Chicagoland area. I interviewed with The Hartford, CNA, and Liberty Mutual. The job market was tough, and I felt fortunate for the chance to interview with these companies. The Hartford position was in Underwriting and I knew I was going up against candidates with good experience. The CNA job was in sales, and I really wasn't interested in a sales position. Liberty Mutual, a company based in Boston, was looking to expand more in the Midwest and were hiring entry level positions in Workers Compensation. I wanted the underwriting position, but I thought that my best chance was with Liberty Mutual.

After two interviews with Liberty, I was offered a Claims Adjuster position. I remember getting a call on a Friday afternoon in early January and accepting the job. I had friends that were still looking for jobs in their area of study and hadn't found what they were looking for. I was grateful. After telling my mom and my grandma, who happened to be visiting at the time, I went to the to an Adoration Chapel at the local parish and prayed a rosary out of gratitude.

During my time on bedrest and crutches, a lot of my friends came over to visit. They would come over to watch a ballgame or a movie, and when I moved on to crutches, my friends dragged me out of the house for a lunch, a movie, or a bar for a couple of beers. I remember one night my buddies dragged me out to the Chicago neighborhood of Wrigleyville (not my favorite place in the world being a White Sox fan). To say the least it was hard to get around crowded bars on crutches, but to be in company of my good friends was something I missed. While rehabilitating, I didn't have any money to spend and my friends paid for me when we went out so many times. I decided that when I get my first paycheck at my new job, I wanted to do something for my friends who where so gracious to me. So, when that first paycheck came, I took about six of my closest friends out for steak dinners.

The Liberty Mutual corporate office was located in Schaumburg, a Northwest suburb of Chicago. Coming from the south suburbs, my commute was a good hour away. The job was demanding, and I often found myself staying after my shift to complete my work. I'd leave the house at 6:30 A.M. and frequently would not get home until around 7:30 P.M. It's one thing to have those kinds of hours when you are passionate about your job, but making phone calls, sending faxes, reading medical reports, and entering claim logs was taking its toll after a while. Liberty had a Team model with three case managers and a nurse for each team. Groups of four each had an assigned cubicle, and we each had our own corner. I was never comfortable and felt like a little mouse trapped in a maze without an exit. My first boss at Liberty was a good guy named Dustin. He was honest and humble, and I wanted to prove he made a good decision hiring me. I stayed late when needed and took pride in my job.

Only three months after I started, Dustin was promoted to another office and we were getting a new Team Leader. Dustin deserved the promotion. He was a hard worker with integrity, and while I was happy for him, I wish he hadn't left. My next boss was Bruce, and after a couple weeks I quickly realized that it makes a big difference who you work for. Bruce was the opposite of Dustin. He was not confident in himself, and felt he had to hide that fact by exerting an authoritative persona with my team, especially me, being fresh out of college. I just couldn't take him seriously. He always wore a white shirt and tie, but without an undershirt. He often sweat through his shirt, which looked anything but professional.

He talked down to me a couple times and my teammates noticed. Everyone that knows me well, knows that I am laid back and easygoing, but I'm also not a pushover and I have never been afraid to stand up for myself. After having had enough, I went into his office to clear the air and tell him I didn't appreciate how he talked to me. After that, things got better, but I really started dreading going to work every day. My co-worker and team-mate Matt was about ten years older than me. He hated his job and in the few years he'd been there, he hadn't been promoted to a higher level than me and he didn't really care.

I remember when our team was flying out to Lincoln, Nebraska for a meeting with one of our clients, Goodyear Tire. Matt "overslept" and missed the flight. He just wasn't motivated, and I was starting to understand his frustration. I arrived at the airport early, but I saw Bruce at the terminal from a distance keeping a lookout for Matt and me, so I decided to wait at a different terminal so he wouldn't see me. I had about 30 minutes before our plane was boarding, and I'm sorry to admit it, but I kind of enjoyed watching Bruce looking all around in panic for Matt and me. When the plane announced its boarding call, only then did I emerge to Bruce's surprise and relief. I realized that I didn't want to get to the point where Matt had gotten too. I couldn't imagine going to work every day to a job I dreaded. Also, having gone through a health scare of my own, I looked at time so much differently now.

The writing was on the wall. I felt it was time to pursue what my heart was telling me for a few years now and make plans to become a teacher. Even during my time at Liberty, I started volunteering at Midtown Center again as a mentor for inner-city junior high students. Every time I went down there, that desire to teach kept tugging at my soul and I couldn't ignore it anymore. In the Fall of 2003, I applied to Loyola University's Master of Education program and I decided that if I was accepted, I would leave Liberty and begin graduate school.

This was now two years after I had had an epiphany talking with Professor Travers on the day the power went out in Champaign. I thank God for that appointment. During my senior year in college, the State of Illinois announced it would require all students who wanted to sit for the CPA exam to have a minimum of 150 credit hours. My graduating class would be the first class that had to meet this requirement, so The University of Illinois had a seminar about options to meet the 150 hours. They talked about a master's degree in accounting, an MBA, and a one-year certificate of accountancy program. After the seminar I asked one of the Accounting professors if a Master of Education would fulfill the requirement. He paused and looked at me in bewilderment, and then asked, "Well I guess you could, but why would you want to do that?" When I graduated, U of I was the top ranked Accounting school in the country, and I knew if I took a job in Accounting, I would be making some good money. But my heart wasn't in accounting or business for that matter.

I applied to Loyola University Chicago and got accepted to start the 2004 Winter semester, so by December I gave Liberty Mutual my two-week notice. My dad had some concerns. At this time there were still people out of work and here I was leaving a good job to take on more debt in graduate school. My dad made a good point. I knew I was taking a risk, and I also knew that if I never took a leap of faith, I'd live the rest of my life thinking what if? The time was now while I was still young enough to pursue a career in education.

Spending a year at Liberty Mutual taught me a lot, however. It taught me that a career in business wasn't what I was meant to pursue, but more importantly, it gave me a great appreciation for the sacrifices my father had made. My dad spent his entire career in workers compensation, the same field that I toiled in during my year in the corporate world.

My dad had some decent years working in the profession, but mostly I knew he disliked his job. He graduated from Loyola University with a degree in History and secondary education. He wanted to become a teacher himself, but during that time there were no openings, and being newly married he took a job in insurance. My parents then started a family and my Dad was never able to leave his insurance job. He worked at a job he disliked but did so with little complaint all because there was something more important in life – raising a family. I left Liberty with a newfound appreciation for the sacrifices my Dad had made for my siblings and me. Some things are worth the sacrifice.

8

The Backup Plan is the Plan

During my time recovering at home after major surgery, I watched a few movies, but the one movie that I watched over and over again was *Rudy*. I just love that movie. There are some many character lessons in the movie, and I show my students at least clips of *Rudy,* if not the whole movie each year. The lessons include perseverance, hard work, and overcoming adversity. Nowadays when I ask my students if they have ever seen the movie, nearly 90% say they haven't. After seeing the film, nearly all enjoy it and a few will even ask me for other recommendations.

When I was watching that movie on bedrest, I had a sense of regret that although I played high school baseball, I had never put much effort into playing collegiate baseball. While I was a senior in high school, I did have an offer to play Division III baseball at a small college but ended up deciding to attend UIC as a freshman. I felt that I let an opportunity slip away.

During the Spring of 2003, while I was still working at Liberty Mutual, I would grab my glove and a rubber baseball on a Saturday and head to a local school where I would throw the ball against the wall and practice long toss to strengthen my arm.

Ever since I was a little boy, I dreamt of playing in the major leagues. I was no different from kids today who dream of playing in the Major Leagues or the NBA or NFL. I've always told students that it is good to have dreams, even ones like that, but I always emphasized having a backup plan. For instance, I was once told that roughly 5% of high school baseball players make it to A level minor leagues, 5% of those move on to AA, 5% of those move on to AAA, 5% of those make the major leagues, and 5% of those actually are able to stay in the majors. If you do that math, it turns out that the chance of having a major league career is 1 out of about 3 million. By the summer of 2003, with all the throwing I had been doing, I had increased my fastball velocity from the high 60's to touching 80 mph. I knew the Major Leagues weren't in my future, but I went to an MLB try-out at St. Xavier University in Chicago. Maybe there was a bit of wishful thinking, but in my heart of hearts I knew the truth. There were all kinds of scouts from different teams including the White Sox, Cubs, Blue Jays, Dodgers, Orioles, and Angels. All the pitchers that were there had to get into line and we waited our turn to throw in the bullpen. When it was my turn, I got up there and threw as hard as I could. I was accurate, but after only two fastballs the scouts put away their radar guns. Each pitcher met briefly with the head scout after their turn was up and when it was my turn, the scout in the nicest way possible just told me, "Son, you have a slow arm."

Some kids with these lofty dreams are absolutely devasted when that day comes, the day they are told they are not good enough, and what's worse is that some fathers take it much harder. Many players just don't realize how difficult it is to reach that elite level.

When I look back at that day, it wasn't a tragedy for me at all, and I got over that fact that I wasn't a major league player as soon as the scout told me so. Years later I would realize that the only real tragedy would have been if I had not left Liberty Mutual to become a teacher.

When I started graduate school at Loyola, I learned that although they didn't have a Division I baseball team, they did have a club baseball team. The team didn't allow graduate students to play during their spring season, but they did for the few games they played in the Fall. I came out for team in that first spring semester and practiced with them. By the fall I had proven myself enough to play, and I couldn't help but think of watching *Rudy* two years ago wanting to play baseball at the collegiate level. Obviously, Loyola University is not Notre Dame, but playing for them was fun and I wanted to be a part of the team. Our lone tournament was held at Michigan State University in Lansing. The teams included Michigan State, Ferris State, and Central Michigan. I came in out of the bullpen against Central Michigan. Club baseball does have school rankings and CMU was ranked in the top 10 in the country. Even though this was not a big stage, I was nervous. I wanted to pitch well for my team, but my nerves got a hold of me and I even committed a balk. I ended up pitching two innings, and although I allowed one inherited runner to score, I induced two double plays and had a strikeout. We ended up losing the game, but I was happy to have kept my team in the game.

A couple years after graduate school, one of my good friends asked me to join a men's league baseball team. I joined and pitched and played the infield for several years. I played on a team named the Rhinos and I've met some lifelong friends and had a lot of fun playing the game I love.

Most every kid who loves sports will end up dreaming of playing collegiately or professionally. That is a natural emotion and there is nothing wrong with feeling that way. I tell students of my own that I would dream of becoming a big leaguer when I was in middle school, but I also tell kids to have a backup plan. While I've had several athletes that I've coached compete in collegiate sports, and there are a few kids in our junior high over the years that have eventually been drafted into the Majors later in their lives, those are the exceptions and not the rule. The message is to give all you can to fulfill your dream within reason, but also to have a good backup plan, because chances are your backup plan will become your career. Playing sports should be fun, but in the same way the career path you take should also be something that you enjoy. Each of us have to look at the talents that we were given and choose a career that brings out the best in ourselves and in others. If we do that, regardless of the profession, we'll definitely be happy and fulfilled.

9

Jesus Take the Wheel

Early in my teaching career, my friend George and I decided to drive out west as far as Southern Utah and Arizona during my spring break. George and I had drove out west a couple years prior when I was still in graduate school and we were both amazed by the beauty and the majestic mountains and scenery. George has been one of my closest friends in life. He has a great personality and has an infectious genuineness about him. We had a lot of fun on those trips and have often reminisced about our ventures out to National Parks and cities in the American West.

On this trip out West, we traveled to Moab, Utah visiting Arches National Park and Monument Valley in northeast Arizona. After spending a few days out there, we had started heading back to Chicago. We decided to go back home through a more Southern route and part of that included passing through New Mexico. George and I took turns driving and it was my turn as we drove in New Mexico near Albuquerque. George and I are both Christians, as he is a non-denominational Christian and me a Catholic. Of all my friends, I consider George one of the most devout Christians that I know. Well while I was driving in New Mexico, George took out his Bible and began reading it to himself. I made a remark to him that we are driving through some beautiful scenery and here you are with your nose in the Bible. I made fun of him and gave him a hard time. He just ignored me and kept reading.

We were not on an interstate highway, but on a local highway that had two lanes on both the right and left side of the road. Within minutes, a hailstorm unexpectedly passed though in the middle of the desert. The road became slick and I lost complete control of the car. My little Honda Civic started spinning around and around, 360˚ turn after 360˚ turn, and I could do nothing to control the car. The car spun to the left on to oncoming traffic and then back to the right before finally coming to a stop on the shoulder of the right side of the road. Miraculously, my car was untouched. George and I just looked at each other. What had just happened? While my car was spinning back and forth and left and right, there were no cars within roughly 300 yards oncoming on the left, and no cars roughly 200 yards behind me. After the car found it's resting place on the right shoulder, we noticed several cars passing both forwards and backwards. If I had lost control of the car just seconds later, I don't know if either George or I would live to tell about it. All these thoughts had shaken me up a bit, and thankfully George gave me a break from driving.

This whole thing happened only minutes after I was just giving George a hard time about reading his Bible in the car. Was this just a coincidence? While I can't prove it, I have come to believe that God was telling me something. Maybe He was telling me I should be reading the Bible too, that I should put all of my trust in Him.

Only months prior to our trip out West, there was a song released by Carrie Underwood called, *"Jesus, Take The Wheel."* The song was very popular, and I remember thinking of how stupid the lyrics sounded. And here I was, thinking that Jesus may have taken control of my car.

Life is a precious gift and this experience in New Mexico taught me one thing for sure; and that is life can be taken away at any time without warning. When it is my time to pass from this life, I hope that my soul will be ready, and I hope I will have the opportunity to say goodbye to family and loved ones beforehand, but there is no guarantee. Tragic accidents do happen, and life can be gone in seconds. This whole experience showed me that. Every day I wake up is a gift, and I am grateful for every day I have. This was a reminder to me to live a life with the purpose and meaning that God has given me.

10

Finding Bernadette

Less than a year after I visited France, I went back. I was having a difficult year. I had recently gone through a tough breakup with a girlfriend. In addition, I had just switched school districts, and was not happy where I was at. For the first time in my teaching career, I did not look forward to going to work each day. While I did have some great students, I had too many that made it nearly impossible to effectively teach, let alone make any lasting impact.

During the course of the year, I continued to attend Sunday Mass, but truthfully, I was just going through the motions. Maybe all this stemmed from going through a breakup and regretting switching schools, but I started to question my Faith, and even question God's existence. I started asking myself questions. Was God real? Did what I do in life matter? Did my life and anyone's life for that matter have meaning? Was Christianity correct in its premise that God revealed Himself to the world through Christ's death and resurrection? Were the teachings of the Catholic Church correct and trustworthy? These are questions that many of us at some point in life have, even cradle Christians and Catholics, and usually these questions become louder during early adulthood.

I wanted to search for clarity about what I really believed. While I never considered myself an agnostic at all, I had similar questions that many agnostics had, but sadly I think there are some self-proclaimed agnostics that never really make a lasting effort to find answers, to find truth. Many agnostics will only consider intellectual arguments for or against God, however when doing so they completely discount looking for God spiritually. I wanted clarity to my search in finding truth both spiritually and intellectually. I decided to book a trip to France again for my spring break. I knew it was expensive, but I felt something tugging at me telling me I needed to get back there. One of the reasons I wanted to go was to travel back to Lourdes again. The previous year when I was in Lourdes, I experienced a deep sense of peace in my soul that I felt desperate to find again. I was hoping that by being there some of my restless questions would be answered.

I spent 3 nights in Lourdes and again almost upon arrival, I felt much peace just being there. I felt that same sense of gratitude I did on my first visit. Those thoughts of thanksgiving to God and a love for Mary started to overwhelm me.

During one of the apparitions to Bernadette in Lourdes, Our Lady said, "Go and drink from the spring and wash yourself there."[9] Pilgrims to Lourdes have the opportunity to do just that, and they can even bathe in a stone bath filled with spring water. After washing in the spring water, healings have been reported in some cases. On my first day in Lourdes, I did go to the bathhouse like I did the previous year, and I noticed there is a volunteer crew that aids pilgrims both into the bathhouse and also into the spring water. After I left, I suddenly had this realization that I wanted to volunteer with the other volunteers and help pilgrims that desired to wash in the spring water.

The bathhouse is operational for two sessions each day, one in the morning and one in the afternoon. The next day as the volunteer crew was getting ready for their morning shift, I asked the head volunteer what I had to do to be able to become a volunteer. He said in his Italian accent, that the volunteers had to make arrangements even months prior to visiting Lourdes. He said the hospital in Lourdes is in charge of putting together volunteer crews, so if I wanted to have an opportunity to volunteer for a day, I would have to check with them. In Lourdes, there are two hospital buildings for pilgrims that are suffering from illness. Many hospital guests are confined to a wheelchair. These hospitals are also in charge of staffing volunteers including nurses and other volunteer workers, including those who help at the baths. I went to both buildings and asked if I could possibly volunteer that day. The people I spoke to spoke only French, and although I tried to explain the best I could, I was told it wasn't possible. I didn't give up. I really felt that I wanted to, and even had to volunteer. God had allowed my life to continue after cancer, and this was at least one small way that I could express by gratitude. I was determined, and I went back to the first hospital building. I asked if I could speak to the person in charge of the volunteers. Fortunately, the man whom I spoke with was British and spoke English. I explained my situation of how my grandma made a promise that if I was healed from cancer, she would take me to Lourdes, and it would mean the world to me if I could volunteer just one shift. He understood my desire and situation and made an exception for me to volunteer with the other volunteers for that afternoon's shift. He also did something that I didn't expect or ask for. That night for the torchlight procession, he made arrangements for me to lead one decade of the rosary. Each night at the conclusion of the torchlight procession, the rosary is prayed with each decade said in a different language. I would be saying a decade in English outside the basilica in front a few thousand pilgrims.

Volunteering at the bathhouse was an experience I will never forget. Volunteers arrived early and we got our instructions, but before opening the bathhouse, all the volunteers prayed for the pilgrims and disabled who were about to enter. One side of the bathhouse is for men and the other is for women. I was assigned to monitor the line of women outside entering the baths. When a pilgrim had left the baths, a message was relayed to me that I should let the next person in line enter. Once in the room with the stone bath filled with water, the whole process is done with great modesty. Obviously, being a man, I did not enter the women's changing side and the actual rooms with the baths. However, the process is similar in that men and women are wrapped in a towel and then gently lowered by volunteers into the stone baths filled with spring water. After each pilgrim is lowered into the bath water, the extremely cold water is not drained. Amazingly, as long as the baths of Lourdes water have been at the shrine, there are no known cases of someone contracting an illness from the water. There is a certain faith and trust in God that all pilgrims have.

In the crew that I was assigned to, there was a French woman working inside the bathhouse who would relay when it was time to send in another pilgrim into the baths. There was also a Spanish man helping me line up people outside. Together we did not speak each other's languages, which made things interesting, but we managed just fine. Witnessing pilgrims come and go into the baths, you can see faces of desperation. Some parents bring in their children hoping for a cure to a disease, and for many it feels like this is a last resort. It's heartbreaking in some ways, because while in some cases, miraculous cures do happen, the vast majority of times, a miracle is not granted. I do remember one little girl that was in my line. She was maybe 7 or 8 years old and her sister was pushing her in a wheelchair. She was obviously suffering from palsy, but she had this big infectious smile on her face. Her family was English, and when she arrived by me, her sister told me that her little sister wanted to give me a hug and kiss. I happily obliged. I am not sure what happened with that sweet little girl. Most likely she was not cured, but I can imagine that she left smiling. In seeing all these pilgrims, many of them with desperate cases, I couldn't help but feel even more grateful for my own life. After my surgery and testing, the only minor aliment from my illness that I live with is that after being on my feet for a long period of time, my foot will be callused and sometimes painful to stand on. This is absolutely nothing, and the little pain I get here and there is actually a grateful reminder that things could have been much worse. There will always be someone who has things worse off than you, and that is one message I tell my students every year. Knowing that, we can all be grateful for the blessings we do have in life. There is no need to put focus and energy on things that you don't have, which can only add to your difficulties.

I left Lourdes and spent the last few nights of my spring vacation in Paris. I was able to do some sightseeing in Paris and I enjoyed it, but that was not my sole purpose. While I was in Lourdes the year before, I read much about Bernadette. I learned there was more to her story than what happened in Lourdes. Later in life, Bernadette became a nun as a member of the Sisters of Charity located in Nevers, France.[10] St. Bernadette is known by Catholics for the apparitions of the Virgin Mary in Lourdes, but many are unaware of her Christian humility. During her time in Nevers as a nun, there was one sister she lived with that despised her and felt that Bernadette had made up all of the 18 times that Mary appeared to her for her own personal gain. During her time at the convent in Nevers, Bernadette, who already suffered from poor health, contracted tuberculosis, which would eventually take her life in 1879. While unknowingly suffering from tuberculosis, Bernadette continued to complete her daily chores and duties without complaint. Eventually, the same nun who felt that Bernadette was a spectacle would beg for Bernadette's forgiveness, which Bernadette freely gave her.

There are also stories of Bernadette that showed God's desire to work miracles through her. One such story goes that a woman brought her crippled small boy who was unable to walk to the convent. The woman felt that if Bernadette would just touch her son, the boy would be healed. The Mother Superior called for Bernadette, now Sister Marie-Bernard at that time, and asked her to take the child to the garden while she and the boy's mother talk. Bernadette, unaware of the child's disability, took the child to the garden, but after finding the boy too heavy to carry, she set the boy down and the boy happily ran to his mother.[11]

The miraculous stories of St. Bernadette fascinated me, but what I was most curious about was the fact that St. Bernadette's body had never decomposed, and you could even see her lying in state in a glass coffin at the same convent in Nevers. This was the biggest reason I traveled to France. I had seen pictures of her incorrupt body, but I had to see her with my own eyes.

I took a 2-hour train ride from Paris to Nevers, which is in Central France. There in the convent's chapel lies Bernadette's incorrupt body. When I arrived, I had the entire chapel to myself. I was able to kneel right beside her coffin. I was in awe. She was 35 when she died, but seeing her right in front of me, I thought she looked even younger. How could this be? Right then and there I was forced to reconcile the fact that science had no explanation for her incorrupt body. Any doubts I had about God vanished. I knew in my heart, and with my eyes, that God was real. As I prayed silently in the chapel, I realized the truth in Christianity, and I vowed that I would remain Catholic until the day I died.

Years later, I learned more about the details of how Bernadette's incorrupt body was discovered and studied. Her incorrupt body was discovered during the process of her beautification, which is the final step before canonization. One of the rites that the Catholic Church does for sainthood candidates is exhume their body and any mortal remains that are found are placed in a church for veneration. Bernadette's body was exhumed nearly 50 years after her death. Since she was buried in a cemetery that was known to be very damp (the moisture accelerates the decomposition process), the Church was just hoping that a portion of her skeletal remains could still be salvaged for relics. When her body was exhumed, it was found that her body was completely intact and had not decomposed whatsoever. Much of her clothing had disintegrated and some of the metal that made up her rosary had completely rusted away.[12]

When this happened, the Church had to act with caution. When word got out about Bernadette's body, the Church did not want to be accused with staging a miracle to artificially increase the faith. What they decided to do was to hire an atheist forensic scientist who performed an examination of Bernadette's body in attempt to provide a scientific explanation of why her body had not decayed. When the pathologist made an incision into the abdomen, not only did the body not have any smell of decomposition, but all the internal organs had not decomposed. The pathologist even noted in his report that the liver had fresh blood dripping from it. In his final report, the doctor wrote that he could not find any scientific explanation for the state of Bernadette's body, and furthermore he noted that he could find no evidence that her body had any artificial chemicals that would induce the body's current state. Shortly after submitting his final report, the scientist converted to Catholicism.[13]

Science must be held in high regard. We all rely on scientific laws and advances such as what kinds of food are heathy for our bodies and what medicines will combat disease. But science is really only the means by which God used for creation and human life, and in miracles like that of Bernadette. God shows us from time to time that He has dominion over it, and he can always break the laws of something that He himself has created.

Nowadays, there are many stories of young adults that say they were raised Catholic or Christian, but after some time, they have lost their faith and often may be heard saying something like, "I used to believe that, but now I believe in science." The irony in a statement like this is that believers in God also believe in science, and if there was intellectual honesty on the side of non-believers, they would have to admit that science does not disprove God's existence. For instance, for those who believe that the Big Bang Theory proves that God does not exist, they are denying the same science that proves that it is impossible for something to be created from nothing. I believe that that something had a Creator, God, and that we do not exist out of pure chance without any meaning to our lives. Whether you are a believer or not, either way you are taking a leap of faith, and for me, after seeing Bernadette's body in person, some 130 years after her death, I am on the side that believes that God does indeed exist. For some, believing in science without religion, especially for our young people, has become just that, a religion in itself. Those that only believe in science, have to reconcile with the fact that science does not tell us what is good and evil, what to value in life, and it does not provide any wisdom in finding true meaning, love, and beauty. Living up to the religious demands of faith, as I can attest to as a Catholic, is very difficult. In reality, it is impossible as we are all imperfect, but at the heart of religion we are taught to keep getting up when we fall, to strive for perfection, and to become the best person we can be for ourselves and others. The biggest difference between those who believe in religion and those who believe in science without religion, is that religion makes demands upon its faithful, while science does not. While I am far from perfect, having faith in God has taught me that there is a certain nobility in trying to get up when I fall, in learning from my mistakes, and trying to be a better person every day.

The story of Bernadette's incorrupt body is a reminder for me. One of the things I brought back from France was a postcard with a picture of Bernadette as a young woman. I've kept that postcard on my wall along with a couple of other things: copy of the results of a blood test taken during my last oncology appointment and also a name tag from the day I volunteered at the baths in Lourdes. A few years ago, my brother Kevin, took a picture of that postcard on my wall without me knowing of it. He has an artistic friend that has a talent for painting, and he had that postcard made into a beautiful painting. The irony of the painting is that the artist actually found a wooden frame-like design near a couple of large steel garbage boxes. He painted his canvas of Bernadette on that. Seeing that Bernadette had seen Our Lady on a dumping ground in Lourdes, I don't think it was any coincidence the wooden frame was found outside of a garbage can. Regardless, when I leave for work in the morning and come home at night, I see that painting, my test results, and the volunteer name tag from Lourdes. For me, this is a constant reminder to be grateful not only for my life, but for the restoration of my faith, while also a reminder to live out my faith through service to others.

11

The Grass Is Not Always Greener

While I was at graduate school at Loyola, I immediately felt that I had made the right decision in leaving the corporate world for Education. I enjoyed my classes and my professors. One of my math education professors, Dr. Diane Schiller, hired me for two months to be a 7th grade math permanent substitute teacher at a nearby school through a grant that Chicago Public Schools had with Loyola. I really enjoyed working with the students.

Later as a student teacher, I had a wonderful experience. My cooperating teacher, Sue Burke, was an amazing teacher and person, and I couldn't have had a better teacher to be paired up with. Sue has had a difficult life. She lost her son while he was in his mid-twenties in a car accident. She had a picture of him at her desk and he even looked like me. It is interesting how God put me in her classroom. Sue and I became friends and she and her husband even came to my graduation from Loyola. After all my years now in education, I consider her one of the finest teachers that I have ever worked with and she is a credit to her profession.

When I graduated from Loyola, finding a good teaching job at the time was difficult. I ended up taking a 7th grade math teaching job at school called Summit Hill on the far southwest suburbs of Chicago. I felt very fortunate to have a job as many of my Loyola classmates were having a difficult time securing employment. Summit Hill was a great school and had a wonderful surrounding community. I was happy. I was at a great school, had great students, had made friends with many teachers, and was teaching in a brand new junior high facility. During my third year, I became the school's assistant baseball coach and I really enjoyed coaching the game I loved.

I had always thought that one day I would be married and I wanted to make enough money to raise a family someday. The pay at Summit Hill was competitive, but when a math teaching position opened up at a nearby community, I noticed that the salary was higher and family healthcare was better. When I was thinking of applying for the job, I was dating someone who I felt I could see myself possibly marrying. I applied for the job and went through the interview process. At this time, my relationship had ended, but I was still thinking I would someday be a father and would have to think of these things at some point. Even though I was at a school I absolutely loved, I took the job.

In my mind I was thinking that that my new school district, which was nearby my old district, would be just as good as the school I had left. After about a month or so, I realized that I had made a terrible mistake. The staff I worked with was very welcoming and I respected the teachers I worked with, but the biggest difference was the student behavior.

I have high expectations for my students. Simply put, I expect students to conduct themselves using the golden rule, to treat others as you would like to be treated. During the course of my teaching career, classroom management hasn't been an issue. I've found that middle school aged students especially want to be treated as adults. Twelve, thirteen, and fourteen year-olds hate being treated like little children and I have always respected that. I approached my students the same way as I always had, but it seemed a number of them weren't getting the message. I had to schedule and assign detentions and I occasionally had students stay with me after school. The students were not used to having negative consequences associated with their behavior. The behavior and the climate in the school was getting bad enough where teachers stopped writing detentions and expecting any consequences. They were tired and had gotten to the point where their school day was all about survival instead. I empathized with them. However, I still felt that I had to hold kids accountable, and that if I didn't they would go through life as adults thinking that life was all about them and what they wanted all the time.

There were a few students who would yell and even swear at me. Some even threatened to inflict bodily harm on me. This was all new to me. I didn't blame kids for their behavior. It is not easy raising children, especially these days. There are more temptations, more instant gratification, and more of a self-center view of life. Our modern culture in many ways has seemed to have forgetten the important things in life like strong relationships, family, faith, and a sense of service that elevates our humanity. Without these things, we can't expect to be happy and I've realized that happiness stems from gratitude, but also from self-control and discipline. To make my point of the importance of self-control, all you have to think about is a toddler unhappy and crying because they don't want to share, don't want to eat their vegetables, or just don't get their way. To have that lack of discipline as an adult is frightening.

Now maybe this group of students I had were just a rough and tumble group at the school and things would get better. I thought long and hard about this, but this did not seem to be the case. After these experiences, I had a great sense of appreciation for those teachers who teach in difficult districts. I've seen the movies based on true stories where heroic teachers make incredible differences. I'm not saying I was at a school that could not rebound with the right leadership and culture. Every school with the right leadership can be saved in my opinion. However, the year had taken a lot out of me physically, mentally, emotionally, and spiritually. I knew that if I stayed much longer, my love and desire to teach would be gone.

When I saw the writing on the wall, I went to visit my old principal, Beth, late in October. Of all the bosses in all the jobs I have had, Beth was the without doubt the best. She had high expectations, and although she was at times demanding, she has great integrity and leadership skills. She definitely got the best from her staff, and I can say that I'm a better teacher today for having worked for her. When I went to visit her back at Summit Hill, the first thing that I said to her was that I made a mistake and that I should never have left. I told her that if any teaching opportunity ever comes up, I hope that she would consider giving me a chance to interview.

As the school year progressed, I became more and more certain that I would not come back to the current school I was at. I got along well with my current principal and thought she was a very caring person. She wasn't the reason I was leaving. That year in April, all non-tenured teachers in the district were told that due to budget concerns, our jobs couldn't be guaranteed for the following year. After a month however, they came back and told me my teaching contract for next year was ready to be signed. I was honest with them and told them that I had since been looking for another job and that I was not ready to sign at the time. I was told that they would give me another month to consider it, and after another month came and went I still told them I needed more time. Just before the end of the school year, Beth had let me know that a position may be available at Summit Hill next year, but there was nothing posted and no job title was provided yet. I was hopeful, but nothing was certain. I didn't want another teaching job outside of Summit Hill. When I taught at Summit Hill, I felt like I was home being in that school and community.

When the end of the school year came, my current school district asked me one final time to sign a contract for next year. Once again even without another job secured for next year, I didn't sign it and advised them to post my position. I was prepared to do anything, and I was also aware of the fact that if I didn't end up at Summit Hill again, there was a real chance I would leave education.

Shortly after that, Beth called me and invited me to apply for a Math and Technology teaching position for next school year. I was really excited, but I didn't take it for granted that I would get the job. The position would require incorporating computer technology while supplementing current math curriculum. I had maybe a week to prepare some ideas and I put a lot of thought and effort into creating math projects that students would enjoy and also enhance the school's math goals.

I applied for the position and was called for an interview. I was very prepared and had many ideas of how I would implement the unique teaching requirements. A lot of my ideas revolved around using Microsoft Office in real world math projects. I wasn't the only candidate interviewed and had to make the most of the opportunity. I ended up getting the job and was just so grateful to be back, but also I had a greater sense of appreciation for Summit Hill.

The expression "don't burn any bridges," comes to mind. When I left Summit Hill, I left in gratitude for the school district that gave me my first teaching job and was so supportive throughout my time there. If I left my job in a less than professional way, I wouldn't have had a chance to be brought back, and I may have left education all together. I found out later that Beth had created the Math and Technology position for me. The junior high computer teacher had left the school for an administration job, and the only way to get me back in the school was to create a math with technology course since I didn't have the computer certification. You can't put a price on being appreciated at work, and I've never forgot what Beth did for me.

I realized that I had been chasing a job with a slightly higher salary and benefits, and I forgot just what I was leaving behind. Many people in this world are constantly searching for something better. Maybe it's a better job, a better girlfriend/boyfriend, a better house or car, a better life in some way. One of my favorite quotes I have read to students over the years is, "now and then it's good to pause in our pursuit of happiness, and just be happy," by Guillaume Apollinaire. It's human nature to desire more, to want something better for you and your loved ones. Even wealthy, famous, and powerful people with great success are never completely satisfied, in fact we read stories of them going in and out of drug rehab or battling depression. But in this very fact is proof of God's existence, in that we as human beings are not meant to stay on Earth permanently. The human heart yearns for perfection and complete satisfaction, and only through a perfect God with *perfect love* can we ultimately realize this.

I have heard that you will never see a U-Haul truck behind a hearse, meaning obviously we can't take anything with us when we die. When we do go to funerals of those who have lived well, we don't hear about certain elaborate possessions that they accumulated, but we do hear how that person treated others and how they gave of themselves. Our real never fading treasure is certainly not in a temporary Earth, but in Heaven with God for eternity.

12

Roots

Walter Payton once said that "if you forget your roots, you've lost sight of everything." For someone like Walter Payton, the Chicago Bear's greatest player who had the city by his fingertips, a statement like that is a testament to his character and humility. All throughout Payton's playing career and life after retirement, he was always known as someone genuine and giving of himself, especially to those "regular" people. It was this demeanor that warrants the nickname "Sweetness." How many times do we see people in the public eye gain notoriety, fame, or wealth and it quickly goes to their head. They forget where they came from and sometimes treat those around them like second-class citizens.

I am just a regular guy and no better than anyone else around me, but I still have never forgotten the roots of my family background. On both sides of my family, my heritage stems from humble Irish family farms. On my dad's side, my great grandmother Jane McGee was born in Larne, County Antrim in Northern Ireland. On a sunny day she could see Scotland from the farm, but seeking an opportunity at a better life, she, at only 17 years of age, worked up enough courage to sail for America in 1916. On the morning of her departure, she and her 15 year-old sister Elizabeth, who accompanied her across the Atlantic, agreed that if the ship was delayed for any reason, they would take it as a sign that they should remain in Ireland. The ship was on-time. My great-grandma and her sister were sponsored in the U.S. by the family of a neighbor in Larne and ended up staying in Jamestown, North Dakota. Only a year and a half later tragedy would strike and Jane's sister would die during the Spanish flu epidemic. Somehow my great grandmother survived and persevered and she later married and settled in Chicago. Jane would only travel back home to see her family once more in her life. To this day, I cherish my great grandmother and remember her fondly. I didn't realize the depth of her struggles until later, and even after all the hardships she endured in life, in my memories of her, she was always joyful, and happy and elated to be around her great grandchildren.

On my mother's side, my grandma Mary grew up in a two-room Irish cottage house on a farm outside of Kiltimagh, a small town located In County Mayo, Ireland. Like my great grandmother, my grandma had to look outside Ireland for a better life. At age thirteen, she lived with a wealthy family for three years, doing household chores and cleaning. At age 16, she went across the Irish Sea to England, where she studied to become a nurse, and after finishing nursing school, she eventually left for the United States with her two younger sisters and landed in Chicago, home to a number of Irish immigrants. My grandma arrived in the United States already an American citizen as her father, my great grandfather, fought for the United States during World War I, earning American citizenship for him and his future children. My grandma's sisters only lasted maybe a year in the U.S. before becoming homesick, but my grandma, stubborn as ever, was determined to make it in America. And she did. She had a successful career in nursing, married my grandfather, became a mother of four children, and she and my grandfather owned a beautiful house on Chicago's Southside.

Looking back at her life, although my grandma had fond memories of her childhood in Ireland, she had a great appreciation for England after being given a chance to attend nursing school there; but she had an even greater admiration for the opportunity to make a life in America. My grandma was proud to be American. My mom and her siblings were taught growing up that they were not Irish, but American. Even on St. Patrick's Day, when my mom's class was asked by her teacher who in the class was Irish, my mom wouldn't raise her hand. The teacher, who knew my grandmother and her Irish brogue, said, "Well Linda, you're Irish!" My Mom however, replied, "No I'm not. I'm American." My grandma was so grateful to be an American where she was given the chance at the American Dream. She was an independent woman who knew the value of hard work and sacrifice. I still remember her telling me several times, "once you depend on the government for your freedom, you are no longer free." How true. Everything my grandma earned and attained in life depended on herself and her work-ethic. She took nothing for granted and was grateful for every opportunity.

Eventually, I finally got a chance to visit Ireland and see my family roots. I was able to connect with relatives on both sides of my family and I saw the humble beginnings of the farms that both my great grandmother and grandmother grew up on. In my grandma's case, she really grew up in what we'd consider today as great poverty. Her parents and her four siblings all lived in a two-room cottage and growing up they all had responsibilities and chores to do on the farm.

The view of the Irish countryside from my grandmother's home in County Mayo. The photo was taken upon my visit in 2010.

Knowing my family history, especially the plight of my grandmother, has provided me with much perspective and gratitude for all the blessings I have. Today, I live in a modest home in the suburbs of Chicago, but in comparison to my grandmother's upbringing, I live in great luxury. Sometimes it takes seeing how little others had to appreciate all the gifts and blessings we have today. This is certainly the case with me.

While in Ireland, I also spent time touring the country, but I especially took time visiting the surrounding area where my grandmother was from in County Mayo. I visited a couple of my grandma's former neighbors, the Kelly's (no relation to my grandma's maiden name of Kelly). Before I left for Ireland, my grandma made sure to tell me to bring over a bottle of Jameson whiskey to Pack Kelly, who still lived on the same farmland. Before my visit was over Pack gave me what he called a "drop" of whiskey when it turned out to be a small glass filled to the top, equivalent to probably four shots. I was overwhelmed to say the least, but not wanting to be rude I obliged and joined him for a drink. Another neighboring family of my grandma's were the Ryan's. Their family owns a pub in town named Ryan's Pub. I met Tim Ryan at the pub one night where he told me stories of growing up with my grandma and her family. I enjoyed my time immensely and learning more and more about my grandma and her siblings. Tim was a seasoned conversationalist and was quite used to telling stories over pints at the pub. I enjoyed the evening with him so much that I lost track of pints. I'm sure Tim felt just fine the next morning, but I had a terrible headache the next day and I quickly realized I was not as seasoned in the conversational arts as I thought I was.

The main street in Kiltimagh, County Mayo, Ireland.
It's a town like many in Ireland and I enjoyed my time in Ryan's Pub,
stilled owned by a family who were neighbors with my grandma.

Only five miles from my grandma's home is the Catholic shrine of
Knock, where Our Lady appeared with St. Joseph and St. John the Evangelist
in 1879 to several local townspeople. I decided to walk the five-mile trek to
Knock from Kiltimagh. It turned out to be a bit dangerous walking along
the very narrow Irish road, and on the return trip, I made sure to take the
bus. I enjoyed visiting Knock and found the shrine to be very peaceful.
While there I thought more of my grandma and I remembered my time I
spent living with her in her Chicago home while attending the University
of Illinois at Chicago for two years. Every night I would see her kneeling
at her bed praying her rosary and I couldn't help but think that Mary's
appearance at Knock had something to do with her devotion to Our Lady
and the rosary. My grandma gave me a great example of prayer, especially
with the rosary, and that still stays with me today. While at Knock, I also
went to confession, and I'm sure I confessed that I had probably had too
much to drink the other night with Tim at Ryan's Pub.

The statue of Mary at the foot of Croagh Patrick.

Another stop I made in County Mayo was the coastal musical village of Westport located near Clew Bay. During the evenings Irish session music plays regularly in many of the pubs. I thoroughly enjoyed it, but I what I really wanted to do was climb Croagh Patrick, a mountain near the coast overlooking the bay. Saint Patrick is said to have fasted on the top of the mountain for 40 days. While on my trip I spoke to many of the Irish throughout the country and they said that for them, climbing Croagh Patrick is something that the Irish people hope to do before they die. While today it is not considered a spiritual journey for everyone, I still thought of it as such. At the foot of the mountain there is a beautiful stature of Our Lady with the inscription, "Come back to my Son." I remember hiking up the mountain taking roughly 3-4 hours, enough time to spend contemplating God in prayer, and as I made the trek, I definitely felt it was a spiritual pilgrimage.

A statue of St. Patrick at the trailhead path
leading to the top of Croagh Patrick

My time in Ireland reinforced my family's humble beginnings and knowing its extent only gave me more reason to be grateful for my own quality of life. I myself grew up in a three-bedroom townhome with my sister and two brothers. Growing up, my siblings and I knew we were not wealthy or as well-to-do as others, but we were happy and knew we were blessed more than others simply because we grew up in a loving home. Little getaways to local vacation spots such as the Wisconsin Dells or Lake Geneva meant the world to us and we were grateful for them. We knew of others in school who were fortunate enough to go on elaborate vacations, but although we'd have loved to have vacations likes those, not all the kids we went to school with were as fortunate to have parents like we had, who raised us with love while passing on their Catholic faith and trust in God.

If you are like me, maybe at some point you have been asked what you would do with your life if you won the lottery? The question's purpose is one that attempts to get you to see that if money wasn't a factor, what are you passionate enough about to devote your life to? How will you pursue happiness instead of dollar signs? What is never asked is that if you won the lottery, would you change how you treat others? I'm sure we'd all answer that question saying that we'd never allow money or fame to change us. But if that were true, why do we see that many times this is not the case with those with great wealth? Unfortunately, there will be people who will treat others differently once they have come into money or success, but the call to love your neighbor as yourself still remains for everyone.

Many of my friends have worked hard and have done very well for themselves. Because of their hard work and sacrifice, they have earned the right to have a nicer home or to take a beautiful vacation. My friendship with them however, hasn't changed one bit in the least because they haven't forgotten their roots and they don't think of themselves as better than anyone else. They still live their life with gratitude and now a greater generosity than before. Money can change us if we are not careful to handle it appropriately, but a test of character is how you act in times of both good and bad fortune.

As someone who believes in God, the roots of each of our lives all have one thing in common: we are all created by God and made in His image and likeness (Genesis 1:26). Knowing this, no matter what our present lot in life, we are all called to come back to our roots and eventually to our true home in Heaven with our Creator. Christ Himself was born into poverty and lived a modest life as a carpenter. If God had desired to, He could have chosen to enter into our humanity in a lot of different ways, but He chose to enter the world in humility and knowing this helps us to keep our own lives in perspective.

13

Unlucky in Love

In my life I have been lucky in so many ways, but when it has come to finding love I have not been so fortunate. Some of the reason for my misfortune is surely due to mistakes that I have made, but I have also had my share of heartache too.

In all my experiences with dating, I have learned lessons in integrity, getting through heartbreak, and finding the value and appreciation in the single life. Dating for young people today is probably more complicated than any other time in history, and hopefully in sharing some of my stories there will be some benefit to current and future generations.

One thing I have learned, no matter how difficult or painful it is to end a relationship, it is important to maintain personal integrity. I especially have been a work in progress when it comes to trying to live up to my Catholic Faith, but I accept all the teachings of the Church and consider myself a practicing Catholic. In many of the relationships I have had, being a practicing Catholic has made it challenging to find someone. While I realize that every relationship will have personality differences, I think sharing the same core values is a prerequisite for a fulfilling and lasting marriage. I could write story after story about women who broke things off with me because I wasn't willing to compromise the teachings of my faith.

I once dated a girl that I really liked in my twenties. She was beautiful, sweet, fun, and we had a lot in common. After about a month or two, she could tell that I took my faith seriously and asked me what I thought about the Catholic teaching on artificial contraception. I gave her an honest answer, and told her that after going through cancer, my faith in God and the teachings of the Catholic Church were something that I had to have complete trust in. That date turned out to be our last. This is a difficult teaching to accept for many people, Catholics included, but I had to be true to myself even if it meant losing someone I really cared about. Looking back, although I was hurt, I was not angry or upset with her. I knew that this was something that nearly all people in my generation had been taught or made to believe in college, and I was not about to go pointing fingers at anyone who didn't share my belief. This was something we disagreed on and we just had to go our separate ways. Unfortunately, today most of the general public is not aware of the harmful effects of artificial contraception such as an increase risk of cervical cancer, breast cancer[14], and blood clots.[15] If people knew the statistics, I think they'd have a different outlook.

Another similar example was probably more difficult for me to accept. In my late twenties, I met someone I really started to fall for. She was very pretty and full of life and we had a fast connection. After about a month or so, she told me that I was moving too slow. At the time I was coming off a tough breakup and wasn't looking to just jump into something quick.

As a few weeks passed, she told me what she had really meant by "taking things too slow." She told me that she couldn't see herself marrying someone without knowing how it is in the bedroom. I initially didn't know what to think. I really liked this girl and had really enjoyed our time together. I wish I could tell you that I broke it off right then and there, but instead I took some time to think it over.

As I write this, I am still a virgin and have made a commitment to God and myself to wait to have sex until marriage. If I never marry, I will, with the grace of God, remain a virgin. It hasn't been easy to say the least, and I am not perfect by any stretch of the imagination, but there is truth, beauty, and even romance in chastity. This is not an easy subject to talk about, but I am not embarrassed for saving myself for marriage, but on the contrary I'm proud of it. We live in a society where modesty and chastity are mocked and belittled and I just don't understand the reason why. I think there is honor, integrity, and dignity in chastity, and I wish more young people gave it more thought.

I called one of my friends, who didn't always share my opinions, but knew me well, respected me, and wanted the best for me. I told him of my dilemma and that I had serious thoughts about giving up my commitment to virginity until marriage. He didn't hesitate in his response and simply said, "She's not the girl for you." In my heart of hearts, I knew that all along, but I just needed to hear that from a friend I could trust to have my best interest. A true friend is not someone who will just tell you to go with the flow or do what feels good or makes you happy, but a true friend is someone who challenges you to be the best person you can be, and unafraid to tell you the truth. A friend like that is priceless.

As I thought of this situation more, my mind and my conscience became clearer. I felt and knew that you cannot just give your soul to anyone and really there is no such thing as casual sex unless you are unconcerned or unaware of God's design for sexuality. I knew that if I had given myself to her in this way, it would have meant giving her my entire self, including body and soul, whereas she felt that sex was simply just a physical act and just standard in all relationships. Once this became clear, I told her that I wanted to wait to have sex but continue to date and see what happens. I wanted to make it clear that I was not looking for someone that was a virgin, but someone that would just be willing to accept me for who I was and what I believed. She ended up considering that for a while, but ultimately, she couldn't accept my conviction and we had no choice but to breakup. I didn't have any hard feelings towards her. We were both looking for happiness, but I just felt she was looking for it in the wrong places, the same places that our society says to look. I respected her for her honesty with me and couldn't help but wonder how many other relationships I've had that ended for similar reasons that I wasn't aware of.

I remember reading a story in Pat Williams' *Coach Wooden: Seven Principles That Shaped His Life and Will Change Yours*. Williams relates a story he heard about a father teaching his son how to shave. After showing his son the necessary steps in shaving his face, he left the bathroom sink saying, "It's a lot easier to shave if you don't mind looking at the face in the mirror."[16] The lesson is a reminder that every day we want to live in a way that has personal integrity and character. If we do so, we won't feel embarrassed or ashamed to look ourselves in the mirror by the life we are living and the decisions we make. With that said however, I want to make it clear that by nature we are all not perfect and we will make mistakes and we will at times hurt others and ourselves. When we do make those mistakes, we must always remember to make amends, sincerely apologize if necessary, to start over, and most importantly, realize the infinite mercy of God to a contrite heart. When I think of my decision to breakup in this instance, I thought of myself having to live up to that idea of looking myself in the mirror. I couldn't wake up every morning knowing that I wasn't being true to myself and more importantly untrue to my faith.

While stories like mine are probably more common when the roles are reversed and men are the ones pushing women for premarital sex, regardless, there is a universal truth in human nature here, especially in the desires of women. We all have a human desire to be loved and to love. Biologically speaking, men are the givers of love, while women are receivers of love. Many women today feel that they must give themselves physically in order to be loved, while many men do not see sex as self-giving, but self-satisfying. When sex is not seen as sacred, self-giving, and without any spiritual or emotional connection, you see what we have today in society.

Many relationships and marriages are broken, and the cycle continues with hardship and heartbreak.

I currently teach religious education for 8th graders at my local Catholic parish. Most kids will end up getting married and one of the things I emphasize to them is the reason a bride wears white and a groom wears black. I tell them that a bride wears white because of her radiant beauty and honor are worth sacrificing for, while a groom wears black to signify death to himself, meaning that he is willing to sacrifice and even die for his bride and his family. Similarly, a husband giving up his life for his bride is like Christ giving up his life for his Church, as the Church has been referred to as the bride of Christ. I think it is safe to say that if more couples looked at relationships in this light, our society would have much stronger marriages and families.

* * *

Like anyone else out there, I have had my heart broken. Of all the heartaches I have went through, it probably hurt me the most when Maggie broke up with me. I met Maggie in a pub in early summer. When I saw her, I just knew that I had to talk to her. I ended up introducing myself and after a while I told her, "I didn't really know what to say to you, but I just wanted to say something." We ended up talking for a while and made plans for a date.

Maggie was everything I wanted in a girl. She was beautiful, yet humble and kind. She had a genuine sweetness about her, and it also didn't hurt that she was Catholic. We started going on frequent dates and I fell for her almost immediately, which doesn't normally happen for me. I didn't care what we did on our dates, I was just happy spending time with her. As the summer was ending, she ended up breaking up with me saying that she just wasn't ready to get into something serious. I was devastated. Even after only a couple months, I knew I loved her. I told her that all I really wanted was for her to be happy and I said that if you ever have a change in heart, to call me whether I'm single or not.

At the time, Maggie was in graduate school and about five years younger than me. Deep down I really felt that she still had real feelings for me. I thought that she was just being honest with me in saying that she was not ready to be serious, and I thought that in a period of time that may change. I decided to give her some space and then after a while I would call her to see how she was doing. After she broke things off, she later ran into one of my friends and she kept asking him how I was and what I've been doing.

I thought that our relationship wasn't over, and that I had to show her that I really loved her, that I missed her, but also that I would meet her where she was at. So after about six weeks I called her. We caught up a bit on the phone but made plans to meet for coffee. When we did go out, it felt great to see her and talk for a while and I knew I still had feelings for her. I still wanted to give her space, and I continued to back off, enough so that she wouldn't take me for granted. For the next couple months, we exchanged a few text messages, and I ran into her a couple times as well. Around Thanksgiving, we made plans to meet again.

I had never told her that I loved her and that I wanted to give this a shot. I decided I would tell her that when I saw her next. This was a big risk, and I knew there was a good chance that she wouldn't feel the same, but I also knew that too much had happened for me not to tell her. I thought that if she really didn't have feelings for me, then why would she meet me for coffee? Why did she ask my friend about me? We made plans to meet for coffee and dessert. While at the table I said, "Maggie, I know that when we met the timing wasn't exactly perfect. I am a few years older, and in my career, while you're still getting through grad school, and not quite ready for a serious relationship. But I want you to know that I love you. I kept trying to tell myself I didn't love you for the longest time, but I do love you

Maggie, I really do. I miss you and if being with you means taking things slow, I'll do that if it means I'm with you."

Maggie started to cry, but eventually she said something like, "I just don't feel the same way." She was trying to tell me more, but I knew it was too painful for her to get it out. I put my hand over hers and said, "I can't remember a time in my life where I've been more happy than the times I've been with you, but I've always been a happy go lucky guy, and if I can't be happy with you, I'll have to find a way to be happy without you." After I said that, her tears started to stop. I felt bad for her because she was really hurt that I was hurt. I can tell you though, I was glad that I told her. I had taken a risk and gave it my best shot and it just didn't work out. I at least had a sense of peace knowing that I gave it everything I had.

I was hurt because the girl that I loved didn't feel the same way. When you think of it though, as much as you might love someone or want to be with someone, you don't want to be with someone that doesn't want to be with you or at least is not sure if they want to be with you.

As much as I was hurt, I never had any feelings of resentment towards Maggie. She is a great person and I honestly wish her well. Nothing in life good comes from anger and resentment. As I told Maggie before, I just wanted her to be happy, and if it wasn't with me, then so be it. I still wanted her happiness. Yes, I was hurt, and it took some time to move on, but I got back on my feet again. Life is a gift and I refuse to waste time moping around and feeling sorry for myself. It's just not a healthy attitude and it won't make me or others around me happy. Life is not always fair and it's never easy, but life is a blessing and it's worth living.

Sometimes I worry about young people who go through a breakup and become depressed or even suicidal. Some get caught up in thinking that this girl or that guy was everything to them and they can't fathom a life without that person. There is much more to life and it's meaning than one person, and as much as things may hurt for a while, all things in life, whether good or bad, will eventually pass. When I myself have been confronted with life's difficulties, I, as a Christian, have often thought of the cross. The trials I have endured are really nothing compared to the suffering and pain that Christ went through, and others in life have endured far worse than a failed relationship. There are thousands upon thousands of people who live every day in chronic illness or physical limitations, with debilitating permanent injuries, or severe burns. When putting things like this in perspective, even the most painful breakups of our youth seem trivial or at least not as bad as we once thought as we get older.

* * *

We've all heard stories about the one that got away, well in this regard I am no different. Mariana was the girl that got away, and in my life, she is my biggest regret.

Maria, my brother John's wife, is from Mexico City. While in college, my brother was teaching a P.E. class at a local catholic grammar school during the same time Maria had left Mexico for Chicago to study English and work as a teacher's aide at the same school. They ended up dating and when Maria went back to Mexico, they found a way to make it work. My brother John, the romantic that he is, would fly back and forth to Mexico when he could to see her. Maria would visit Chicago too, and once she brought with her, Mariana, her best friend. When I met Mariana, I thought she was really pretty and sweet. I later found out that she had a crush on me but was 16 at the time and I was 21, so I didn't think much of it.

Mariana ended up coming to Chicago herself to learn English and she stayed locally with a family. I would see her from time to time, but the the age difference at our ages was too much for me to consider any thought of dating her. As John and Maria continued do date, they got engaged when my brother was 24 and Maria was 18. A year later, the wedding was in Mexico City. While in Mexico, I got to know Mariana better. While I still thought she was beautiful and she was a wonderful person,

I didn't really know how we would make it work from such a distance. I had just begun my teaching career and she was still studying at the university level in Mexico. The following summer Maria's sister got married and my entire family was invited. Mariana was invited too. I was working that summer as a Sports Director at the Midtown Center in Chicago and didn't travel with my family. I arrived a day later, but Mariana agreed to meet me at the airport in Mexico City. From there we took a two-hour bus ride to Cuernavaca, which is located south of Mexico City. It was really nice of Mariana to help me navigate through Mexico and I really enjoyed spending time with her. I got to know her much better that weekend. We enjoyed the wedding together and got to spend more time with her when we returned to Mexico City before I left. I always thought she was beautiful, but now I know that she was one of the sweetest girls I've ever met, not to mention she was very sophisticated and independent. She really had such a big heart. She said she would come to visit Chicago to see my sister-in-law Maria, and spend more time with me.

I really liked Mariana, but I didn't know if my feelings for her were strong enough to start dating with us living in different countries. If we lived closer, I think things would have been different. Over the next couple years, we would e-mail each other here and there and write letters and cards, but we never started dating.

Two years later, Mariana did come to Chicago to visit for a month. I was happy she was coming to visit, and we could spend more time to really get to know each other. Timing is everything. When Mariana came to Chicago, I had already started dating Maggie and things were going really well at the time. Mariana had sacrificed her time to stay in Chicago, but I had a girlfriend that I really cared for during that same time. If she had came a month or two before or a month or two later, things may have been different and I may have fallen in love with Mariana, but that summer was not meant to be.

A couple years later, after it didn't work out with Maggie and I had continued to date other girls without any love in sight, I started to think of that lost opportunity with Mariana. At this time, I was 30 and she was about 25 so the age difference wasn't a factor anymore. The only problem now, Mariana was now in living with her cousins in Spain while in graduate school.

I remember going on dates and coming home thinking, I just miss Mariana. I missed her, and even though she was an ocean away, I wanted to see her. I started e-mailing her again and I told her just how much I missed her. She still had a boyfriend in Mexico at the time, but I thought, hey, she's not married, I needed to give it a shot. I just didn't care about what her circumstances were, I needed to see her. I never fully appreciated how special she was, and I wanted to convince her to give me a shot. By this time, it was fall and I was back teaching. I decided that I would go to Spain on Columbus Day weekend to see her since I had that Monday off and it would give me more time in Europe. I told Mariana that I was going to Madrid that weekend whether she wanted me to come or not. After some time e-mailing back and forth, she finally agreed to see me in Spain. I had booked a flight for Thursday afternoon that would arrive in Madrid Friday morning. It was against our school policy that a teacher take off the day before a long weekend and I didn't want to just call and say I was sick. I wanted to be honest with my Principal on what I was doing and where I would be. I told my Principal Beth at the time what my plan was and she didn't hesitate to approve the day off. I even took a half day Thursday as well.

To some who reads this, I probably sound crazy to spend a lot of money for trip to Spain only for 3 days, but I had to. I knew Mariana at least had some feelings for me. She even confided in Maria that at some point she loved me. I cared deeply about her and I wanted to find out if what I felt was really love and if it was strong enough to somehow make it work with her. I wrote a letter in advance to Mariana before I left. In it, I wrote that I loved her. I wrote that I wasn't a wealthy man, and couldn't give her everything she deserved, but everything I did have was hers. I told her that I wanted to give this a chance.

After I arrived at Madrid's enormous airport, I taxied to my hotel and settled in. As the evening began, I waited for Mariana in the courtyard of the hotel, and when she arrived, she looked even more beautiful than I remembered. Late that evening at dinner I had some cured ham, which was very commonplace for that area in Spain. When Mariana left to take the bus back to her cousins' home, I started to have an allergic reaction to the cured ham. My throat stared to close and I began struggling to breath. Into the early morning, I thought I was going to die. I don't know why I didn't call for an ambulance, but after struggling for a couple hours, my throat started to open, and the difficulty breathing began to subside.

The next day Mariana and I had planned this trip to explore Madrid. When morning arrived, my body was wiped out and I could hardly muster enough energy to make the trip down the stairs from my hotel room to meet Mariana. As much as I wanted to, I was in no shape to leave for Madrid. Mariana and I had breakfast at the hotel and even Mariana could see I was not doing well at all. I ended up going back the hotel room and Mariana graciously stayed with me and took care of me. She was so sweet. I was able to take a nap and in the late afternoon I felt good enough to venture into Madrid with her. We ended up having a wonderful night in the city. We found this beautiful cathedral overlooking the city and were able to attend Mass together.

Fully recovered, we spent Sunday in Toledo, which is a picturesque city not too far from Madrid. Late in the evening we arrived back at the hotel, and it was nearly time for Mariana to leave for the bus. I had the letter I wrote with me. I just wasn't sure if I should give it to her. I knew I loved her, but was I in love? Looking back, I thought I'd just feel some magical spark and that I would have perfect clarity about that she was the one for me. That didn't happened. I realized I loved her, but again I wasn't sure how we could make it work. She would be in Spain for still over a year.

I didn't know when I'd see her next. Regrettably, I didn't give her my letter. I thought that we would just see how things went during the year and then maybe she'd come to Chicago or I'd see her when she returned to Mexico and we could really give a serious relationship a chance.

Just before I left for Spain, I had read a book entitled, *The Wonders of Lourdes*, which included 150 miraculous stories from Lourdes. One of those stories was about King Baudouin of Belgium in 1960. While he was in his late 20s, he went to Lourdes to pray for a wife. A local Bishop in Belgium recommended a Catholic woman within the archdiocese to help find a wife for the young king. She ended up finding a woman in Spain that the King met and fell in love with at first sight.[17] After that they were soon married. I thought that after I had prayed at Lourdes that maybe God was answering my prayer.

About a month after I visited Mariana in Spain, she broke up with her boyfriend in Mexico. For several months we e-mailed each other, and on occasion we would talk on the phone. During that time, she took a break from her job and her schooling to travel and explore Europe. While on her trip she met Tim, who was from Belgium. He fell in love with Mariana immediately. By the time I realized that I did indeed love Mariana very much and wanted to pursue a courtship, it was too late. Now I knew that Tim was the King from Belgium in the story, and Mariana was his Spanish Queen.

When Mariana told me she had met someone, I felt that I had missed my chance. When she finished her schooling in Spain and went back home to Mexico, Tim eventually followed her. They were married soon after.

My biggest regret in life was not pursuing Mariana earlier, before I even went to Spain. God knows I had my chances. By the time I realized that I did love her for everything she is, it was just too late. Tim was deeply in love with her and knew exactly what he wanted when he met her. He loved Mariana enough to move to Mexico, marry her, and make a life there. He risked everything to be with her. Isn't that what love really should be?

To put yourself aside for the sake of the other. I have since got to meet Tim when He and Mariana came to visit Chicago. Believe me it wasn't easy on my heart, but I saw just how much he adored his wife. He's a wonderful guy and they are perfect for each other. It makes me so happy to know that Mariana's husband is a great guy and that they have a wonderful marriage. I'm just happy and at peace that Mariana is happy.

As life goes on, we all will have regrets of some kind, some bigger than others, however, what I've realized is that most of the regrets we will have in life are not really the things we did do, but more likely the things that we didn't do. Knowing this has helped me to live life more deliberately, to have greater faith, and to be more open to taking bigger risks.

* * *

As of this writing, I am single. There are many single people today who look at the single life as burden and some unfortunately are unhappy. As a Catholic, there are three choices for your state in life. Marriage and a family life, religious celibate life, and the single life. Which ever choice you decide, there is a sacrifice.

In marriage, you sacrifice much personal freedom as a spouse, but especially so as a parent. Husbands and wives, fathers and mothers, can't just decide at the drop of a hat to go out with friends or do what you want to do at any given moment. Marriage is covenant between husband, wife, and God and through this there is a lifelong commitment to your spouse and children.

Religious celibate life such as the priesthood is an obvious vow to God to shepherd their flock. Priests give up their personal freedom for the good of each soul. Consider a parish priest getting called in the middle of the night to leave his home and administer late rites to a dying parishioner in a hospital. A priest takes the place of Christ on Earth in providing life-saving sacraments of the Church in Baptism, Reconciliation, and Holy

Communion. Catholics completely rely on the sacrifices made by priests for these beautiful graces. A priest makes the ultimate sacrifice of giving up his desire to marry and giving up much of his personal freedom as well. Many who are not Catholic question how a priest can remain celibate throughout his whole life. Every married man makes a life-long commitment to fidelity, and a husband must say no to every woman except his wife. A priest on the other hand must make the same commitment, only that he has to say no to just one more woman.

The single life has its sacrifices as well. Many that are currently single, may remain single their entire life. The realization that marriage is not something that Gods has blessed you with can indeed be painful to grasp.

In my life myself, I've have never closed the door to marriage. If that is something that may happen in the future for me, then great, but if it is not, then that is okay too. I have always felt that I'd rather be single than marry the wrong woman for the wrong reason. I have dated many girls whom I thought were very attractive, but in the end, we didn't share enough common values. A meaningful relationship needs core values in common in order to thrive. I have also dated girls who I have shared my faith and values, but there just was not a spark. In the end, in my opinion, there needs to be both core values and a spark of attractiveness and chemistry. Whether I ever marry or not, I am still happy and grateful for the life I have.

One of the gifts of the single life is greater personal freedom. Singles have a greater capacity and freedom to volunteer themselves for the good of their Church, community, and other charitable causes. Even though single, I have tried to make the best of my time in improving my relationship with God, but also making time to volunteer to my Church, community, and worthwhile causes. If I were married or a priest, I would not have the necessary freedom to make myself as available to others. I do not look at this a burden, but a great gift.

14

Fatima

During the summer of 2014, I decided to travel to Portugal for a week. I spent a day in Northwest Spain and a couple days in Lisbon and its surrounding area, but the primary reason for my trip was to visit Fatima, a town about 100 miles north of Lisbon. Fatima, like Lourdes, is home to one of the most well-known Marian Apparition sites approved by the Catholic Church. After having been to Lourdes, I began to take my faith more seriously. In addition to reading books for fun such as biographies, sports, and history, I started reading books about Mary and the history of the Catholic faith.

As I learned about Fatima, I became more and more intrigued. My father, who recently has given a few talks on the Apparitions at Fatima has always encouraged my siblings and I to heed the message of Fatima in our own lives. He has become so knowledgeable about Our Lady's appearance at Fatima that he is considered the Fatima expert at his local parish.

I felt that Mary's message at Fatima was important to Catholics, and I felt a strong enough desire to take a little pilgrimage there. With that said, I feel I should try and explain what happened in Fatima in 1917. In a period of six consecutive months from May to October 1917, Our

Lady appeared in Fatima, Portugal to three poor shepherd children named Lucia dos Santos and brother and sister Francisco and Jacinta Marto. The Blessed Mother appeared to the children in a pasture outside the small village of Fatima, where the kids were tending to their families' grazing sheep. Mary appeared to the children six times and in her appearances, the Blessed Mother pleaded for the children to offer sacrifices and prayers for the sins committed against her Immaculate Heart, while she also especially encouraged them to pray the Rosary daily. When the townspeople heard that the three children were witnessing a vision of Mary, crowds began to grow every thirteenth of the month, the dates of Our Lady's scheduled visits. Like Bernadette in Lourdes, no one else but the children could see Our Lady and naturally many became skeptical, which included Lucia's own mother. In one of the apparitions, Mary herself promised to provide a sign on her last visit in October so that her presence and message could be authenticated.

During the Apparition in July, Our Lady gave the children three secrets. In the first secret, Mary gave the children a frightening vision of Hell. After the vision, Our Lady explained to the children that Hell is where poor sinners go. Mary explained that "God wishes to establish in the world devotion to my Immaculate Heart. If what I say to you is done, many souls will be saved and there will be peace."[18] Our Lady asked the children to pray for sinners as many of them go to hell simply because there are not enough people who pray for their conversion.

In the second secret, Mary told the children that "the war is going to end; but if people do not cease offending God, a worse one will break out during the pontificate of Pius XI. When you see a night illuminated by an unknown light, know that this is the great sign given to you by God that He is about to punish the world for its crimes, by means of war, famine, and persecutions of the Church and of the Holy Father."[19] The first war mentioned obviously refers to the current war that was ongoing in 1917, World War I. The second war Mary referred to is considered World War II. Pius XI's papacy took place from 1922 to February of 1939, and some critics of Our Lady's prophecy claim that World War II didn't begin until Germany invaded Poland on September 1st, 1939. However, the fighting began before that as Japan had already invaded Manchuria in 1937 and Russia in 1938. By March of 1938, Germany had already annexed Austria with occupied troops. A great sign was indeed also given to the world before World War II. Father Andrew Apostali, C.F.R. in his book, *Fatima for Today* describes it this way:

> *After mentioning that a worse war would happen if people did not stop offending God, Our Lady said that it would be preceded by an unknown light in the night sky. This sign occurred between January 25 and 26, 1938. It consisted of an extraordinary aurora borealis that illuminated the night skies of Europe and parts of America for almost five hours. Lucia, a nun at the time, regarded it as the God-given sign that the next world war was near.*[20]

In addition to a second world war, the second secret also included more. Mary also requested that Russia be consecrated to her Immaculate Heart and she also asked that the faithful make reparation for sins committed against her Immaculate Heart on the First Saturdays (more on this later). Furthermore, Our Lady warned that if her requests are heeded, Russia will be converted and there will be a period of peace, but if not Russia and will spread the errors of communism throughout the world. In the end, she gave hope stating that the Holy Father will consecrate Russia to her, a period of peace will be granted, and her Immaculate Heart will triumph.

On March 25, 1984, Pope John Paul II, now Saint John Paul the Great, in unison with bishops throughout the world, did in fact carry out the consecration, including Russia. On May 13, 1984, the anniversary of the first apparition in Fatima (May 13, 1917), there was a fluke explosion that destroyed the Soviet Union's main munitions storage depot for its largest fleet. Later, on December 13, 1984, another explosion occurred in Siberia that destroyed the Soviet Union's ammunition base.[21] As we know the Soviet Union was dissolved in 1991, but what you may not know is that since that time Christianity has grown greatly, so much so that since the Soviet Union was dismantled, Russia has opened up 30,000 Russian Orthodox Churches, which has led many to believe that as Our Lady predicted, Russia has been converted or at the very least is much on their way to a Christian renewal.[22]

The third secret, which was also given to the children in July, was another vision. This time the children saw an Angel with a flaming sword that looked as if it would set the world on fire, however the flames died out once they came in contact with the light that radiated from Our Lady. Lucia mentions that the Angel cried out "Penance, Penance, Penance!"[23] The children were then shown a vision of a bishop dressed in White as well as other bishops, priests, and other religious souls. The bishop in white, whom the children identified as the Pope passed through a city in ruins while praying for corpses of souls along the way. He made his way to the top of a mountain and once at the top he kneeled before a cross. While doing so he was seen being shot by a group of soldiers.[24]

After an assassination attempt was made on Pope John Paul II on May 13, 1981, again on the anniversary date of the first apparition of Fatima, he asked to read the third secret of Fatima. After doing so he believed that he was the bishop in white, but he felt that Our Lady of Fatima had intervened that fateful day and spared his life. A year and a half after the assassination attempt, the Pope visited the shooter, a trained assassin named Mehmet Ali Agca, who was now in prison. Agca was perplexed that the Pope was still alive and asked the Holy Father, "I know I was aiming right. I know that the bullet was a killer. So why aren't you dead?"[25] The Holy Father famously would answer believing that "one had pulled the trigger; another guided the bullet."[26] The Pope had kept the bullet that invaded his body. When removed, doctors discovered that it was just millimeters from a major artery near his heart. When the Pope visited Fatima, he gave thanks to Mary's intercession and, miraculously, the same bullet that was dislodged from the Holy Father's body, now fit perfectly in the center of the crown of the statue of Our Lady of Fatima, which is kept in chapel located on the apparition site.

The third secret's vision of a city in ruins filled with the corpses of souls was also sadly prophetic. After research commissioned by Pope John Paul II in 2000, it was discovered that "the 20th century had produced double the number of Christian martyrs than all the previous 19 centuries put together."[27]

During the last apparition, October 13th, 1917, Mary did honor her promise and provided the estimated 70,000 people present with a sign. In this apparition, Our Lady again appeared only visible to the children, but this time she was with St. Joseph and the Infant Jesus. She asked that a church be built at the site where her love, compassion, and protection may be given. She also identified herself as the Lady of the Rosary. Although the thousands of people could not see the presence of the Holy Family, all who were there witnessed what is known today as "the Miracle of the Sun." Leading up to the very moment Mary appeared, it had rained constantly for over a day before and conditions were extremely damp, but once the apparition began, everything including the ground and all who were there became immediately and completely dry. At the end of the apparition, the sun began to spin wildly and started changing colors. Eyewitness accounts stated that they were able to look at the sun constantly without hurting their eyes. Eventually, the sun began to shake and tremble so ferociously that many thought they were going to die, and people started confessing their sins aloud fearing their death. Right as this time did the apparition finally end.[28]

Going back to the second apparition on June 13, 1917, Lucia asked Our Lady if she would take them to Heaven. Mary answered:

Yes, I will take Jacinta and Francisco soon. But you are to stay here some time longer. Jesus wishes to make use of you to make me known and loved. He wants to establish in the world devotion to my Immaculate Heart.[29]

After the last apparition in October, Jacinta and Francisco did die soon after from the influenza pandemic. Francisco passed away in 1919 while Jacinta died shortly after in 1920. Lucia did learn to read and write and later became a nun. She wrote several memoirs at the requests of the Church and Our Lady appeared to her several more times throughout her life. As seen from Mary's words in the third apparition on June 13, Christ Himself desired that the message of Fatima be spread throughout the world and Lucia's writings have provided the Church as well as all those who desire to learn more about Mary's message of penance, prayer, and conversion.

There is one more final thing I want to include about Fatima. On August 6th, 1945, a B-29 bomber dropped the atomic bomb over Hiroshima, Japan. The explosion as we know was deadly. Those that lived within a mile and a half radius of the explosion died instantly. Those in the surrounding area died days later from the effects of the radiation. In the end over 100,000 people died. A Jesuit Catholic Church named after Our Lady's Assumption was only 8 blocks from the blast. The eight Jesuit Missionary priests who lived in the house next to the Church all survived the bombing with no side effects. Over the next thirty years, over 200 scientists examined the eight Jesuit survivors and could not come up with a scientific explanation for why these men had survived without any ill effects whatsoever. Later when Fr. Schiffer, who had survived the bombing, was asked why he and his fellow missionaries survived, he explained, "We believe that we survived because we were living the message of Fatima. We lived and prayed the rosary daily in that house."[30]

The prophetic nature of Our Lady's Apparitions at Fatima is indeed a lot to take in, but once I learned of them, they definitely had my attention.

The main message of Fatima was really not drastically different from that of Lourdes in that Heaven was asking for repentance and a call to seek forgiveness through penance, but also our Mother in Heaven is asking us to pray for the conversion of sinners, especially through small sacrifices and the recitation of the Rosary.

Lucia later became a nun, and in 1925, while in a convent in Pontevedra, Spain, Mary again appeared to Lucia. Our Lady announced that in order to console her Immaculate Heart, she was requesting that souls make the First Saturday devotions to her. The First Saturday devotion specifies that for five first Saturdays of the month, souls should:

1.   Go to Confession within the week of the First Saturday

2.   Receive Holy Communion

3.   Say Fives decades of the Rosary

4.   Meditate for fifteen minutes on the decades of the Rosary.

If the faithful complete the First Saturday devotion, it was revealed to Lucia that she promises to "assist them at the hour of their death and provide all the graces necessary for their salvation of their soul."[31]

* * *

By my 2014 visit to Fatima, I had recently completed a First Saturday devotion. To this day, I have tried my best to keep the First Saturday requirement on each first Saturday of each month. Doing so has provided me with peace while strengthening my faith and trust in God. I now feel that saying the Rosary and meditating on its mysteries has led me to a closer relationship with Christ and a deeper love of Mary. For my life at least, I think that without Mary's guidance towards Christ, I'd really be lost. I wish that more people would give the Rosary a chance as I am confident that if they only prayed it every day for maybe a month, their lives would dramatically change and they would have a sense of peace and trust like never before. If you don't think so, then what does it hurt to try?

When I booked my trip to Portugal, I booked it around a Joe Satriani concert I wanted to see in Vigo, Spain. From Vigo, I took a bus to Porto, Portugal. Porto, a truly beautiful city, had three bus stops in it and as I didn't bring my cell phone with me to Europe (After traveling to different places, I have found that I don't mind getting lost. It makes the adventure more fun!), I had to guess which stop to get off at in Porto in order to get the correct bus to Fatima. As it turned out, I guessed correctly and made the correct transfer! I arrived in Portugal in the middle of the week. It was peaceful and not very crowded, but all the people there were friendly and accommodating. Portugal is known for being very accepting of Americans and I had that feeling not only in Fatima, but in Lisbon too.

At the shrine in Fatima, there is small chapel on the site of Mary's appearance now over a hundred years ago. Like Lourdes there is also a beautiful picturesque basilica within the grounds as well as a museum that chronicles the three prophetic secrets Our Lady gave Lucia, Francisco, and Jacinta. Another aspect of the shrine is that there is a marble pathway leading to the apparition site that is maybe 150 to 200 yards long. Many of the pilgrims that I saw in Fatima, in an act of humility and contrition, made their way along the path on their knees all the way to the Apparition Chapel. One night while I was there, I decided to do the same, and as I prayed my Rosary along the way, my petition to Our Lady was "Mary, don't let me go." I was asking Mary to protect me throughout my life under her mantle, and every day since then I feel as though Mary has protected me from great harm while I have also felt encouragement to get up when I fall and keep moving with her guidance on a path leading to God.

15

The Good Shepherd

Jerry Shepherd was one of the biggest reasons I ended up becoming a teacher. Jerry was my high school English and Religion teacher at my high school, Northridge Prep, an all-boys school in Niles, IL. My high school was run by a Personal Prelature Catholic Institution called Opus Dei, which is Latin for "Work of God." Opus Dei was founded by Saint Josemaria Escriva, who worked to establish an order dedicated to sanctifying your daily work and ordinary duties for God. Although there are many priests in the Prelature, many of the members of Opus Dei are not in fact priests, but single men and women who dedicate their life to evangelization. They are not monks or hermits, but instead give their lives to God through their ordinary work, but also focus much of their free time to apostolate in some capacity.

Jerry Shepherd was one such man. I always imagined those who committed their life to God in such a way to have this aura of holiness around them. Jerry was indeed a holy man. He attended daily mass, had a great love for Our Lady, and was devoted to the rosary, but there was an ordinary realness about him that his students, friends, and colleagues admired. He was completely dedicated to his Catholic faith, but he lived in a humble and genuine way that made you realize that anyone and everyone

could work towards holiness. How real was Jerry? He swore, smoked cig-
arettes, drank beer, and loved pizza and potato chips. He was overweight,
and during every school day it seemed like his dress shirts were constantly
coming untucked, and as the school day wore on, his tie seemed to get
looser and looser. He grew up in Boston and had a heavy New England
accent, and his students would do impression after impression of him, all
trying to do their best Dr. Shepherd imitation. I heard a story once that
really epitomized the person he was. Jerry was once invited to have dinner at one of the homes of a Northridge student. Well on this day, I guess
Jerry didn't have time to eat his lunch during the day, as teachers in their
on-the-go job often must do. When he arrived at the house and sat down,
he pulled out a sandwich from his pocket and ate it leaving some crumbs
on his pants and maybe some on the ground. That was Jerry. He was genuine and authentically himself, and people loved him for it.

During my junior and senior years in high school, Jerry taught
English Literature and Religion. As I mentioned, he did swear from time to
time, and if one my classmates was acting up, Jerry would sometimes lose
his temper with the boy and he wasn't be afraid to use the f-word here and
there. Imagine in a room of twenty-five 17 and 18 years-olds witnessing
their teacher berating a student with a litany of swears and f-bombs. We
loved it, and it was nearly impossible to contain our laughter! Later, if one
of my friends was on the receiving end of a Shepherd scolding, Jerry would
often apologize to him the next day, even if he didn't have to. All of his
students loved him and respected him for that. This is something that, as a
teacher, I have used this approach in my classroom, minus the f-bombs of
course. If I do feel I have gone too far in scolding a student, or even if I feel
that the student may have deserved it, I will apologize soon and talk with
the child about how I still care for them and just want them to give their
best. As I witnessed from Jerry's example, I have found that every time I
do that, students greatly appreciate it, and most of the time students will
admit that they were wrong and apologize. In all honesty, in Jerry's classes,

we really didn't act up much at all. We had so much respect for him that we wanted to give him our very best. We just didn't want to disappoint him.

Jerry was a brilliant man. He completed his undergraduate work at Harvard University and eventually earned a PhD. at Washington University- St. Louis. While at Harvard he was involved in a student actors guild and even performed in several plays alongside Tommy Lee Jones, who was also a student at Harvard at the time. At Washington University, Jerry completed his dissertation on Melville's *Moby Dick*. He had a great passion for literature, and a fondness of Shakespeare especially. Once I was at a wedding of one of my friends, and a fellow Northridge alum and Jerry were also in attendance. At one point during the night, Jerry and his former student were going back and forth for an hour quoting verbatim lines of their favorite Shakespeare plays. Jerry could have done many different things in his life. He could have had a career in theater or become great writer. He definitely could have been an English Professor instead of a high school teacher. He did write and publish several short stories and even some books, but his love in life was being a teacher and working with young adults. He was brilliant, but he never talked down to anyone. In fact, if I hadn't known already, I would not have known his educational pedigree and literary accomplishments. He was completely humble and down to earth.

After high school, I got to know Jerry as a friend. There are several Opus Dei centers throughout the country and one of them was in Urbana, IL on the campus of the University of Illinois. When I was a junior at U of I, Jerry was in town for my 21st birthday. He tagged along with many of my college friends and joined us for a couple of beers at a local pub. Jerry was also a big sports fan, especially baseball and basketball. Being from Boston, he loved his Red Sox and Celtics. Once or twice a month, Jerry would host alumni open gym sessions at Northridge where he would do his best Larry Bird impersonation. After finishing my bachelor's degree, I moved back home to the Chicago area, and I was able to make most of the open gyms that Jerry organized. Jerry was actually a pretty decent player, despite what you might think. After the games however, he and the alum would gather for a beer, potato chips, or pizza. He enjoyed the basketball, the camaraderie, the pizza and beer, but this was Jerry's subtle way of encouraging us in our spiritual life. He would encourage us to go to Mass, to develop a prayer life, and to keep the sacraments.

Later on, as I got older and into my teaching career, Jerry would meet alumni nearly once or twice a month at one of his favorite Irish pubs, Molly Malone's in River Forest, a western suburb of Chicago. Jerry loved conversation, and it seemed whenever you where around him, he treated you like you were the most important person in the world and would give you his undivided attention. It was true that Jerry enjoyed having a couple of beers, but this was not the reason Jerry met his friends at pubs. Jerry, like myself, was an Irish-American, and like any good Irishman, we understand that beer tastes better with friends. It is well known that the Irish love their tea and their pints. When I was visiting relatives in both Ireland and England, I was constantly being invited in for tea or meeting up with cousins in pubs. It wasn't that they all loved tea and beer so much, but that they love being together with family and friends, and what better way to converse with a friend than over a beer or a cup of tea. Interesting enough, Irish beers such as Guinness, do not have a high alcohol content, so the Irish can afford to have maybe a couple extra pints for longer conversations! Another interesting fact I discovered in Ireland was that if I didn't want to have a pint at the moment, I could order a cup of tea, and the bar tender and patrons would not think anything of it. When I'd order a cup of tea among friends at local pubs in the States, I would be sure to receive some odd looks from some bar tenders, while I definitely became the brunt of jokes from my friends.

I would look forward to spending time with Jerry. Sometimes, it would be just Jerry and I, and we'd share Irish jokes, talk sports, faith, and even literature. He would often ask me about girls I was dating and give his best relationship advice. Although Jerry, as a member of Opus Dei, made a commitment to embrace celibacy in his way of following Christ, Jerry always claimed that he was a ladies' man and he had to fight them off back in his heyday. Jerry knew everyone at the local taverns, and would ask waitresses and bartenders alike, how they were doing and what was new in their life. When he retired from teaching at the high school, he took a job as the Director of the Midtown Center for Boys in Chicago. When he took the job, Jerry recruited people he'd met at local pubs and eateries to become volunteer tutors for young students at Midtown. He just had this genuineness about him that you could not help but admire. Once you got to know Jerry, you realized he was a devout Catholic, but he never forced that upon anyone. He spoke of his faith very casually and he listened and respected people of all backgrounds and all faiths. This was a characteristic that I think Jerry always had in him, as I can attest to from my high school years at Northridge. Although the religious component of Northridge was entrusted to the Catholic Prelature of Opus Dei, there were students from all different faiths including Protestants and Muslims as well. For Muslim students who attended Northridge, Jerry himself made his own office available to them daily during their mid-day prayer time. He loved his Catholic faith, but also was accommodating and respectful to others in theirs. Jerry had something in him that people wanted for themselves, even newly met people he'd come across around town and in the pubs. He lived his life in a deliberate way, and everyone he met, regardless of where they were in their own life, respected him and his faith; And for everyone who crossed his path, Jerry saw them as a child of God. Only God knows how many lives he changed and impacted.

Jerry was proud of his students and he cared deeply for them far beyond their high school years. He took the time to e-mail every one of his former students on their birthday to wish them well. He was so loved and admired by his students that he was in attendance in weddings of many alumni. Obviously, with Jerry's educational background and love for the Arts, he took special pride when one of his students excelled in the Arts. David Krump was one of my classmates and baseball teammates at Northridge. David had a brilliant literary mind and Jerry knew this. After his sophomore year, David's family moved out of state and unfortunately had to leave Northridge. After a year away from Northridge, Jerry encouraged David's family to make arrangements for him to finish his high school Senior year back at Northridge under Jerry's guidance. Jerry saw so much potential in David that he had the high school grant him a scholarship, and David ended up living with a relative who still lived in the Chicago area. Jerry's intuition was proven right, and in good part to Jerry's tutelage, David went on to great success. After studying at a small liberal arts college, David earned the Ruth Lilly Poetry Fellowship, which is given to only a couple of the most promising poets in the United States under the age of 30. David was awarded this prestigious award and went on to graduate school at the University of Oxford in England. There was no one more proud of David than Jerry. One of his students had achieved the pinnacle in poetry. As time when on, David continued work in the Arts and even wrote a couple of plays that received some notoriety. When David's plays were shown, Jerry was there beaming with pride.

Jerry was proud of all of his students' accomplishments, but there was another one of his students, Jamie Muller, that gave Jerry great satisfaction and pride. Jamie, a student in Jerry's religion classes, went on to become a Catholic priest in the Archdiocese of Chicago. During Jamie's ordination, Jerry was there, again beaming with pride. In the cases of both Jamie and David, Jerry was particularly proud of these students because they had pursued something in which was dear to his heart, his love the Arts and his Catholic Faith.

As Jerry approached his late fifties, he was diagnosed with bladder cancer. Jerry, ever the comedian, had a great outlook on his treatment and prognosis. I remember him telling me once that one of the nurses assigned to his case spoke to him in a manner similar to how a teacher speaks to a young child. While I had some wonderful nurses when I was going through cancer, there were a few here and there that would talk to me as if I was unaware of how serious the illness was, so having experienced that I could relate to what Jerry was saying. Anyway, there was one nurse in particular that advised him to cut back on his drinking. Jerry drank, but never in dangerous amounts. When he saw the same nurse again for his next doctor's appointment, he told her, "I thought about what you said last week about cutting down on the drinking, and you'd be happy to know that I only had about 7 beers last night." He said the nurse had this utter look of shock on her face, and only then did Jerry tell her he was joking. Jerry would go through chemotherapy, and in time his cancer went in remission and his life went back to normal.

About five or six years later, Jerry would be plagued again, this time with a new cancer. Unfortunately, this cancer was in an inoperable area, and after a while, chemotherapy proved to be ineffective. Jerry would try other treatment options and even flew back and forth to the East coast for trial therapies, but after about a year of this, he was starting to fade. He started to lose weight and lose his hair, but through it all he remained upbeat. Even during this time, Jerry and I still made plans to go out and watch a ball game at a pub. He still wanted to be a good friend to everyone, even while fighting for his life.

I remember about two months before Jerry died, he and I went out to watch a Yankees/Red Sox game on television at a local bar. As we parted that night, he told me that he didn't think he would win the battle this time. By this time, the cancer was dramatically attacking his body. He was becoming more frail and had lost even more weight. I knew it didn't look good, but I just always thought that he'd find a way to beat it like he had before. As he always did with all his friends, he gave me a hug, and said, "Love ya bro." I saw Jerry one last time in his home about three weeks before he passed. By this time he was pretty much confined to a bed. When I was there, he was eating lunch and spilled some soup on himself. When he did this, he blurted out the f-word, and I was a bit relieved knowing that Jerry still had his sense of humor and personality. Uncle Jerry, as his old students called him, passed away on October 2nd, 2016. October 2nd is the anniversary of the founding of the Prelature of Opus Dei of which Jerry devoted his life to. Everyone who knew Jerry found the date of his passing to be of no coincidence at all. It's interesting how many saintly people leave this earth on meaningful dates in the life of the Church, and I felt the timing of his death was a beautiful sign that Jerry was with our Lord in Heaven.

There were thousands of people who attended his wake and funeral. People from all walks of life were there: former students, friends, family, colleagues, and even bar tenders and waitresses from the local pubs came to pay their respects. During Jerry's last days, I wrote down all the Irish jokes we'd told each other over the years and emailed them to him only weeks before he passed. To my surprise, a few of the jokes had been printed out and were posted at his wake for his friends to read. He wanted people to remember his jovial and genuine nature, but also, especially for those who attended his funeral at the beautiful basilica of St. Mary of the Angels in Chicago, his deep faith and love of God.

Jerry was a friend like no other. On the day of his funeral, I took the day off work. We are fortunate in life if we have good role-models to lead us on the right path. I have been blessed to have a few wonderful role-models, but there was no one better than Jerry. He was a role-model that influenced my career path, but also more importantly a friend who impacted my life and my faith in a way that I will never forget. On the day of the funeral, I wrote a John Wooden poem on my classroom whiteboard for my students to see:

> At times when I am feeling low,
>
> I hear from a friend and then
>
> My worries start to go away
>
> And I am on the mend.

> In spite of all that doctors know,
>
> And their studies never end,
>
> The best cure of all when spirits fall
>
> Is a kind note from a friend.
>
> -John Wooden[32]

The wake and funeral were crowded with people, most of them Jerry's friends and former students. You couldn't find a seat at the funeral mass which was held at St. Mary of the Angels in Chicago, a Church that holds roughly 5,000 people. In the days after Jerry died, Northridge Prep High School and the Midtown Center created a website where those who knew Jerry could share their memories. I took some time to think about how his life had impacted mine and so many others, and posted the following:

"One life can make a difference and everyone should try." – John F. Kennedy. A fitting quote for a man like Jerry Shepherd. Jerry made an impact on so many people in this life and I am eternally grateful to have called him my friend. He impacted my life immensely and is one of the biggest reasons I decided to become a teacher.

Whenever you spoke with him, he treated you like you were the most important person in the world, and he did this being one of the most brilliant people I knew, yet probably the most humble.

I know he was a member of Opus Dei, but I once told him he had a Jesuit heart. St. Francis Xavier, speaking of apostolate, said, "I go in at their door, but I am careful to make them come out at mine. I interest myself in what interests them, that I may lead them to interest themselves in the things of God." Jerry had countless people whom he met in pubs and around town that took him up on tutoring kids at Midtown. He changed more lives than we will ever know and is an example of someone who fought the good fight, finished the race, and kept the faith. He was a role-model, a mentor, a local hero, a comedian, a teacher, and a faithful friend I will always remember in my heart.

A Dream, A Speech, and the Results

When friends and loved ones pass away, how often do we think of them? The death of a spouse, a parent, or a sibling, can most definitely leave lasting memories and thoughts throughout a lifetime, but how often do we remember friends or colleagues after they are gone? If we are honest, we'd probably say in most cases a few weeks or a few months. To this day, years after Jerry has passed, I still think of him often. I miss his friendship, but the example he left me in living his faith and living for others around him has provided me with a life to model. In early June of 2017, I still hadn't forgotten Jerry. At the end of each school year, I give my students a parting speech, trying to impart some wisdom while encouraging them to place value on character for their journey ahead. I write about the contents of this speech later in the chapter entitled *Seven Things to Do.*

Every year I have given the speech, it is well-received by students, but this year the impact was like no other. The day of the speech was scheduled for the last day of school. With end of the year locker clean outs and celebrations, the last day of class was the only day I could schedule the character talk. The last days of school are hectic and all that are on the minds of kids is summer vacation, while the last thing they are expecting is listening to a 30-minute speech.

The night before the speech I went to bed like no other night, but I woke in the middle of the night in a panic thinking I had overslept. I quickly realized it was around 3 A.M., plenty of time before school began at nearly 8 o'clock. Realizing it was the day of my speech, I said a little prayer to myself asking, "Lord, when I am in front of the class today, let them see You, and not me." I then added, "Jerry, help me out today."

I drifted back to sleep, and this time I had a dream I will never forget. In the dream I walked into this pub filled to capacity. There wasn't a seat in the house. I saw a man in bright white and there was Jerry right next to him. They were both standing near the bar, while everyone else was sitting. I didn't recognize him and couldn't tell who this person was, but I was drawn to him first and gave him a long emotional hug. Next to him, there was Jerry who I did recognize, and I hugged him as well, but this time my legs had given out from beneath me and I began to cry uncontrollably while Jerry was holding me up. When I woke up, it was time to get ready for work, but the dream was still fresh in my memory like it had actually happened.

That day, I gave my speech like any years past, but I got this impression that it went better than usual, that kids really took the words to heart. They listened intently and several students thanked me over and over again for it. After the day was over, and relief set in that another school year was finished, one of our school counselors stopped by my classroom. She said that whatever I told them in the classroom had really made an impact. Not aware that she even knew that I had given a speech to my classes, she told me that she was busy the entire day with kids coming in and out of her office wanting to talk after they had listened to my little speech. Kids were telling her that they wanted to make a difference in the world, that they wanted to repair friendships and their relationship with their parents, that they wanted to live a better life. I couldn't believe what I was hearing. Like I mentioned, this was the last day of school. Teachers were scheduling movies and classroom reward days, and this was a day that counselors and social workers could relax a bit from all the heavy lifting they had done throughout the year, but here was a counselor telling me that she didn't have a break all day.

I knew that God had answered the short prayer that I made that morning. I also knew that the man in bright white at that divine pub in my dream was Christ. As much as I loved and admired Jerry, there was as reason I was drawn to that bright figure in my dream. I am convinced that God used me as an instrument that day, and I have no doubt that Jerry was with me the too. I've never had another dream about Jerry ever since, but I still to think of him from time to time. The impact he made on my life will last forever. He has helped me be a better teacher, a better man, and like the dream showed me, he has helped me put Christ first.

16

Father and a Friend

I can't imagine going through my Christian faith alone. St Paul reminds us Christians to "encourage one another and to build each other up" (Thessalonians 5:11). Especially in this time in our world, Christians very much need encouragement to press on in faith. I've been very fortunate to have many role-models in my life that have set examples for me while encouraging me in my walk with God. I can think of numerous people that have provided me with wonderful examples of living their faith including my parents, good teachers like Jerry Shepherd, and also family members and friends. There is however, one person who I see on a regular basis that has given me tremendous hope, encouragement, and discernment for God's design for my life.

Father Peter Armenio is a priest like no other. He is an Opus Dei priest and was a part-time chaplain at my high school, Northridge Prep, as well as the chaplain of Northridge's sister school, The Willows Academy. I always liked Fr. Peter in high school. He had this an incredible down to earth demeanor, yet I knew he was on fire for Christ and the Catholic Church. Father Peter is a man beloved by so many. In some ways, he's almost like a rock star in our local community here in the Chicago area. If people know he will be saying Mass or giving a talk , there are bound to be higher attendances for sure. As I write this, I can see him saying that in no way this is true, but I know that it is. When people witness someone living out their faith and God's calling, they can't help but be drawn to their holiness and sincerity. Fr. Peter even served as chaplain of the Chicago Bears for a number of years and still has good friendships with former players and coaches to this day. It is not uncommon for Fr. Peter to get a call from a player or coach asking for help or advice as people from all walks of life recognize his genuine concern for others. Long after high school, I began to take my Catholic faith more serious and I contacted Father Peter. I asked him if he'd be willing to give me spiritual direction, and for many years now, Father Peter has provided me with spiritual guidance in my life.

Every few months, I make an appointment with Father Peter and over the years he has not only become my spiritual director, but also a close friend that I cherish dearly. As a catholic with a spiritual director like Father Peter, I take his advice and guidance like I am hearing it from Christ Himself. Fr. Peter has helped me persevere in my vocation as a teacher. Like many catholic men who try to take their faith serious, I have considered the priesthood and have taken sometime to explore it, but the more and more I discerned it, I realized that my calling in life wasn't to be a priest, but to be a teacher. Father Peter never pressured the priesthood on me, and although he has helped many young men enter the priesthood, he felt that being a teacher and providing kids with a Christian example was what God was asking of me. Knowing that he felt that way gave me the confirmation that I felt in my heart for years. I am very much at peace with my life as a teacher and coach working with young adults.

Fr. Peter is an Italian-American from New York City and he very much appreciates his Italian heritage. For me, being of Irish decent, he has told me that the Italians and Irish are both emotional, but the difference is that the Italians freely let out their emotions regularly while the Irish hold it in, however, when it comes out, it really comes out! Although, I'm not Italian, Father and I both have a love for and devotion to Padre

Pio, a famous Italian priest and one of the most beloved modern saints in the Church, having lived in the 20th century and only having been more recently canonized in 2002. Fr. Peter has a personal connection to Padre Pio. During his childhood in New York, his family was friends with another family whose son was deathly ill, and his Italian Catholic family were all praying for a miracle that he would survive. Father's Peter's own father, who was from Sicily, traveled to Padre Pio's Monastery in San Giovanni Rotundo, Italy in the 1960's to see Padre Pio and ask him to pray for the boy to survive. Padre Pio was well-known for his spiritual gifts such as reading hearts of penitents during Confession, bilocation, healings, and he was also a priest with the stigmata of Christ. Traveling to Italy to see Padre Pio was nothing uncommon to Catholics throughout the world, so going to see Padre Pio in order to ask him to help this boy was nothing out of the ordinary, especially for Italian Catholics. In the end, the boy did not survive, however, the boy's mother and father always felt that God, through the person of Padre Pio, answered their prayers in a different way. Without any doubt, the boy's parents feel that Father Peter's vocation to the priesthood was a direct result of Padre Pio's intercession and ultimately God's will. Father told me that story and he feels the same way as those parents. He self-admittedly was a troubled youth with little regard for religion, and he attributes his calling to the priesthood to Padre Pio. Whenever I hear of or read about one of the countless miraculous stories about Padre Pio, I always remember to tell Father about it when I see him, and over the years we have shared many amazing stories of our beloved saint.

Another common bond we have is that we are both cancer survivors. As I've mentioned earlier, going through cancer has given me a greater appreciation for life and a realization that time is a precious blessing. I haven't met a cancer survivor who was unhappy in life, and it is no surprise that Fr. Peter also views life as a gift, and his gratitude for life only increased after surviving a serious illness. Two of my closest mentors in my own life have been Jerry Shepherd and Father Peter, and maybe it's not a coincidence that they too have gone through cancer. Positive attitudes and hope are qualities that are in great need today, and to know Father Peter, one is surely drawn to the hope he brings to the lives of others.

Father is an incredibly busy guy. He is a priest and has many obligations and commitments to his flock but also to the Prelature of Opus Dei. He often travels for engagements throughout the country. When he is in town, he has many priestly duties and countless other people whom he provides spiritual direction to as well. Over the years, I've come to appreciate just how busy he is, and like any of us, he gets tired and needs a break, although he rarely admits it. Being a priest will not make him immune from becoming tired, and realizing this, I started bringing a couple of beers with me for us to enjoy during our time in spiritual direction. Becoming closer friends over the years, Fr. Peter and I now schedule my spiritual direction meetings for his last time slot of the evening, so he and I can chat a little more and enjoy a beer together. There are times when I have brought four beers just in case he wanted to have a second one. I've told Father that Padre Pio would enjoy a beer in the courtyard at San Giovanni Rotundo nearly every day, and that on special occasions he would even have two! Father Peter however is a very disciplined man and only once did he have a beer and a half, which naturally occurred on Padre Pio's feast day. Everyone, clergy or not, deserve and need a chance to relax and enjoy the camaraderie in sharing a beer or a cup of coffee over a conversation with a friend. It makes me happy to know that he thinks enough of our friendship to share a pint together. In 2013, when the Catholic College of Cardinals went to the Vatican to discern who would be chosen as the next pope to succeed Pope Benedict XVI, I joked that if I had a vote, I'd vote for him. Many people aren't aware of this, but when discerning who will become the next pope, the future pope doesn't have to be a Cardinal as most people assume. The only requirement is that he be a priest, so when I joked about Fr. Peter being voted the next Pontiff, he said that even if he were Pope, he'd still make time to have a beer with me. By the way, Fr. Peter would be an awesome pope!

I find it funny how many people, Catholics included, consider priests so different from everyone else. I've known some great priests over the years, and they are all regular people, imperfect like you and me, working to make improvements in their own lives to become better people. All the priests I know have a sincere humility about them, which helps them to empathize and encourage each of us in our own spiritual struggle. Spiritual direction is meant for a mentor, preferably a priest, to aid and encourage their mentee in their faith. Those who have a priest for a spiritual director are able to receive the grace of Reconciliation, and I have gone to Confession to Fr. Peter several times. Fr. Peter always encourages me to keep the sacraments, go deeper in my prayer life, and to live my Catholic Faith more deliberately with a focus on being a witness to Christ in my daily life. Father has a deep love for Christ and His Mother. His insight on the life of Christ and the Blessed Virgin has helped me into a deeper relationship with our Lord and Our Lady. He constantly reminds me as well as all those that see him for direction that the goal in life is to be a saint. He's right. We are all called to be saints. A saint is someone who makes it to heaven. Some saints are canonized and celebrated in the life of the Church, but most are not. So to get to heaven we must strive to become a saint, and sainthood simply requires that we say yes to God, however difficult that may be at times. Those that know Father Peter will tell you the same thing, that his love of God is contagious and he truly is living his vocation in an inspiring way, and I know that he is living the life of a saint.

It is important to have friends to push us to be better and grow in our faith. While, I have the best of mentors in Fr. Peter, I also have a support group of friends in which we encourage each other in our faith. It could be as simple as asking for prayers or just being able to talk to someone who shares the same love of God. Not all my friends who are in my little circle of faithful people are Catholic, but there is common love of Christ, and having that connection means so much in a world that seems to put less and less importance on having relationship with God. Knowing that I have friends that I can count on and trust to encourage me through life's difficulties and trials makes all the difference, and I encourage christians everywhere to find people whom can be counted on to encourage you in your faith journey. Even if you have only one person that shares your faith in God, it is far better than going it alone.

17

Seven Things to Do

I'm a big fan of John Wooden. Wooden is most well known as the former men's head basketball coach at UCLA. During the end of his coaching career, he had led UCLA to 10 NCAA national championships in a span of 12 years, a feat that I believe will never be repeated. Over the years I have read several books about John Wooden and his coaching philosophy. When we think of basketball coaches today, we often think of a coach yelling and screaming on the sidelines at referees or their own players. Wooden never resorted to such tactics. He didn't have to. He always was able to get the most out of all his players and because they had such respect and love for their coach, his players gave him all they had on the court, but more importantly strove to be good citizens and people in their own lives. Wooden, who grew up on a farm in Indiana, was the opposite of flashy. He obviously had a brilliant mind for basketball, but more so he was admired and loved in that he was incredibly humble and true to himself and his values. He was a man of absolute integrity.

At the end of each school year, I give a character speech to my students. The speech covers a variety of topics from advice for overcoming peer pressure in high school to what is most important in life. One of the main focuses that I make in my character talk with students stems from something I learned when reading about John Wooden. When John Wooden had graduated from elementary school after finishing the 8th grade, his father gave him a little card that read: "Seven Things to Do." Underneath the title was a list of those seven things. They read:

1. *Be true to yourself.*

2. *Help others.*

3. *Make each day your masterpiece.*

4. *Drink deeply from good books, especially the Bible.*

5. *Make friendship a fine art.*

6. *Build a shelter against a rainy day by the life you live.*

7. *Pray for guidance and count and give thanks for your blessings every day.*

When Wooden's father gave him this little card filled with treasure, he simply told his son, "Try to live up to these."[33]

When I first read this, I found all of these lines to be universally true and a wonderful guide to live by. A good part of my character speech for the past ten years has included these Seven Things To Do. In fact, I make little bookmarks with these written on them, have them laminated, and pass them out to my students. Obviously, teaching in a public school, I knew that I could not tell my students to read the Bible or even to pray. So, in a way to get around that, I write for line #4 to "Drink deeply from good books", and for line #7, I write "Ask for guidance" instead of pray (more on this later). After I read and have taken time to ponder Wooden's Seven Things to Do, I realized that all respectable religions, and all of us under natural law, find these lines of wisdom as universal pillars of truth. I really wanted to pass this life wisdom to my students. In the lines below I will do my best to explain how I present them to my students in my annual character talk.

- **Be True to Yourself**. In this life, now more than ever, you will be pressured to do things you know are contrary to yourself, your beliefs, and your faith. In high school and college, you will be pressured with alcohol, drugs, sex, etc. Be tough and stick to what you know is right, even if you are alone. People will respect and admire you for it. And if you do fail, because we are all imperfect and make mistakes, don't forget to apologize and start over again. It is never too late to start over again.

- **Help Others**. In everything we do, are we doing it to help others or ourselves? I try and think of this question often and know I need to work on this every day. One of my favorite quotes by Martin Luther King is "Life's most persistent and urgent question is: What are you doing for others?" Helping others and giving of ourselves gives us real meaning and purpose in life. Again, at the end of our lives, people will forget your individual accomplishments, but they will always remember how you treated them and helped them. If you want to be happy in life, we must help others, so volunteer your time and yourself for good.

- **Make Each Day Your Masterpiece**. Be grateful for your life and every day you have. This is one that hits home with me. As a cancer survivor, there was a time when I didn't know if I'd live another 3 months...but I did, and as bad as things may be on any given day, try and just be happy to be alive and make the most of your days. No one knows when their time on Earth will be over. Every day we have a choice to make the most of our time here. Use your time wisely. Roberto Clemente, a Hall of Fame baseball player, put it well when he said, "If you have an opportunity to make a difference in the world, and you don't do it, you are wasting your time on this Earth." Also, do your friends and loved ones know that you love them? If you haven't told them so, don't wait another day.

- **Drink Deeply from Good Books**. If you really want to grow as a person and reach your full potential, read. Reading is one of life's greatest joys. Don't forget that there are many intelligent people in the world, but intelligence does not always mean they are wise. In choosing books to read, make sure to choose books that will not only grow your mind, but choose books and stories that will inspire you to be a better person and live a better life.

- **Make Friendship a Fine Art**. You can never have enough friends. I am lucky to have friends with different interests, and this has also helped me grow. Also, don't forget to be friends to those that need a friend the most. A true friend will challenge you to be a better person, to be the best version of yourself. They will encourage you when you need it, but also tell you when you are wrong. Remember however if you must give a critique of a friend, for every criticism, there should be at least five compliments. Real friends will also do kind things for you, so if you are always the one to do things for someone and they are not doing things for you, they are not your friend. You are worth more than all the stars in the sky, and definitely more valuable than all the likes on a social media site, so choose friends wisely.

- **Build a Shelter against a Rainy Day by the Life you Live**. You will have bad days, terrible days. Things will happen beyond your control, but don't ever lose heart. Stay cheerful. Keep smiling. Laughter can be the best medicine. Many people today often complain about the things they don't have in life instead of being grateful for the things they do have. I think there is a lot we can learn by the motto of: Stop trying to find ways to be happy, and just be happy, and "The most indispensable part of happiness is gratitude" (Dennis Prager). Additionally, every goal will have setbacks and roadblocks along the way, so when they do happen, don't lose sight of where you are striving to be, and don't forget about maintaining your moral character. Remember when things get difficult, take one day at a time. When things get more difficult, take one hour at a time. And when things get incredibly difficult, take one minute at a time, but keep moving forward.

- **Ask for Guidance, Count and Give Thanks for your Blessings Each Day**. As bad as things may be, there will always be someone who has it worse off. Just think of walking in a hospital and seeing people that are fighting for each breath. Be grateful for the blessings you have. Ask those people who have your best interest at heart for advice when you need it. I do say to my students that if you are someone that prays, I have found much peace and guidance through prayer.

- The junior high I teach at holds a National Junior Honor Society induction ceremony every spring. One year, the students got to pick who they wanted to speak at the ceremony. I was taken back when the kids voted for me to give the speech. They each had filled out a voting paper of sorts and had to explain who they picked and why they chose this person. I got to read the notes that the kids wrote, and I have to say that I got a little emotional reading them. Like every teacher, we sometimes wonder if any of the things we say to kids is ever listened to, and to read these notes, gave me much joy. In my speech, I revolved it around Wooden's Seven Things to Do. There were about 200 kids in attendance and a gym full of family members, which made me a bit nervous, but I was so grateful and happy to do it. Afterwards, many of the parents had told me how much they appreciated what I had said and that they felt it wasn't just for kids, but for the entire audience. It was nice to hear that, and I feel that God was with me when I was at the microphone.

Over the years, I have run into several former students in high school, college, or even out of college. I always enjoy seeing my former students and finding out how they are doing. When I do see students, some of them have actually told me that they still have that little card I gave them years ago. I am sure many of my students won't exactly remember learning slope-intercept form or scientific notation, but they will remember how you treated them, and they will remember if you had any impact on their life. I've tried to make an impact on all my students and knowing that I made a difference in some of their lives helps me realize I believe I chose the right vocation as a teacher, and for that I am eternally grateful.

18

The Parent Lottery

I have been given countless blessings in my life, but one of the greatest gifts I have been given may be my parents. Both my parents provided me with examples of hard work, faith, and compassion for others.

To this day, I do not think I have heard my mom ever say an unkind word about anyone. Ever. I wish I could say that I have followed her example perfectly, but unfortunately, I have not and still have a lot of work to do. She taught me not to judge someone because if we were in that person's shoes, there is no telling how we might react. No matter what was going on in life, my mom always remains positive and hopeful even in the most difficult circumstances. She always finds reasons for hope, and when you think about it, it is impossible to live without hope in your life.

My mom was a nurse by trade, but after giving birth to my oldest sibling, my sister Jenny, she decided to stay at home. While having a parent stay at home today has become more and more difficult for families to achieve, I believe it still has great benefits on children. And while my mom didn't receive a paycheck for raising a family, her job was more demanding than anything found outside the home. My dad earned a middle-class salary, and we were not wealthy by any stretch of the imagination. My family of one sister and two brothers all lived in a three-bedroom townhome. My parents decided that having my mother at home would be the best way to raise children, and for that decision and sacrifice, I am eternally grateful. We were not wealthy, but we really didn't know it because we were happy. My mom raised us well. Cooking meals, taking us out to the library, helping us with schoolwork, taking us to and from little league practice, and pitching whiffle balls to me and my brother were just a few of the things she did for us. For our family, local vacations spots like the Wisconsin Dells or a trip to a theme park were exciting adventures for my siblings and me. My parents gave me a wonderful childhood.

My siblings and I had our fair share of childhood fights and arguments, and I was usually behind them all with my mom, God bless her, trying her best to monitor the chaos. I remember that when I was in real trouble, my Mom would say, "just wait to your dad gets home," and when he did, I would likely be grounded. I wasn't exactly a terror, but I was the child in my family that my parents were probably most concerned about. Growing up, I was selfish and I pathetically wanted my way all the time. I constantly fought my brother, and even my sister. My parents were right to worry, and they probably prayed for me more than my other siblings, and for good reason. With time, I began to grow up and my parents' prayers started to pay off.

Probably the greatest gift both my parents passed on to their children is the gift of faith. Sadly today, many who have grown up going to Church no longer practice their faith. Amazingly, all of my siblings today have kept their faith and attend church on a regular basis. How did that happen? It's hard to answer that, as I know many faithful parents who did everything right, and still their children have left the Church. My parents for one modeled the faith that they believed in by the way they lived. Going to Mass, praying, and keeping the teachings of the Church were something that they took to heart, and their example was evident to us. Another big factor was that my parents sent us to a wonderful Catholic high school. Catholic school, as you may know, is very expensive, and my dad really couldn't afford it, but somehow, he found a way to send us. In doing so, my parents sacrificed having a bigger home, a better car, nicer vacations, and a more comfortable life in general. We attended a Catholic high school run by a Personal Prelature of Opus Dei, and while the school gave students a traditional Catholic education, we also got an excellent academic education that well-prepared us for college.

My dad always had his priorities straight. He lived his life for my mom and his children. In our world today, we are seeing fewer and fewer examples of fathers with that kind of self-giving love. If we had more loving fathers, I don't think it's hard to argue that our society and our families would be better for it. Fathers make such a big difference in the life of a family. My dad worked very hard at a job that he did not especially like because he saw a greater purpose in providing for his family. He was very much present in our family. He was always there for big family events and also more regular ones, like attending my baseball games, even all throughout high school.

I learned even more about the kind of man my dad was when he retired from his 38 years in the Insurance industry. I set up a retirement party for him at a local pub in the south suburbs of Chicago. Many of his coworkers attended and some came in from out of state to celebrate with us. I invited the attendees to feel free to give toasts and little speeches about my dad. The speeches and stories shared about my dad lasted for over an hour. I knew that my dad lived his faith out in his daily life, but it meant a lot to hear story after story about how his coworkers loved and respected him and how he worked hard, always maintained his integrity, and was charitable to all he encountered along the way. There was one story mentioned about how my dad had to fire someone that apparently after repeated warnings was not taking their job seriously. The Assistant Manager at his office who witnessed the whole event, told the story about how my dad was so delicate in handling and explaining the situation to this man about his termination that afterwards the man actually thanked my dad. There is a certain dignity that my father has, and I knew he lived the same way whether at work or at home. A quote from Maya Angelou reminds me of my dad when she said, "You can be kind and true and fair and generous and just, and even merciful, occasionally. But to be that thing time after time, you have to really have courage."[34]

I am blessed to have two wonderful parents, but one of the things I have realized in my teaching career is that not all of my students are as fortunate as I was to grow up with such a stable and loving home. I believe it is a calling to be a teacher. Teaching is not just a paycheck and a way to make a living, but good teachers realize that they must be positive role-models for their students. Teachers nowadays are more than just teachers, and even more than just role-models. Teachers that answer the call now may be required to wear different hats at different times, and in some ways I act very much like a parent. I know that for some of my students, the most important person I could be for them is a father figure or a trusted male role-model in their life. I remember on at least two different occasions during my career, I have had a young middle school boy, while in tears, ask to talk with me after class because their parents were going through a divorce. In both cases the father had been unfaithful to their mother, and their relationship with their father had become distant or even not non-existent. These boys were holding all this pain in for so long. They were trying to be strong for their mom who was hurting, and they, being only adolescents, had reached a breaking point. As my heart sank for them, I just said, "Some day you will get married, and when you do, you are going to be a great dad and a great husband." After I said that, in both cases, the boys were visibly comforted, and I hope I gave them some measure of peace. In circumstances like these, I've always told kids that I would pray for them. Kids appreciate a gesture like this knowing that there is someone out there who cares, and I am very grateful that students think enough of me that they feel they can trust and talk to me about things they may be going through. Coach John Wooden is known for saying that "The best thing a father can do for their children is love their mother." I often quote him in my class and make a note of this particular one. Looking back at my childhood, I was so fortunate to have witnessed just how much my father loved my mother and their love for each other reflected in their love for us children. Not every child has been given this beautiful gift in their life, but even though some kids will undergo their own family trials, they all have the choice to shape their own future family out of self-giving love.

19

Goompa

As I have mentioned before, I have been incredibly fortunate to have great role-models in my life and in my own family. One of those role-models has been my grandfather, and the way my grandfather lived his life provided me with a wonderful example of how to live mine.

For as long as I remember, my grandpa was known as "Goompa." He had watched the movie *Mr. Hobbs Takes a Vacation*, and Jimmy Stewart, who starred in the picture, played a grandfather who was lovingly referred to as "Goompa." When my grandfather, Raymond Hagen, became a grandfather, he had already made up his mind that he wanted to be called "Goompa", and my siblings and I have never known him as anything else.

When he was only seventeen years old growing up on Chicago's southside, he heroically answered our country's call and enlisted in the United States Navy during World War II. His brother Roy had enlisted in the Navy at 18 years-old, and my grandpa wanted to follow in his older brother's footsteps. Needing to be 18 to enlist in the military, my grandpa had to convince his parents to give their signature of approval for him to be eligible for the Navy. When asked why he joined the war effort, he would say the same thing you may have heard from nearly everyone who volunteered, "It was the right thing to do." He definitely had a sense of service and honor and lived his entire life for something bigger than himself.

My grandpa was a Navy signalman on a small tugboat in the Pacific. He once told me that his little tugboat had gotten within range of a German submarine, but the submarine moved past the small American boat, not wanting to waste a torpedo on such a small ship. During the war, he actually met his brother at sea, who was on a much larger ship in the Pacific. In the ever-expansive Pacific Ocean, their ships actually crossed paths and my grandpa even got to visit his older brother on his ship for an hour. What were the odds of that!

There is one story however that has stayed with me throughout my entire life. The story goes that my grandpa's boat docked in Shanghai and the crew had a few days in the city. His crewmen explored the city and when they came across a Shanghai brothel, the entire crew all went in except my grandpa as he waited outside. My grandpa was a man of integrity. He had met my grandma while stationed in Boston, and during the war they had been writing letters for some time. My grandparents would marry shortly after the war and he would not betray her trust, and he expected the same of her. Looking back, one could have made a different decision that day. Who would ever know? But he was wise enough to know that he would know, and God would know, and that was all that mattered. They say that character is what you do when no one is watching. My grandpa had the highest character.

We lost my grandpa just recently. He was just short of 92 years of age. He was married for 68 years and my grandparents knew each other for 73. Marriages like that today are extremely rare, but I had the good fortune to witness one. In my grandpa's lifetime, I never once saw him get upset or say anything bad about anyone. He had a very humble nature, and a quiet confidence in God. Throughout his life he also had a special innocence about him. He would always assume the best in everyone, or at the very least, not pass judgement on someone. In today's world, innocence is not thought of as the something sacred that should be preserved, but too often, many of today's youth have lost a sense of innocence in the current climate we live in. My grandfather maintained and protected his innocence as something to treasure his entire life.

I have never been a very emotional man, but I became very emotional at my grandpa's funeral. I was a pallbearer at the funeral, and while processing out of the church, for the first time in my life, I had no control over my emotions. I sobbed uncontrollably. He had that kind of impact on me. He was a holy man, not because he ever thought he was better than anyone or thought he knew more than anyone, but because he was genuinely good, true to himself, and true to God, and I am forever grateful for his example.

20

Planting Seeds

As I have gotten older in life, I started to begin taking my faith more seriously. I had always gone to Mass on Sundays, but as I reached my 30's, I started going every Saturday morning during the school year. I began to desire more. I started keeping the First Five Saturdays Devotion revealed by Our Lady of Fatima. This included going to Mass on Saturday, making a confession, praying the rosary, and keeping Our Lady company for 15 minutes on the first Saturday of each month for 5 months. After a while, I started reading a couple chapters of the Bible a day, and then, during the summer, with more free time, I started to go to daily Mass.

I started to fall in love with the Catholic Church. I also started going to Confession more often. When asked why I go so frequently, it's definitely not because I am a saint, it's the exact opposite, that I'm a sinner in need of God's grace. As I started to renew my faith, I began to fully realize that I was far from perfect and that I needed to work on making improvements in my life. I was in my early to mid-thirties, and while I wasn't old, I wasn't getting any younger. Naturally with age, we realize the inescapability of death, and start to question what eventually lies ahead for each of us after our earthly lives are over. Eternity is forever, and I wanted to live in a way pleasing to God, and while I, as a Catholic, believe in a loving and merciful God, I also believe in a perfectly just God. While, not wanting to live eternity in Hell is surely not the best reason to love God, it sure does get our attention. I knew that God was asking more of me than just to go through the motions. As a Catholic, we believe in showing our faith in God through works as read in the Book of James, and I felt God was asking me to give more of myself.

After a while, I began to feel a tug on my heart to become a catechist. By this time, I had been a math teacher for about ten years, but I had the realization that teaching kids about their Catholic faith was much more important than students being able to graph slope-intercept form or solve multi-step equations. Yes, I was trying to be a role-model as a public-school teacher, but in being a catechist, I could teach freely about the love of Christ and share my Catholic faith. I could never have that autonomy in a public school. One summer afternoon, I decided to stop by the local parish within my school community. Many of the Catholic families that were part of my school community attended the parish, and I wanted to teach catechism to some of the same kids that I taught math to. I felt if my students had respected me in my math classroom, then they would also respect me in a religious education setting too, and hopefully come to the idea that practicing their religion brings fulfillment to life. When I stopped by the Religious Ed. office and asked the parish's Religious Ed. Director, Sandi, if she needed any catechists (all churches are always looking for catechists), I think she was a little taken back. Most catechists are parents who have kids in the program, but here out of nowhere walks in some guy asking to teach CCD. Directors have to make sure that catechists are in good standing with the Church, and Sandi took this seriously. I explained how I was a teacher in the area, but I felt the desire to teach kids what really mattered most in life, faith in God. I told her that I was trying to take my faith more and more serious, and that I was actually going to confession to the pastor of the church. I thought to myself, the pastor can vouch for me, and then I remembered, he's the same priest who knows all my sins and maybe he'd say no!

I was assigned 8th grade. Confirmation year! It's a lot of pressure to teach a sacramental year, but I was happy that Sandi had confidence in me. It's no secret today that our youth are finding their Christian faith less and less important in their daily lives. Attendance of Catholic Sunday mass has been steadily declining in our country, and this to a great extent includes our youth. In a recent Pew Research study, nearly 80% of Catholics who leave the faith do so by age 23.[35] And sadly, many students in Catholic religious education programs do not have any more contact with the church after Confirmation. I think most people that leave the Church really don't know what they are leaving behind. In a small way, I wanted to help kids realize that the thing that will give them the greatest sense of meaning and purpose in life is found in faith. Undoubtedly, kids will have big questions about life, about their belief in God, about what is important and what is not important. In being a catechist to 8th graders, I could attempt to provide answers and guidance for some of life's biggest questions.

* * *

Most of my students, and likely many Catholic adults, are unaware of some extraordinary events that have occurred in our church's history. I was always fascinated with stories of miracles that defied science or stories of heroic courage and virtue in the lives of many of our Catholic saints. I've always tried to incorporate these kinds of stories into my religious education lessons.

I make it a point to tell students of stories of Eucharistic miracles. In a Pew Research survey in 2019, it was found that just one-third of Catholics actually believe that the bread and wine consecrated at Mass are actually transformed into the body and blood of Christ.[36] One Eucharistic miracle I make sure I tell my students about is the Miracle of Lanciano, Italy. This took place around the year 700 and is considered the church's first known Eucharistic miracle. The miracle took place while a priest, who doubted the real presence of the body and blood of Christ in the bread and wine, was saying Mass in a monastery chapel. During the consecration, the bread miraculously turned into human flesh and the wine into blood right in front of his eyes and that of the attendees of the Mass. To this day the miracle is preserved in the chapel and you can see it 1,300 years later. In 1970, Pope Paul VI ordered experiments to be done on this Eucharistic miracle. The examination revealed that the tissue was determined to be from the human heart wall, with type AB blood (universal donor), and the scientist who performed the analysis found no traces of any agents used for preservation of the flesh.[37]

There have been many Eucharistic miracles that have occurred throughout the Church's history, but a recent one in 1996 which I only just learned about peaked my curiosity. In 1996, in a parish in Buenos Aires, a woman discovered a consecrated host that she found discarded in the back of the church, and she then alerted the pastor of the church. As is standard protocol in a situation like this, the priest placed the host in a dish of water to be dissolved. After about a week, he checked to see the progress of the host, but when he did, he saw that the host had turned into human flesh. The priest contacted the archdiocese and spoke to Bishop Bergoglio, who as we know would later become Pope Francis. Bishop Bergoglio ordered the priest to take pictures of the host and leave it as is.[38]

Three years later when Bishop Bergoglio was made a Cardinal, he ordered that samples from the flesh be taken for study, and they were taken to Dr. Frederick Zugibe, prominent forensic scientist in New York. They sent him the samples not telling him where they had come from, and just asked him to explain what the samples were. The results he found were astounding. Dr. Zugibe reported that the samples were human flesh tissue from the heart wall with a high concentration of white blood cells. Zugibe noted in his report that the white blood cells were embedded deeply in the tissue, which indicated that the body of whom this tissue belonged to had been under significant trauma. To further add to the dismay, Dr. Zugibe remarked that while examining the sample under a microscope, the cells were still alive and moving. He questioned those who sent him the sample and asked how old the sample was. When he was told the sample was three years old, Dr. Zugibe couldn't make sense of the phenomenon and noted that something like this would be impossible as he explained that white blood cells die within minutes, yet these were still alive after three years! Only then was Dr. Zugibe told that the specimen had come from a consecrated host. Zugibe was a devout Catholic and this for him reaffirmed his faith, but as a pathologist, he noted that there is no scientific explanation for what he had discovered.[39]

Amazingly, the story continues. Later, when Cardinal Bergoglio became Pope Francis, he had the results of the tests compared from both studies, the flesh taken from Lanciano in 1970 and the flesh taken from Buenos Aires in 1996. The conclusion was that the samples had come from the same person![40]

In telling my religious education students this, I do so to show them that that piece of bread they receive at Communion truly is the body of Christ. I ask them to be reverent when they enter a Catholic church, because the presence of Christ is truly in the consecrated host in the tabernacle. Every religious education session starts in church, and the entire group of students gather there before heading to class. I make sure my students genuflect while in the presence of the Body of Christ. I'm sure there are many people out there who see Catholics as lunatics who kneel down in front a piece of bread. I can't say I blame them for being skeptical. I mean wouldn't you have to be crazy to believe such a thing? For much of my life, I had real doubts about the real presence of Christ in the bread and wine. I went to Communion every Sunday not really sure what I was actually receiving. Even as I began to grow in my faith, I still had these doubts, but it wasn't until I started researching on my own and reading books about Eucharistic miracles that I finally came to the point where I am today.

Many young adult Catholics today are also largely unaware of heroic lives of many of the saints in the Church. Since St. Bernadette is close to my heart, I do share her story of the miracles of Lourdes and her incorrupt body that can even be seen today. When I show kids pictures of her body currently visible in a glass coffin in Nevers, France, students are stunned to learn that this isn't science fiction.

Besides Bernadette, there are a couple other saints I always remember to tell them about. One saint that I discuss with them is Maximillian Kolbe. When asked whether we'd give our lives for our family, our loved ones, or our friends, most Christians would do so without thinking twice. But how many of us would give our life for a complete stranger? Without question, many of us would at the very least hesitate, and that is the response I get when I first pose the question to my students, but sacrificing his life for a perfect stranger is exactly what St. Maximilian Kolbe did.

In the eighth-grade academic curriclum, students learn about World War II in their Social Studies classes, and are genuinely interested in learning more about a challenging, yet fascinating time in our world. Maximilian Kolbe was a Polish priest during the Nazi occupation of Poland. He ran a Catholic publishing house through a monastery and from there circulated a newsletter entitled *The Knights of Mary Immaculate*. The newsletter encouraged the faithful while it also attacked and exposed the evils of the Nazi regime. He and his fellow friars used their monastery to also house an estimated two to three thousand refugees, mostly Jews, who were seeking safety from Nazi persecution. In February of 1941, Kolbe was arrested and jailed and later sent to the Auschwitz concentration camp. While there, he heard confessions and even said Mass using smuggled bread. In July of 1941, after a prisoner's escape, 10 men were chosen at random to be isolated inside separate quarters and then staved to death. One of the men chosen, Franciszek Gajowniczek, who was married with children, pleaded with the Nazi guards to spare his life. When Maximilian saw this, he persuaded the guards to let him take the man's place. After three weeks, Kolbe and three prisoners were still alive. On the eve of the feast of the Assumption of Mary on August 14th, Maximilian and the remaining three prisoners were killed with injections of carbolic acid.[41] Remarkably, in 1982, when Maximilian was made a saint in the Catholic Church, Franciszek Gajowniczek, the prisoner whom he traded places with, was in attendance.[42]

The other saint whose story I share is of the short life of St. Maria Goretti. Maria is the youngest saint in the Catholic Church, dying in 1902, just shy of 12 years old. Maria's family and another poor family, the Serenelli's, shared rented farmland in Central Italy near Nettuno. Both families shared the land and the workload as tenant farmers struggling to make ends meet. Hardship ensued when Maria's father died suddenly of malaria. Her father had taken care of the farming responsibilities, while Maria's mother tended to the home and took care of their six children. After her father's death, in order to survive, Maria's mother had to take her husband's place working in the fields, while Maria took her mother's place in the home, taking care of her five siblings.

Around this time, twenty-year-old Alessandro Serenelli, Maria's neighbor, started to develop an impure liking to Maria, even threatening to assault her. Without her father to protect her, and with her mother working in the fields, Maria was left vulnerable. One day, while Maria was sewing a shirt in her the home, Alessandro left the fields and pursued Maria in her home and attempted to assault her. Maria fought off his advances, and in frustration Alessandro stabbed her 9 times with a sharp farming instrument. While Maria fell to the floor unconscious, Alessandro locked the door behind him and went to a nearby room. Later when Maria regained consciousness, she began to open the latch of the door in an attempt to cry out for help. Alessandro heard the sound of the door latch and proceeded to stab her again 5 more times.

Eventually, on the verge of death, she was found and taken to the hospital. A parish priest met her in the hospital and asked little Maria if she would offer her suffering for the salvation of sinners, and Maria agreed. In attempt to save her life, doctors performed surgery to stop the internal bleeding and repair the perforations in her body. Because Maria had already lost so much blood, doctors had to perform the surgery without any anesthesia, as they felt her heart was not strong enough to endure it without forcing cardiac arrest. Maria would feel every painful and anguishing movement of that surgery, and she had decided to offer it up to God. Maria would eventually die, but before she did, she said to the priest, "I forgive Alessandro Serenelli, and I want him with me in heaven forever."[43]

I only learned of her story just a few years ago, and when I heard that she forgave her killer, and even wished he join her in heaven, I really couldn't wrap my head around it. It just seemed inconceivable that someone could have that amount of peace and forgiveness in her heart, even towards the man who would cause her death. However, there was a parallel in her last words to the last words of Christ on the cross when he said, "Father, forgive them, for they don't know what they are doing" (Luke 23:34). In Maria's last wish, she was modeling the example that Christ Himself gave.

The story, however, does not end with her death. Alessandro was sentenced to 30 years in prison, and the only reason he was not given life imprisonment was because he was considered a minor at the time. For the first six years of his sentence, Alessandro was an extremely violent prisoner, so violent that during that time, he was kept in isolation from other inmates. One night however, Maria appeared to him in a dream. She appeared to Alessandro in a garden and without speaking, she handed him 14 white flowers, one by one, marking the 14 times that she was stabbed. Maria was giving Alessandro a clear message: I forgive you.[44]

From that time on, Alessandro began a transformation. He asked for a priest and confessed to Maria's murder. While in prison, Alessandro began to read the Bible and even spread his new-found faith to his fellow inmates. He was even released from prison three years early because he had become a completely different person. When he was released, Alessandro eventually went to visit Maria's mother, Assunta, on Christmas Eve, 1932. When he knocked on the door, he asked Assunta if she knew who he was, and she replied that she did. He then asked, "Do you forgive me?" Assunta then said, "God has forgiven you; Maria has forgiven you; how can I not forgive you?"[45] That night the two of them went to Christmas Eve Mass together. After prison, Alessandro went on to live a holy life himself, living in a Franciscan monastery working for the friars in differing compacities including even working with students in a local catholic school. Later, when Maria Goretti was canonized a saint in 1950, both Assunta and Alessandro were present to witness the joyful event.[46]

There are many reasons I choose to tell kids of this story. For one, it's an incredible story about a modern saint, but this moreover is a story of forgiveness. Many today are fearful of going to Confession, and some are so much so that they avoid it for tens of years, sometimes sadly, their entire life. They are afraid or embarrassed to admit their faults and shortcomings. I tell them that if someone like Alessandro can go to Confession with all he had done, we should have nothing to fear. I don't want my students to fear Reconciliation. I want them to embrace it and make frequent Confession a part of their life, as I realize that Confession has provided me with the grace to persevere in faith. I also highlight how Maria and her mother embraced forgiveness. If there ever was anyone who had a right not to forgive, it was Maria and her mother Assunta, yet they did choose to forgive because they followed Christ, and He asks us to forgive as he did. People in life hold life-long grudges for things far less than what happened in this story, but there is a peace given to everyone who chooses to forgive.

* * *

All of our 8th graders in religious education are required to attend a day long retreat at my parish. Towards the end of the retreat, students are given letters of encouragement from family, relatives, teachers, and friends. I also give a letter to my students and to other religious education students whom I had in my math class or students I have coached at my school. The letter is similar to the character talk I give my students in the public school, but this time I am able to share my Catholic faith. The letter I write is seen below:

I want to encourage you to truly live your Faith each day. You may know that I admire Coach John Wooden and his Seven Things to Do. The letter I'm writing to you centers around the Seven Things to Do, but with a Catholic perspective. I will do my best to explain them below...

- ***Be True to Yourself****. In this life, now more than ever, you will be pressured to do things you know are contrary to yourself, your beliefs, and your faith. Be tough and stick to your faith, even if you are alone. People will respect and admire you for it; And if you do fail, because we are all imperfect, don't forget the beauty of Confession, one of the greatest parts of our Faith and humbling realization that we needs God's help to live as He intended.*

- ***Help Others****. In everything we do, are we doing it to help others or ourselves? I try and think of this question often and know I need to work on this every day. This is one of the biggest attractions to the Catholic Church...the Church, more than any other religion has been the most charitable...helping the poor, the sick, the disabled, the old, the lonely, the marginalized, the vulnerable, the unborn, and all of society's unwanted. Mother Teresa and her life is really what Christ meant when he said, "whatever you do for the least of my brethren, you did it to me" (Matthew 25:40). I also like Martin Luther King's quote of "Life's most persistent and urgent question is: What are you doing for others?"*

- ***Make Each Day Your Masterpiece****. Be grateful for your life and every day you have. This is one that hits home with me. As a cancer survivor, there was a time when I didn't know if I'd live another 3 months...but I did, and as bad as things may be on any given day, try and just be happy to be alive and make the most of* your days. Baseball Hall of Famer Roberto Clemente once said, "If you have an opportunity to make a difference in the world, and you don't do it, you are wasting your time on this Earth."

- **Drink Deeply from Good Books, especially the Bible.** *If you really want to grow both spiritually and intellectually and reach your potential, read. Reading is one of life's greatest joys. I have made a list for you of some of my favorite books. I hope you'll enjoy them as much as I have. Don't forget that there are many intelligent people in the world, but intelligence does not always mean they are wise. In reading God's word, we are also given wisdom.*

- **Make Friendship a Fine Art.** *You can never have enough friends. I am lucky to have friends with different interests and this has also helped me grow. Don't forget to be a friend to those that need a friend the most. A true friend will challenge you to be a better person, to be the best version of yourself. They will encourage you when you need it, but also tell you when you are wrong. They will also do kind things for you, so if you are always the one to do things for someone and they are not doing things for you, they are not your friend.*

- **Build a Shelter against a Rainy Day by the Life you Live.** *You will have bad days, terrible days. Things will happen beyond your control, but don't ever lose heart. Stay cheerful. Keep smiling. Laughter can be the best medicine. Don't forget the suffering Christ endured, the pain that Mary had to go through when she witnessed her Son die on the cross. Stay close to Mary and you will always be near Jesus. Many people today often complain about the things they don't have in life instead of being grateful for the things they do have. I think there is a lot we can learn by the motto of: Stop trying to find ways to be happy, and just be happy, and "The most indispensable part of happiness is gratitude" (Dennis Prager).*

- *Pray for Guidance, Count and Give Thanks for your Blessings Each Day. As bad as things may be, there will always be someone who has it worse off. Be grateful for what you have. Keep prayer at the center of your life and you won't lose perspective. If you need advice, pray and ask someone you love and trust for help...don't be afraid to ask God and your parents for help and guidance.*

One more thing. Everyone will have doubts about their faith. I am no different. For about two years during my late 20's, I seriously contemplated leaving the Church. As I have mentioned, I'm a cancer survivor. During my treatment, my Irish grandma prayed and prayed and prayed for my healing. She made a promise to Our Lady of Lourdes that if I was healed, she would take me to Lourdes, France. I was healed through what I believe were the prayers of so many including my grandma. She wasn't able to make the trip, but years later I made the pilgrimage to Lourdes in 2008. The next year, 2009, when I was having my doubts, I remembered Lourdes and St. Bernadette. During my Spring Break, I went back to France to see Bernadette. When she died, her body was exhumed twice, and both times her body remained incorrupt. Her body still remains incorrupt in a glass case above ground in Nevers, France (I was not able to get there during my first visit). That's where I went in 2009. I had to see her for myself and amazingly, she looked like a 25-year-old girl. Science has no explanation for this. Amazingly after Bernadette's body was exhumed, the Vatican hired an atheist doctor to study her body nearly 50 years after her death. When the doctor made an incision into her abdominal cavity, amazingly fresh blood was found in her body. After completing his analysis, the doctor became a Catholic. It's mysteries like this that helped strengthen my faith and I am forever indebted to Our Lady of Lourdes and St. Bernadette.

Another point...in today's world many people will spend their whole life searching for its meaning. In one word, the meaning of life is love. Whatever you do, do it out of love, with love, and for love. Remember that "God is Love"

(1 John 4:8) and if you live for love, you are living for God and putting God first in your life. Always put God first in your life at all times, and remember what Christ said, "What profit would there be for one to gain the whole world and forfeit his life?" (Matthew 16:26).

All my Best,
Mr. Hagen

The last part of the letter includes some book and movie recommendations:

Some Good Books (In no particular order)

Before I Go – Peter Kreeft

Because God is Real – Peter Kreeft

Have a Little Faith – Mitch Albom

This is a Soul – Marilyn Berger

Saint John Paul the Great – Jason Evert

Unbroken – Laura Hillenbrand

Don't Give Up, Don't Give In: Lesson from an Extraordinary Life – Louis Zamperini with David Resin

The Last Lecture – Randy Pausch

A Lifetime of Observation and Reflections On and Off the Court – John Wooden with Steve Jamison

Safe at Home – Bob Muzikowski

Terry Fox – Leslie Scriverner

Running for My Life – Lopez Lomong

Mere Christianity – C.S. Lewis

The Glories of Mary – St. Alphonsus Liguori

Gifted Hands – Dr. Ben Carson

No Turning Back – Fr. Donald Calloway

Eucharistic Miracles – Joan Carroll Cruz

Rome Sweet Home – Scott Hahn

Fatima for Today: An Urgent Marian Message of Hope – Fr. Andrew Apostoli

Gangland to Promised Land – John Pridmore

Reason to Believe – Ron Tesoriero

When God Winks at You: How God Speaks Directly to You through the Power of Coincidence – SQuire Rushnell

Broken Mary – Kevin Matthews

Life Lessons: Fifty Things I've Learned in My First 50 Years – Patrick Madrid

Grateful American – Gary Sinise

A Pope and a President – Paul Kengor

Movies

Bella

The Song of Bernadette

The Scarlet and the Black

The Way

For Greater Glory

October Baby

Cinderella Man

McFarland, USA

Mully

Gifted Hands

Unbroken

Unbroken 2

Hacksaw Ridge

The Case for Christ

Deciding to become a catechist hasn't been easy. Teaching is not a job that I can just leave work after the last bell every day and head home. There is grading, lesson planning, tutoring after school, and endless paperwork. The teaching profession is demanding, and coaching only adds to my responsibilities. It seems every week when I am scheduled to go to the church and teach CCD, I dread it. I'm tired and I would rather just go home and relax a bit. But somehow, God gives me the strength to continue and after nearly every class, I feel better that I was there.

What makes it difficult however, is that I know I am teaching a handful of kids that don't really want to be there. They are there because their parents are making them go, wanting them to get confirmed. It can be daunting and frustrating at times. I can tell some kids have never taken going to CCD serious. I can't say that in my years as a catechist that all my students have a new appreciation for their Catholic faith. Some, no matter what I try to do, seem utterly disinterested. However, there are a number of them that I can see a wonderful transformation in their outlook towards their faith and life in general. I once got a letter from one of my former religious ed students. He told me that he had dreaded going to CCD and basically looked at it as a complete waste in time. He was angry, mischievous in school, and in a dark place. But he wrote that things started to change. After some time, he started to listen and even look forward to coming to religious education class. By the end of the year, he had become a completely different person no longer angry at the world and even told me he looked forward to attending Mass with his family and that he would remain Catholic until the end. I got emotional reading his letter. I knew that his transformation had nothing to do with me. God had decided to open this young man's heart, and God was just using me to do so. I realized that even though some of my students may go through the confirmation class without having been impacted, some of my students do open their hearts and minds, and knowing that God is using me for that keeps me going.

When the Religious Ed. year is over, there really are three major things that I want my students to take away form my class. The first is a love of the Eucharist and commitment to Mass. The second is a commitment to frequent Confession to help us through the storms of life and for perseverance in our attempts to make lasting improvements. Thirdly, is a devotion to Mary, specifically through praying the rosary. If you were to study the lives of the saints, I think you'd find that all of them had these three loves and commitments in their lives, and if we can live by these, the saints could do no better.

21

I'd Rather Tie Shoes

After I had left Summit Hill, I had also left my position as an assistant baseball coach. We had a great team the year I had left and had many talented players coming back for their 8th grade year. The year that I did leave however, the baseball team won the Illinois State Championship. I would joke that all they had to do was to get rid of me! When I came back to Summit Hill, I volunteered with the baseball team as a pitching coach and enjoyed coaching baseball again and working with young players. We had a successful year, and actually had a 3rd place finish at the State Tournament. The head coach of the team, Fred Pufahl, is one of the best coaches that you'll find at any level of competition. During his own coaching tenure, he's had a string of seven consecutive seasons where his baseball teams have made it to the state tournament, and of those years his teams have claimed two state championships. Summit Hill has been fortunate to have him teaching and coaching at the junior high, as his talent as a coach in my opinion is so high that I believe he could have chosen to coach at high levels in high school or even college or higher, but yet he remains happy and content in middle school. I learned a lot from coaching with Fred and have taken much from him with me in my career. What is more important than all the success that Fred had on the field, is that he is someone his players can look up to as a role model and provides an example of a loving husband and father.

After a year of being back at Summit Hill, I got a call over the summer from my principal, Beth Lind, telling me that she needed a girls' softball coach. I was a bit surprised. Having only coached boys' teams throughout my life, I wasn't sure if and how I could coach a team of girls. I told Beth that I would need a day or two to think about it. After some thought I decided to take the job. Seeing Fred coach baseball and giving his players a positive male role-model to look up to, I felt that being a positive male role-model for young girls would be just as important. While I was never considered a coach that would yell at players, to some extent I'd have to modify my coaching style. Having taught at this point for 5 years, I've made it a point to watch some of my students, both boys and girls, play their games on one of our school sports teams during their season. After watching some of my female students play softball, basketball, and volleyball, I knew that these girls were very athletic and wanted to compete at a high level. I was impressed.

There are some major differences between softball and baseball, but there was much I could take from my experience in baseball and transfer it to softball. Obviously fast-pitch softball in much different from baseball. In softball compared to baseball, there are different hitting techniques, base-stealing rules, and various defense strategies. I needed to learn the different nuances, so I quickly checked out some softball instruction books at the local library and read up on things I thought I could use. There are differences also in coaching girls as opposed to boys. When I first started out, a coach once told me that boys need to win to feel good, but girls need to feel good to win. There is indeed a lot of truth to that statement and I've tried to remember that wisdom as I continue to coach.

That first-year coaching softball was one of my favorite years coaching in any sport. We had a very talented team. Over the years, I've learned the hard way that sometimes girls can have some drama during the season, but this first year, all the girls got along and supported each other. As time has gone by, I am more aware of drama ensuing on the team, and for the most part our coaching staff has been able to stop any major issues before they begin, but still drama can sneak up on you at times. That first team I had however, the girls were a joy to coach, and I'll never forget that season.

I still remember all the kids on that first team, but there are a few that I will always have fond memories of. One the girls I'll never forget was a girl named Haley. She was maybe 4'11" at best. She played shortstop and hit 3rd in our lineup. But don't let her smaller stature fool you, Haley was a tough girl, smart hitter, and tough out in the lineup. During our regional playoffs that season, I remember Haley ripped a double in a big spot in one of our first postseason games. After she was standing on second base, she called timeout and ran over to me as I was coaching from the third base line. She then said, "Mr. Hagen, can you tie my shoe?" We ended up winning the game and advancing, but the win didn't consume my thoughts so much as Haley calling timeout did. This was still early in my career as a teacher and memories of my stint at Liberty Mutual were still not too far in my past. As I thought of tying Haley's shoe, I was overwhelmed with gratitude for the job I had teaching and coaching young adults. If hadn't made the decision to leave the corporate world, although I'd have move money, I'd still be stuck in a cubicle behind a computer at some desk. Instead, I was tying a girl's shoe in the middle of a junior high softball game, and I wouldn't trade that for anything. I realized how much I loved what I was doing, and I knew in my heart that my profession as a teacher and a coach was what God wanted me to do with my life.

As years have passed, some of my players have gone on to play collegiate softball. Recently, I was able to see Haley's last college softball game, and it's moments like those that would have been lost had I decided to never pursue a career in education. While money has its importance, devoting your life to something you love will give you a peace and contentment like nothing else.

I've now coached softball for ten years and counting, and over the years I still hear from players now and again. Sometimes, former players or their parents will update me on current game schedules in high school and in some cases college, and I try and catch local high school games when possible. Over the years, I still do keep in touch with players and their families. One such player is Molly, who again was on that first team I coached. Molly is one of three daughters in her family, and over the years, I've noticed that some of the best girls that I've coached have one thing in common, they have no brothers. Maybe their dads, who didn't have any sons, just wanted someone to play ball with and encouraged their daughters just a little bit more to take on softball. Regardless of whether that's true, in my career, I've seen it over and over again, that families of all daughters are where some of the most talented players I've coached have come from.

Not only did Molly play softball for me for two years, but she was a student in my honors math class as well as a player on our state chess team, and a good player at that. In Illinois, the junior high softball season begins in late July, weeks before school actually begins. We begin each season with a weeklong softball camp, and while in high school, and even in college, Molly would help out at the camp and when able, even help coach during our games. I've become friends with her parents, who are wonderful people, and when Molly was a player for me in junior high, her mom even told me that she considered me the big brother that Molly never had. I don't have a younger sister in my family, and similarly I've always thought of Molly as the kid sister I never had. I've written college recommendations for Molly, provided references for scholarships, and as Molly has gone on to play collegiate softball, I have even been interviewed for her university's student newspaper. Molly is probably the most decorated softball player that has come out of Summit Hill. She has gone on to be an All-Conference Shortstop at Division 1 softball program, and I'm really proud of her. To me, Molly represents the best in what our world needs. She is remarkably talented, yet she remains humble. She is also hard-working and committed to service. Knowing Molly's family and her Catholic faith, like any good big brother would do, I make sure to remind her to continue to attend Mass and keep the faith when I see her. Recently I was able to attend her Senior Weekend at her University. I promised her I'd make the trip out to see her play before she graduated. I saw her play her final regular season home stand, and I couldn't help but think of my time coaching softball all these years. How quickly time passes. I thought of young Molly as a 7th grader and watching her compete at such a high level in her final collegiate year forced me to reflect on a decade of coaching girls' softball. I thought of all the girls I've coached over the years and realized that even coaching the game for a couple of months can have a lasting impact on both players and coaches. I felt so fortunate to have been a coach and to have an opportunity to influence the lives of my young players.

The relationships that I have developed with my former players are dear to me, and again all of them wouldn't have been possible had I not left the corporate world for a career in teaching and coaching. Coaching girls' softball has been a blessing, and I am eternally grateful to my old principal Beth Lind for nudging me in that direction.

A Championship Season

In all my years coaching team sports, it has never been a goal of mine to win a state championship. In professional sports I completely understand the idea of setting goals to win championships, but at the junior high, high school, and even the college level, the primary goal of a coach should be to help kids develop good character and grow to become better people, all the while becoming better players. In coaching young adults, winning simply isn't everything. There are so many life lessons and character traits that players can take from playing team sports including: sacrificing yourself for the good of the team, perseverance, hard-work, sportsmanship, teamwork, humility, and having faith in each other.

In my first season coaching softball, I coached the team by myself without a full-time assistant. I did have some former students that were in high school help out when they could and they really helped me better learn the game, but for the most part I was on my own. It was tough managing all aspects of the game from lineups and substitutions, giving signs, calling pitches, and coaching players from situation to situation. It's a lot to take in and by the end of games, I'm mentally drained. Later I coached with a friend and retired teacher as an assistant for one year, and I even had some dads help out from time to time, but finding a permanent assistant was tough. About halfway through my career, Summit Hill hired a new teacher, Scott Chromcak, who had been a softball coach at his prior school. I got to know Scott and I immediately felt that he had a genuine nature about him. We would talk sports and coaching softball, and I realized we had a lot of the same coaching philosophies and a common goal to compete at a high level, make the game fun for all players, and help kids grow in character. Scott was also great with his students. Eventually, we started having conversations about the possibility of being an assistant coach for the team.

Scott started off as an assistant, however we'd talk through everything aspect of the game from signs, game strategies, and making out lineups. For three years prior to 2018, Scott was an assistant softball coach. We had some very good teams, but we always ended up getting knocked out early in the playoffs. After each season, we talked about ways to improve for the future, but in the end, we really still believed in our philosophy and what were trying to do. One of the things we both felt strongly about was giving every player a chance to play. We didn't get caught up in winning at all costs like some youth coaches do. As the pressure to win climbs in high school, junior high may be the last chance players have to showcase their talents. Junior high sports are not the end all be all, and I wanted to make an effort for all my players to feel a part of the team and have opportunities to contribute. Every season as a softball coach, I'd give players opportunities to play during the regular season, but once in the playoffs, I'd put together the lineup that I felt would give us the best chance to win. Scott was completely on board.

Before the 2018 season began, I decided that Scott and I would be co-head coaches. I gave up coaching third base and Scott was now in charge of giving batters and runners signs. He also was in charge of defense alignments. I was still calling pitches and making in game substitutions including pitching changes. Both of us made the lineups together. Sharing the head coaching responsibilities made me a better coach. I've always felt that head coaches are only as good as their staff and Scott was such a talented coach that I didn't want to waste his insight and everything he brought to the table. We were able to give greater focus and concentration to different aspects of the game and talk through strategies and ideas in game situations. Coaches at the highest levels in sports often have endless searches throughout the country in attempt to try and find the right staff to work with towards a common goal, and here Scott and I had a cohesive unit in the same school. Furthermore, not only did our coaching philosophies match, but Scott is a wonderful husband and father and his life is an important example to our team as well.

Another thing that Scott and I had in common was a commitment to having fun. After each game during our huddles, we always gave out jolly ranchers to each of our players. For each girl, we would make a comment on something positive that player did during the game. Yes, if we played poorly, missed signs, or even had a bad attitude, there have been times when Scott and I would decide not to reward the kids with jolly ranchers if they didn't deserve them. Sports should be fun, and if they weren't fun, we wouldn't want to play them. Coaches who yell at their players constantly, especially junior high girls, rarely get the best out of their players. Kids can be challenged to raise their game for sure but putting the fear of failure in them is not a way to coach, but to intimidate. Scott and I for sure motivate and challenge our players to be at their best and to continue to improve from one game to the next, but you can still do all that while having fun and it sure makes the season more enjoyable for everyone.

Scott and I celebrating our big win! (I'm on the left)

Our 2018 team was stacked. Our lineup top to bottom was loaded with hitters. Our defense was rock solid, and our pitching staff was stellar. Players that came in off the bench were great as well. Our best player, our starting pitcher, was also probably our hardest worker, as well as a fierce competitor and role-model on and off the field. When your best player leads by example, coaching the team becomes so much easier. I knew we had a great team and a real chance to go deep into the season, but I wasn't going to and didn't mention any goal to win a state championship. I've had many talented teams over the years that I felt had the same chance to go deep and win a state championship, but ended up getting beat. As in single game elimination playoffs, anything can happen and in any given game any team can beat you. Scott and I didn't want our team to get complacent and expect to win just by showing up, and we ended up using the slogan of "no finish line," modeled from Loyola University's run to the Men's Basketball Final Four. There was no finish line in that we wanted to keep getting better day after day, game after game, and go as far in our season as possible.

Our 2018 season was incredible! Of the 27 wins the team had, 14 of them were come from behind victories. The girls just had this never say die attitude no matter what the situation and they had a perseverance and grit about them unlike any team I've ever coached. Before each game I'd give them a quote to help them mentally prepare for what they were about to do. I'd give them quotes from famous athletes like Michael Jordan or Kareem Abdul-Jabbar about the willingness to sacrifice or overcome obstacles. I always liked John's Wooden's mindset in his belief, passed down to him from his college basketball coach Piggy Lambert, that "the team that makes the most mistakes usually wins, because doers make mistakes."[47] With this one, I wanted the girls to be aggressive and not to be afraid of failure. It also very much applies to life in that no matter how hard we try, we'll never reach perfection and we will make mistakes, but the real issue is what we choose to do about it when mistakes occur. We have no choice but to continue to move forward and learn from our own mistakes instead of blaming others or letting mistakes be your downfall.

When the playoffs began, I remember quoting Coach Sue Enquist, the storied UCLA Softball Coach. She says, "I want my team to be more detached from the wins and losses and be more focused on doing the little things well. When you focus on getting the win, it can suffocate you, especially during the playoffs when the pressure gets thick."[48] Focusing on the little things is always the best approach. Thinking about winning the game or achieving your ultimate goal lessens the focus on what needs to be done at the moment. In softball this is as simple as taking one pitch at a time. Similarly in our lives, we can't control what will happen in the future, but we can only focus our energy and efforts on the present by taking things one step at a time towards improvement and growth. Anything worth pursuing has a first step to take and if we are to reach our goals, we have to pay attention to those little details, however small they may be.

As I mentioned before, Scott and I have fun coaching our softball teams, but for us competing isn't all fun and games. We both want to put each player in the best possible situation to succeed, and we both want to win. After we won our quarterfinal game at the state tournament, our girls ran to the pitcher's circle and jumped up and down and while they were celebrating, I yelled out at them, "Why are you celebrating? We haven't won anything yet." You might think that this was a little extreme of a statement to 13 and 14-year-old softball players, but this mentality wasn't our "no finish line" mantra. If we were going to be the best we could be, we couldn't settle for less than that. As a coach, I've always been quick to remind players that whether we win or a lose, we have to move on from the past and focus on what's ahead.

The Illinois Elementary School Association (IESA) Softball tournament is held over a span of two days that starts with 8 teams. After winning our first game on Friday, we had to win two more games on Saturday to win the state title. By this time in my life, I had gotten into the habit of reading a chapter of the Bible each morning and night. I remember that Saturday morning reading my Bible, and the chapter I happened to be on was Hebrews Chapter 11, and the first line of the chapter reads, "Faith is the realization of what is hoped for and evidence of things not seen." I finished reading the chapter which recounts example after example of how the ancient Jews remained faithful to a God they had not seen, yet they still believed with great faith. I also couldn't help but think of my grandfather, Goompa, who had passed away months before. I ended my prayers that morning asking him to help the team out today and I knew he was watching from above.

In our pregame talk before the day of games started, I reminded the girls to have faith; to have faith in themselves, to have faith in our team, and to have faith in each other. While down 2-0 in our semi-final game, we came roaring back and won convincingly, 10-2. The state championship game was a tight one. Again, we found ourselves down 2-1, but had another one of our comebacks. While up 4-2 in the last inning after getting the first two batters out, I could sense our dugout, including a couple of our assistant coaches, getting excited thinking the game was all but over. Just like in life, we can't assume anything, and sure enough the opposing team quickly put runners on 2nd and 3rd base with the leading run at the plate. I knew we had to continue to compete every pitch and called timeout to tell our girls just that. Down to their last strike, the hitter lined a ball right back at our pitcher, and she was able to bat the ball down, pick it up, and throw to first, nabbing the runner by a half step to claim the state title!

My initial feeling after our team got that last out was relief. I had been so focused all year on trying to get the best out of our players and our team game by game and pitch by pitch, and now I finally was able to breathe a little easier. After feeling relief, I then felt great joy. I was so happy for this team. They were a wonderful group of girls both on and off the field and I was proud to be their coach. I also felt so happy for Scott and I knew that winning a title wouldn't have been possible without him. Letting go of the head coaching reigns and sharing that with Scott remains the best coaching decision I've ever made in my career. Looking back at that season, I don't take the credit. A coach's job is to get the best out of their players and giving a roadmap for each player to work towards making the team the best it could be. I think Scott and I did that, but it was the players that went out and executed. Part of the problem with youth sports today is that too many coaches are quick to take the credit for their team's success. While it's true that coaches do play a part in creating a successful and positive team culture, the players have to buy into it and execute on the field. What I am proud about however, is the culture we created and the sportsmanship we played with. Every player on that team got to contribute playing in games throughout that season, and even in our semi-final game, all 18 players got into the game at one point or another. Throughout the season, the girls played with grace and sportsmanship that made their coaches, parents, and school proud. Thankfully, I've never been so focused on winning that I have forgotten what matters most in coaching kids. What really counts are all the life lessons they learn along the way, and making sure that kids know that they are all important and valuable.

That season will remain in my memory for the rest of my life. I've long felt that kids will always remember good teachers, but good coaches they will never forget. Of course there are exceptions, but from the standpoint of a teacher and a coach, I'd have to say that I probably will remember with more fondness, the memories I've had as a coach more often than as a teacher. When I retire from education someday and look back at my career, I can't help but think of that state championship softball team and feel a deep sense of gratitude that I got to be a part of it.

**Helping coach our softball team to a state title was
one of the most fulfilling and joyous days of my life.**

22

Beat Your Time

Nearly since the beginning of my teaching career, I have also been a track coach in the spring. I ran when I was in junior high school, and later on as an adult, I ran local races for fun and at one point had worked on my endurance enough to run a half-marathon. However, in all honesty I took that first track coaching job because it was an open position, and I needed a little extra cash on top of my teaching salary. I was assigned to coaching distance running for our 7th and 8th grade boys and girls, and as years have passed, I have really enjoyed coaching our young distance runners. Over the years, I have studied distance running strategies, read stories about some great runners, and have developed some of my own workout routines and philosophies for my athletes.

As a distance coach, I like the fact that for most races there is no limit to how many kids can run in the 800 meter (1/2 mile) and 1600 meter (mile) runs. Sprinting races have a set number of lanes on the track that kids run in, and therefore there is a limit to how many kids can run in each event. This is not the case in the 800m and 1600m races, where, after the first 100-meter curve of the race, all runners can run the rest of the race on the inside lanes of the track. Sometimes a large number of runners can be difficult to manage, but in middle school, our coaching staff makes it work, and if necessary we sometimes will add another 800m race to accommodate larger amounts of runners on the track.

Distance running magnifies many great character lessons for young adults. I have been coaching distance runners for 13 years now, and on average I will have roughly 40 boys and girls run in either the 800m or 1600m races. As the season progresses, only the top two boys and two girls from each grade level can run in our conference and sectional races, which at most would be 16 kids if each kid runs only one distance race. That means that roughly 20 to 25 kids will not qualify for those postseason races, but during the regular season there is still plenty to run for. One of the aspects of track that I love the most is that every runner in every race is running with the goal to beat their time from the previous race. It's a continuous personal quest to get better, to put the work in to become faster, to be the best they can be. I like to remind kids not to compare themselves with others on the track and just focus on being at your own personal best. Yes, I still want my runners to compete and model the efforts of our top runners and try to beat them on the track, but more importantly I am interested in their self-improvement. Much like life, I do not want kids jealous of someone else's success. I make it a point for them not to compare themselves to others, and this is a trait needed in life and not just in track. As we know, there will always be someone in life that is better than us or has been given more than we have, but on the contrary, there will always also be someone who is less fortunate. There will always be people suffering much greater than us. For example, imagine those in critical care in a hospital fighting for each breath to survive. For those of us who have our health, we can appreciate not being in such dire circumstances. There is always something to be grateful for in life, and if you are having trouble thinking of something, think about it a little longer. Everyone can find something in life to be grateful for. Many people in life spend time thinking that, if they could just have this or have that, only then will they be happy. Some spend their lives with this line of thinking, instead of taking time to be grateful for all the blessings and gifts that they do have. In having personal running goals, there is also wisdom in not comparing yourselves to others, and just focusing on getting the best out of yourself.

Although distance running in track is more of an individual sport, unlike running on a cross-country team, I treat it as a team sport in many ways. During races that kids on the distance team are not running in, I ask them to watch their teammates run and cheer them on during the races. I also advise my runners to try and be just as happy for their teammates that do win a race as they would be if they themselves had won. This is obviously difficult to do, but if you can live your life with this kind of selflessness, there is a personal peace and a sense of contentment that helps all of us grow as human beings. Nearly every year, my top runners have running partners pushing them throughout the year, and often from race to race, they will take turns beating each other. I remind all my top runners that their success would not be possible without the push they get in practice and during the races from their teammate(s) so be sure to thank them. Again, there are parallels to this thought process in that anything we achieve in life would not be possible without the help and encouragement of others. As a teacher, I have been known to tell my students that "Anything worth anything has never been easy, and no one has ever accomplished anything worthwhile without getting help from someone along the way."

* * *

After many years coaching track, I developed some guidelines and expectations for my distance runners. I felt that there were three major components of running: physical, mental, and spiritual.

First of all, if athletes are to be successful in athletics, they must be physically prepared. Runners, especially distance runners who depend on endurance, must come into season in shape and ready to work. Those less than serious runners who enter the season in poor shape, often take the first month of the season getting into decent competitive running shape. In all my seasons coaching, I can't remember a distance runner who came into camp out of shape and was able to run a competitive time that qualified for our state track meet. As a distance runner, there is no magic switch that you can turn on and run at such a high level. There is no secret at all, it just requires hard work and dedication. I realize that coaching 7th and 8th graders is not the same as coaching college runners and there definitely is a balance needed. For instance, I expect my runners to eat healthy, drink plenty of fluids before races, and electrolytes after, but I am not going to tell them not to have a piece of cake or dessert. Running, like in life, has a balance. There are other runners that I have coached that are so focused on lowering their times, that they push themselves to the other extreme, even to the point of injury. Coaching 13 and 14 year-olds has a delicate physical balance. Too demanding of a training regimen can do serious harm to the health of a growing teenager, and with many of my more competitive runners, I have to constantly weigh their health with reaching their peak performance for the season.

Running, like any sport, has much to do with overcoming mental obstacles as much as it does physical, maybe even more so mental. Most junior high-aged runners are unaware of their own limits of pain and competitiveness on the track. Many will think they have given it their all when they have another gear that they have yet to discover. So much of life can be thought of in the same way. Whether a runner trying to win a race, a student trying to earn an A, or a husband or wife trying to repair a broken marriage, the same question must be asked, have I given my best and done everything I could or have I just been going through the motions? Every goal takes commitment and hard work, but also a willingness to be open to change the course when something needs improvement. A runner trying to reach a goal may need to change a training regimen, a serious student may need to tweak their study habits, and a husband and wife may need to change their priorities to save their marriage, but honest mental courage is unavoidable.

As you can imagine, my best runners were ones that were open to advice and hard work with the desire to learn and improve. As a coach, it's fun watching runners improve throughout the season as they realize that their hard work and mental approach are making a difference. As a coach, I've become a big advocate of quotes, and from time to time I share some of them with my athletes. One of my favorites that applies especially to runners is one from Pete Zamperini, the brother of Louis Zamperini, the famous World War II hero and track Olympian who was made well-known from Laura Hillenbrand's book, which was later made into a major motion picture, *Unbroken*. Before heading to the 1936 Berlin Olympic Games, Pete said to his younger brother, Louis, "A moment of pain is worth a lifetime of glory."[49] I've told my runners this many times over the years. It's a reminder to fight through the minutes of pain on the track to reach your potential. For a runner, there is no worse feeling than finishing the race knowing that you had more to give. Similar in life, I think if we were honest, most of us will regret the things that we didn't do much more so than the things we did. We won't know what our full potential could be if we never are willing to try.

Earlier in my coaching career, I once had an 8th grade girl come out to run track for her very first time. I knew this young lady had talent and already had good conditioning having been a soccer player, but it wasn't until her final race of the year did she realize her potential. On her final mile race during our sectional meet, she pushed herself to her physical limit and was running her best race of the year by far. After crossing the finish line, she was gasping for air with tears in her eyes. She had just taken over a half-minute off her time, and when I told her what she had done, the tears immediately evaporated into a big smile. She had put her mind and body through the grind of four laps, but all the pain and struggles were obviously worth it. She had realized that she had a gift for running, and through dedication to her new found love of running in high school, she would later earn a running scholarship in college. The moment of pain was worth the glory.

The final aspect of running that I devote time to is the spiritual side to competition. It may seem odd to some, but I find it to be just as important as any other. Every season for the sports I coach, I give my students a list of expectations, derived from John Wooden.[50] The list is as follows:

20 Suggestions to Perform to the Best of your Ability

Be a gentleman/lady at all times. (I added the lady part as Wooden coached only men)

Be a team players always.

Be on time whenever time is involved.

Be a good student in all subjects – not just sports.

Be enthusiastic, industrious, loyal, and cooperative.

Be in the best possible condition – physically, mentally, and morally.

Earn the right to be confident.

Keep emotions under control without losing fight and aggressiveness.

Work constantly – improve without becoming satisfied.

Acquire peace of mind by becoming the best you are capable of becoming.

Never criticize, nag, or razz, a teammate.

Never miss or be late for any class or appointment.

Never be selfish, jealous, envious, or egotistical.

Never expect favors.

Never waste time.

Never alibi or make excuses.

Never require repeated criticism for the same mistake.

Never lose faith or patience.

Never grandstand, loaf, sulk, or boast.

Never have reason to be sorry afterward, (but if so apologize*).

*my added modification

The sixth line reads, "Be in the best possible condition – physically, mentally, and morally." I've already discussed the physical and mental aspects, but moral preparedness is of great importance in competing to your best ability. None of us are perfect and we will for sure do things or say things that are harmful to others or ourselves. Kids are no different, especially kids navigating through the uncertainties of middle school. In a fit of adolescent emotion, kids can quickly lose perspective in situations with friends or family. Maybe they called a friend a name or talked back to a parent, but in circumstances like these, the guilt they have from a strained relationship or an ignored conscience will eat at them and impact their ability to focus on competing. When reviewing these expectations, I remind my athletes that if you've done something hurtful to someone, make sure to make a heartfelt apology to that person as soon as possible. Make it a real apology, and not something like, "I'm sorry if you were offended by what I did." Any apology needs to be genuine, like: "I'm sorry I did that to you. What I did was wrong. I hope you can forgive me, and I want to make it up to you." Without making things right, and without having a moral peace of mind, there is no way that you will be able to compete at your highest level.

A final part of the spiritual side of running, is a simple one in saying a prayer before the race. Some of my runners, who know I teach CCD have told me they say a Hail Mary before each race. While I teach in a public school, I can't bring together a huddle of athletes and say a prayer, but I can say to my athletes before getting on the track, "say one you know." Saying a little prayer beforehand can never hurt. Regardless of the situation, those that pray are sure to have an element of peace about them, and what better way to calm your nerves before a race, than a short prayer.

As a coach, I've come to realize the great impact that mental toughness and a sound spiritual mind can have on sports including running, but also life in general. During the track season, I make it a point to show kids the impact of running with mental toughness and purpose, and I make sure to tell them the story of Meb Keflezighi's 2014 Boston Marathon. Meb grew up in Eritrea in a time when the country was fighting a war for independence from a brutal Ethiopian regime. His family fled from Eritrea to Italy, and then eventually to the United States, where Meb would become a naturalized U.S. citizen in 1998. In the 2000's, Meb had solidified himself as a decorated marathon runner taking an *Olympic silver medal* in Athens in 2004 and winning the New York Marathon in 2009. After the tragedy of the 2013 Boston Marathon bombing, Meb made a commitment to win the 2014 Boston Marathon. As a grateful American, he wanted to be the first American to win the Boston Marathon since 1983. The only problem was that by this time Meb was 38 years old, about ten years past his prime as a distance runner. Going into the race, Meb was considered a long shot at best and none of the experts saw him as a serious contender to actually win, but he believed that he could win. He trained all year for the race, was mentally and tactically prepared, and had the determination of the American spirit to help a city and a country that was still healing from the previous year's tragedy. On race day Meb ran with a conviction and purpose. He was leading the marathon in the late stages in a race he had no business winning. Meb, a very spiritual Christian himself, was running for something bigger than himself. Only weeks before his 39th birthday, Meb Keflezighi won the Boston Marathon with a person best time of 2:08.37.[51] Every season now, I show my runners the clip of him winning the Boston Marathon (you can easily find it on YouTube) to the sounds of cheers throughout the city, and I remind them of the importance of mental toughness, will power, and having faith in yourself, even when no one else does.

Nice Guys Finish First

Coaching track has provided some memories that will stay with me for a lifetime. Early in my coaching career, I had a young 7th grade girl named Alison tryout for the track distance team. Alison was a student in our school's self-contained special education classroom. While there are tryouts for the track team, most of the cuts only apply to sprinters, where there is only a limited amount of lanes on the track available for sprinting races. Alison was trying out for the 800m race and she just wowed me with her attitude. She had a number of setbacks she was living with, but she had a desire to be part of the team, and to run the two laps of the 800m race without stopping. I was convinced that she would be an asset to our team.

Having Alison on the team wasn't a sure thing. Some of the other track coaches, whom I have much respect for, had differing opinions. The coaches that differed with me felt that having Alison on the team would be too great a time commitment on my part and that I would not be able to fully commit to coaching and developing my other distance runners. They also felt that I would not be able to effectively supervise the 40-plus distance runners already on the team. They had valid points, and I under-stood the competitive nature of team sports in junior high and high school. Like them, I wanted to compete well with other schools, and I wanted to help develop some very talented runners. I wanted to be fair to them as well. In the end however, the decision to me was easy. Alison was on the team, and I'd find a way to make it work. I remember after the last day of tryouts, Alison's mother picked her up from practice and I told her that she had made the team! Alison was so excited, and her Mom was thrilled. I later found out that that night the family bought Alison some brand new track shoes and the entire family went out to dinner to celebrate her accomplishment of making the team.

Having Alison on the track team was such a blessing! We did have a teacher aide helping and encouraging her, which was great, but there were always distance runners on the team that wanted to volunteer to help Alison in her practice workouts and races. There were three girls in par-ticular that were wonderful. They ran their mile races competitively, but every meet they would volunteer to run the 800m side by side with Alison encouraging her the whole way. Our track team had some talented ath-letes in various races, but the cheers and encouragement Alison got was always the loudest. Parents, teammates, coaches, and opposing teams all cheered and encouraged her in finishing her last lap. For the coaches who had initial reservations about having her on the team, those reservations quickly diminished. Witnessing Alison run inspired many including her teammates. Just the same as every kid on the team, she had the same goals every race to improve her times. Alison was a part of the team, and the three girls who ran along side her befriended her long after junior high where Alison continued to run on the high school track team.

Ever since, Alison joined the team, I've had the good fortune of having boys and girls from our self-contained special education classroom join our distance team and run the 800-meter race. It has been a blessing to coach these athletes and the other kids on the team have embraced it as well. Including students like these on the team has been a valuable lesson for them. They see that everyone has goals to work on and achieve, and that everyone has value. For those runners who volunteer to work with these athletes, they learn one of the most important lessons of all, that in helping others, we are helping ourselves find real happiness, while certainly growing as a person.

* * *

I've coached many runners over the years, and there are several that I'll always remember. One of them was a young lady named Mallory. Mallory was one of the toughest competitors I've ever coached. She was more of a cross-country runner, but ran the mile during track season. She wasn't the fastest runner on the team, but her work-ethic and competitive fire were contagious. As a coach, especially a coach of middle school runners, I try to monitor kids on their health before races. For my more casual runners, some will at times try and get out of having to run hard in practice due to some soreness or mild injury, but for my more serious runners like Mallory, they will do anything to compete in a race and even try and hide or downplay injuries, telling me they are a little sore or "it's not a big deal and I can run with it." Mallory's attitude definitely applies to the latter and before her final race during her 8th grade year, Mallory told me her hip was a little sore, but that she could fight through it and be fine. I'm sure when she told me this she was hiding a limp or was downplaying the pain, but at that moment I didn't think too much of it. Mallory was one tough girl, and knowing her competitive fight, I felt this was pretty normal for her. Well during the final stretch of her last lap of the race, Mallory collapsed maybe 100 meters from the finish line. I ran over to her and she was in such agony. I felt terrible. We had to get a wheelchair to cart her off the field. After the meet, I called her parents and found out that they took her to the hospital and that due to scheduled tests, she'd be in the hospital overnight. The next day I called her mom during my lunch break and found out that a test had revealed that part of Mallory's muscle had detached itself from her hip bone. I felt awful and I couldn't help but feel that I shouldn't have had her run in the race, but her parents, knowing how insistent she could be, didn't blame me. I spoke to Mallory briefly on the phone and told her family I'd stop by the hospital after practice that afternoon.

At track practice that day, I gave the kids an update on Mallory's condition. I told them that she'd recover, but once the kids found out the extent of her injury, they were inspired by her toughness. I had kids write get well cards and notes and I brought them over to the hospital after practice. When I arrived at the hospital, I gave Mallory the cards from our team, but the card that she and her family really appreciated the most was a card from Jonathan. Jonathan was a runner on the team that was in our self-contained special education classroom, and it was his note that gave Mallory the most joy and hope.

In my coaching career, the decision to have students with special needs on our school track team is one of the best coaching decisions I've ever made. The joy and inspiration that they bring to our team is priceless and I couldn't imagine it any other way.

Contrary to what other track coaches across the country may think, having students with special needs will not make your team and runners less successful, but in fact I believe the success I've had as a coach would not be possible without them. During all the years in which I've coached students with special needs, I've also had runners achieve great success. During this time, I have coached every boy and girl that holds our school record for the 1600m and 800m races, including a state champion runner in the Boys' 800-Meter and other school record-holders. I'm not a coach that takes credit for the success of an athlete or a team. I'm not the one running the race or playing the game, but it is satisfying to know that a team or individual can have that kind of success while doing the right thing and including those with special needs. Joe Newton, the famous cross-country coach from York High School in Elmhurst, IL with 28 Illinois State Titles, had the same philosophy in coaching his runners. In a movie made about his team, *The Long Green Line*, the film documents his 2005 state championship season. In the movie however, the most moving part for me is that he worked with a young boy who had some physical disabilities and still had the courage and determination to run, improve, and be an inspiration to the entire team.[52] If an icon like Joe Newton, a man who actually was an assistant marathon coach for the 1988 USA Track and Field Team, could coach all runners of all abilities of all backgrounds, then I think I can try and incorporate the same style at our little junior high school.

Humility and Character in Running

Running is a humbling sport, and knowing this, I've tried to instill a sense of humility in my runners too. Every race is an attempt at perfection. For distance runners, in the race itself, they have to think about the segments of a race: a quick, but relaxed beginning, a middle pace with strategic positioning, and finally knowing when to make your final kick. I always tell my runners to expect the unexpected. In a race, you may get boxed in, you may start your kick too late or too early, and you may just not have a physically good day for a number of reasons. Perfection is impossible to achieve, but important to continue to strive for.

I have been fortunate to have coached so many runners that remain humble even with great success. While I make sure to let them know how proud of them that I am, I've always preached that they continue to work to improve on bettering their time, and to be grateful to teammates that have helped push them along the way. It's funny how the best runners I've coached are some of the nicest kids I've ever come across in my teaching career. There are parallels to trying to improve your time to trying to improve your character. Runners can never reach perfection because it will always be possible to run a faster race. In life, we can never reach perfection, but the efforts we make in trying are the very things that make us a better person.

Every year before our track team heads off to the state track meet, we have a pep rally at school. Each coach gets a few minutes to talk about their athletes. While I make sure to let our school community know of the accomplishments our state distance runners have made, I've made it known in my speeches that these athletic accomplishments aren't everything, but their character is. Years from now, hardly anyone will remember certain athletic feats that you may have had, but instead people will remember how you carried yourself and how you treated others around you.

Everything that goes into running a race just has so many life values that can be taken from it and I've been fortunate to have coached all these years and hope to continue to do so. Recently, I have gotten into the habit of writing my athletes thank you notes at the end of our season. In them, I try and give them goals to think about for 8th grade or high school, but I make sure to end my note with the phrase, "remember to fight the good fight, to finish the race, and keep the faith," which is slightly modified from the Bible in Paul's words before his death (2 Tim 4:7). Everyone of us has the same goal in life, to get to Heaven, and everyone of us will run our own unique race in our attempt to get there. In the race of life, we must have the faith and trust in God in our own paths, and fight to do what it right, even when we can't always see the finish line.

In life's journey, I think Mother Teresa's poem (adapted from Kent Keith) sums it up perfectly:

"People are often unreasonable, irrational, and self-centered. Forgive them anyway.

If you are kind, people may accuse you of selfish, ulterior motives. Be kind anyway.

If you are successful, you will win some unfaithful friends and some genuine enemies. Succeed anyway.

If you are honest and sincere people may deceive you. Be honest and sincere anyway.

What you spend years creating, others could destroy overnight. Create anyway.

If you find serenity and happiness, some may be jealous. Be happy anyway.

The good you do today will often be forgotten. Do good anyway.

Give the best and it will never be enough. Give your best anyway.

In the final analysis, it is between you and God. It was never between you and them anyway."[53]

23

In the End...

When I graduated from the College of Business at the University of Illinois, I was excited for graduation day to finally arrive. I was happy to realize one of my goals and to have my family there to celebrate. I was not excited for our commencement speech, however. By that time, I was already having second thoughts about a career in business, and the keynote speaker was the Vice President of Kraft Foods. Boring!

To my surprise, the speech that she gave nearly 20 years ago has stayed with me. The V.P. didn't use these contemporary business buzz words that I heard year after year. I also don't remember her telling us to follow our dreams or any cliché like that. I remember that she warned the graduates that at the end of our lives when we are on our deathbeds, no one will be saying, "I wish I spent more time at work." Instead people may say something like, "I wish I spent more time with my family. I wish I was a better father or mother. I wish I was a better husband or wife. I wish I was a better person. I wish I gave more to others."

I found this incredible for the V.P. of a major multibillion-dollar company to give hundreds of business students a speech on how our future business careers were not the most important thing in life. Instead family and giving of ourselves is what matters.

As a teacher, I have asked my students what they would like their obituary to say. It's interesting to hear their answers, but sometimes in thinking of the end, we are forced to think of how to best spend our living years. At wakes and funerals, people will remember acts of kindness and love that the deceased showed to them during their lifetime, and stories like those are the ones that provide those grieving with peace. How you treat people in life matters more than anything else and what you devote your time to will define you as a person whether you want it to or not.

In the end, your career cannot save you. Accumulating great wealth, possessions, fame, or worldly influence cannot save you. Only God can save you, and when we have to account for our lives, a question He may ask us is how did we love? Or, how did we use the time we had? One rule I have for my students is for them to live by the golden rule in my classroom, and sadly some kids have never heard the saying, "treat others like you want to be treated." But at its core, we know this echoes what Christ requires of us: "to love your neighbor as yourself." In the end, we will probably be judged by how we lived that message.

Most of us at one point or another have imagined what our funerals would look like. Would many come? Who would be there? What would people say? As I mentioned before, you will never see a U-Haul behind a hearse. Even if you devote your whole life to wealth, you won't be able to take it with you. On the contrary, if you devote your whole life to others, in the next life, you may be reunited with those who you loved enough to sacrifice your time for.

24

Find the One

We've all been to parties and events where there is a person or a few people that don't know many of the guests. Sure when we attend parties, we want to talk to our good friends and catch up with them and their lives, but if those are our good friends, odds are we are probably aware of how they are doing and don't need to converse with them the entire night. Our time could be spent helping make someone new more comfortable.

I haven't always done this in my life, and still often forget to do so, but now when I am at a party, I try to look around and find someone that needs someone. I try and find someone that has no one to talk to, or at least introduce myself and introduce that person to some friends. I can tell you that after doing so, I can really see how that new stranger is so much more comfortable after getting introduced to others and meeting new people. While I understand that some people are very shy, and that the very thought of introducing yourself to a complete stranger may be terrifying for some, this is something that over time, while not being perfect at it, I have gotten better at it, and have even come to enjoy it. After doing so, I know I always feel better that someone else is enjoying themselves too.

I know that at staff parties, staff will often talk to their same group of friends at every event, which is perfectly fine, but getting to know more and more people can only be a good thing and give you a greater appreciation for them and their lives. I am someone that gets along with, or at least tries to get along with, everyone, although this is not always possible. Throughout my career in teaching, I have made some wonderful friendships. Being a math teacher, I am close with our math staff, and being a coach, and I am close with other coaches, but I am also good friends with teachers of a variety of disciplines, and in all honesty, I am more close to some custodians, maintenance staff, and bus drivers than I am with many teachers. This is not a slight on those teachers, but what I have learned is that your profession is only one of hundreds of possible connections in life you may have with someone, and over the years I've enjoyed developing friendships with custodians and bus drivers outside of work that I don't have with other teachers. If I hadn't taken the time to get to know them, I'd would never have had those friendships.

Having gone through junior high and high school, we know there are students that just aren't as popular as others are for one reason or another. Maybe someone is just overlooked because they may be shy and reserved, or someone just looks like they need a friend or someone to talk to. I often tell my students to find someone during lunch that needs a friend and invite them to sit with your friends at your table. In junior high and high school, this can make a world of difference in someone else's life and you may never even know it. For someone going through a difficult time or depression, even a smile can uplift their soul, so imagine what a conversation can do. This logic of thinking doesn't apply to only students, as adults are equally in need of just someone willing to listen and be present.

Friendships can make all the difference in life, especially for teens navigating through the uncertainties of their early life. But whether a teenager or not, when trying to navigate making friendships, Dale Carnegie has some good advice for us all when he wrote, "you can make more friends in two months by becoming interested in other people than you can in two years trying to get other people interested in you."[54]

Living in the Chicago suburbs, I was just old enough to remember the tail end of Walter Payton's storied football career, after reading his auto-biography, *Never Die Easy*, I have come to realize even more so that he was more than just a phenomenal athlete, but also an incredible giving man. He noticed people hurting. There is one story about him told by an assistant in his charity in which he was signing autographs in a mall in a Chicago suburb. After his time was done signing, there were several people that were left without autographs as the line was quite long. Walter Payton, was very popular in Chicago, and for good reason, so getting a chance to meet him and get an autograph was something fans, especially children would do anything for. Well there was one lady who was not able to get the autograph and she began to cry. Walter noticed her and asked his assistant to follow her and see where she goes. The woman went to another store in the mall, and when Walter's assistant found her, she called him, and he came over to meet her to spend time talking with her. It turned out that the woman was waiting line to get an autograph for her grandsons, so Walter got her address and ended up sending her a couple of autographed foot-balls.[55] There's story after story about how Payton always looked out for those in need. He was also one of the few players that would take time and sign autographs for kids, and if you can believe this, he would say that he got more out of the exchange with kids, talking with them and asking them questions, than the kids got out of meeting him.

One story in the book that really gave me the impression of Payton's knack for elevating the overlooked, was a story of how he was scheduled to appear at a fundraising event at a luxurious hotel. At this particular fund-raiser, there where various booths representing charitable organizations, and those in attendance were well-to-do and well-dressed people looking to donate to good charities. When Walter walked into the building, all the people ran towards him. They just wanted to be around the guy, as he was a larger than life figure, especially in Chicago. While the crowds converged on him, Walter simply told the people that he'd be right with them and that he had to say hello to some friends first. Walter had noticed a booth from the Boys and Girls Club and went right over to the booth where there were two kids running the table. He gave them hugs, spent time with them, and told the young boy and girl that he was just so happy that they were at the convention. Before Walter did that, the Boys and Girls Club table hardly had any visitors, but after Walter visited those kids, everyone in the convention wanted to go and talk with them.[56] There will never be another Walter Payton. He was one in a million, but his selfless nature of seeking out those in need and being present to them is a gift that everyone can give someone.

After reading his book, I started to make little changes in my life like trying to make a stranger alone feel more comfortable at a party, but I also tried to be more aware of my surroundings, especially when I am in the city. Next time you go into a more urban area, and notice a homeless man or woman begging for change, take notice of how few people, if any at all, even bother to make eye contact with them. To me it's not the people refusing to give a quarter, but their refusal to even acknowledge their humanity. A simple smile can go along way. Some people will tell me that if you give money to the homeless, how can you be sure that they won't just waste the money on alcohol or something worse? My answer is God knows your heart, and if you are trying to help someone and they take advantage of your goodwill, then they have to live with that, not you. What I have started doing, however, is carrying $5 gift cards to Subway, and if I see someone in need on the streets, I'll just ask them if they like Subway, and if they do, I'll give them the gift card. This definitely isn't enough to change someone's life dramatically, but at the very least it is just another human being present to another human being in a small act of kindness, and that is worth it every time.

25

Be a Role-Model

Everyone who is around children and young adults is a role-model whether they like it or not. Some are good and some are bad, but we are all role-models. Whether you are a parent, a teacher, a coach, an uncle or aunt, or a sibling or friend, the way you live your life is seen, especially by our youth and young adults.

You may have heard the quote from author Michael Levine, "Live your life in the manner you would like your kids to live theirs."[57] I can't think of better advice for parents to live by, but this mantra also applies to anyone who is in position to influence our youth, especially teachers and coaches. Ask yourself the question, if those around me, whether they are your children, students, or players, were to model their life after mine, would our world and society be better for it? While there is no such thing as a perfect role-model, parent, or teacher, I think it's agreed we can learn from our mistakes so that we don't make them again. We know that what counts in life is not so much whether we have made mistakes, but how we respond to them and our commitment to improving our lives for ourselves and those around us. I've read stories about alcoholics who have gotten DUI's and looking back they are happy it happened. They realize that if they had not gotten caught, they could have ended up hurting or even killing someone in an accident. They were on a collision course with death and destruction, and getting a DUI was their wake-up call in hitting rock bottom. After some time, an alcoholic can realize the path they are on, make a commitment to change, and with time go on to share their trial and triumph with those around them.

We can share those mistakes and failures that we have gone through with those young adults around us so they can learn from them as well. What I've found with kids is that they greatly appreciate your honesty and willingness to share something personal. They no longer look at you as a teacher, but as someone that truly cares for them and wants the best for them in their own life.

I think it can be said that success is in great proportion to whether or not our youth have good role-models in their life. Take for instance, the presence of a good father and mother in the lives of children. While there are certainly exceptions, most families with both parents present in the lives' of their children tend to have more loving childhoods and greater success as they become adults. Often, we see that troubled parents can have troubled children, but there are also exceptions to that as well. Children with an absent or unreliable parent can sometimes learn what not to do, what decisions not to make, and they can see that they want things in their life to be different. One of my best friends grew up with parents that were sometimes unreliable or unavailable to him. My own parents acted like parents to him in many ways, and my family has always considered him part of the family. He also had a wonderful aunt and uncle who were wonderful role-models and treated him like he was their own son. As time progressed, he made a decision that when he got older, he wanted to be present to a family of his own someday. He wanted more for his children then his parents had given him. Today he is a wonderful husband and father to his own family, and without positive role-models during his childhood, who really knows what his life would have been like without them.

A positive role-model can make all the difference in someone's life, and in the grand scheme of things, the impact we make on others is life's greatest importance. As Jackie Robinson once said, "a life is not important except in the impact it makes on others."[58] As a teacher, I have made a deliberate effort to be a role model. Being a role-model is more important than students getting high marks on their state tests or ACT's, and definitely more important than getting accepted to a "good" college. As I have mentioned before, what matters most is what kind of person they become. What kind of moral compass do they have? How do they treat others? Do they have courage and conviction to stand up for truth? Will they be ready for the sacrifices that come with life and their possible future as a parent?

I'm one of those teachers that has saved all these little notes from students, and I store them in a box in my basement. Occasionally I'll come across them and take some time and read a few. The ones that mean the most to me are the ones where kids say thank you for helping me become a better person or thank you for making a difference in my life. Sometimes I'll even get an e-mail or a note from a former student in high school or college. Even after all those years, some will take a moment to send me a note of thanks. They'll say things like "I couldn't have made it this far without you," "thank you for all the life lessons," or "thank you for all you have done for me." I read these and obviously I think they are giving me way too much credit. The reason for the success and the people they are becoming has little to do with me, but more likely due to the fact that they have had supportive parents, and probably the biggest reason for their success are the good decisions and sacrifices the students themselves chose to make. A parent or a teacher can give a child advice and wisdom, but in the end, the child must make the decision to listen and make the necessary sacrifice and commitment. If after all these years, a student feels I've made some impact, I am grateful that I played a role in their life, however small it may be.

The letters I get from students have given me a sense of peace in my decision to be a teacher. I feel that teaching is the job that God wanted me to do, and the letters I get from students have helped me realize that. A few years ago, I received a letter out of the blue mailed to me at school from a former student. The student wrote how thankful she was that I was her teacher years ago and wrote that I had made an impact in her life. On the day I received the letter, I had just finished reading a book entitled *33 Days to Merciful Love*. The book, written by Fr. Michael Gaitley, has day-by-day meditations on consecrating your life to the Divine Mercy of Christ. When I got this little note from my former student, I felt as if God was giving me a little signal of grace, letting me know that He is was with me, and present to me and the students in my classroom. I cherish every one of these letters as they add years to my career and help me to continue to move forward and work to be a better role-model for them.

26

Smart, Successful,
Happy, or Good?

Over the years I have become a big fan of Dennis Prager. If you are unaware of Dennis, he has a daily syndicated radio program and is the founder of PragerU and their 5-minute videos. I have found him to have a beautiful outlook on life filled with wisdom on many topics, all the while being grounded by faith and reason.

One of the questions that I've heard Dennis pose on air is this: If you could be certain of having one thing in your life, would you choose to be smart, successful, happy, or good. Dennis Prager said that when he asked this question, he has gotten mixed results, but he feels that there is one best answer. I agree with him and I will do my best to explain how I arrived at it.

Smart

First of all, know that there is a major difference between intelligence and wisdom. In a 2019 report completed by the National Association of Scholars, it was found that out of 173 colleges reviewed, 76 of those schools offered black students segregated graduation ceremonies. One of the schools doing so was even the prestigious Harvard University known as one of the most intellectual and renowned universities in the world.[59] In all the pain and suffering that our country and its citizens have endured to secure to civil rights for all, regardless of race, I fail to see the wisdom in the decision that these universities made. Apparently in the eyes of the intellectual-minded faculty, separate is still equal, regardless of Brown vs. Board of Education. This is an example of how even the most well-educated and intellectual people are capable of making terribly unwise decisions.

Throughout my own education, I have had some very well-educated college professors and teachers; however, just because someone may have intelligence, it does not necessarily mean they are wise or rational. In fact, while I was in college, one of my criminal justice professors argued that prostitution should be legalized because it would promote family life. He felt that a man would be less likely to leave his wife for a prostitute than for another women. It may be true that a man would not leave his wife for a prostitute, but if he is willing to have relations with a prostitute, what in his character would prevent him from having a relationship with another women? How would this be good for the wife and her emotional and physical health? And how would selling your body for money be good for anyone? This is flawed thinking. Here was a professor who was Head of the Criminal Justice Department, a man with a PhD. and multiple degrees, and he made this claim. I believe there is a universal moral code and only through wisdom, not intelligence, can one have clarity on life's biggest questions. Ideally, we would want to be both intelligent and wise, but you can definitely have one without the other. I have found that true wisdom comes from God and all throughout the Bible we read that the beginning of wisdom is fear of the Lord, which in other words is a sense of humility. Although I have made some poor decisions in my own life, I eventually have realized that clarity and right judgement come not from intelligence, but from wisdom, and more specifically wisdom from God which can be found in the Bible.

I imagine that most parents want their children to be smart. What parent wouldn't want that for their child? Being intelligent and capable would ideally mean that their children would not struggle as much in school. There is nothing wrong with this line of thinking. I myself was a good student. I was bright, but there were definitely kids I went to school with who were much smarter than me. I had to work hard for my grades and had to earn every one of them from elementary school throughout college. I can tell you though that there is a certain degree of satisfaction for getting the grades and degrees through hard work, dedication, and sacrifice. If everything was easy to me, it would be less meaningful. One of John Wooden's quotes about this is that, "goals achieved with little effort are seldom worthwhile or lasting."[60] Obviously, highly intelligent people can and do attain goals with hard work and sacrifice, but being very bright leaves yourself open to complacency, and those who become complacent never find meaning or fulfillment in life.

I have coached Special Olympic sports now for about ten years, and I've been around individuals with special needs. One constant about them is that they are usually always happy. These are people with intellectual disabilities and not considered smart by worldly standards, yet they seem like they always have a smile on their face, and they are completely content and at peace in life. Intelligence does not bring happiness, but love does, and in my experience working with those with intellectual disabilities, I can clearly see this. In fact, I can say without a doubt that I have learned much more about the meaning of life from my Special Olympic athletes than they could have possibly learned from me.

Successful

When society thinks of successful people, we usually think of wealth, status, fame, and maybe power. However, why is it that these people with seemingly everything are often reported to suffer from depression, addictions, alcohol dependency, and failed marriages and relationships? They seem like they are never happy for any extended period of time. Obviously, there are exceptions. I'm sure there are some happily grounded actors or actresses in Hollywood or extremely successful fortune 500 CEO's, but it seems a constant that those who seem to have everything are desperately searching for something bigger than themselves. Some of these successful people come to this realization, and run charities or spread some kind of awareness for people in need, but often they are not fully invested and they are in it for the wrong reasons, such as a desire to be liked by the public. There definitely are people who have achieved great success and prestige while genuinely giving back for the right reasons. Take a Gary Sinise for example. He achieved great success in Hollywood and has had prominent roles in some terrific box office hits including *Forest Gump*. He also is a man grounded by faith, family, and service as you may be aware of his wonderful charitable work for veterans and military service men and women. My point is not that success is unimportant, it is that success alone will not provide lasting happiness.

In my classroom, I take one day a year and ask my students to write down their own definition of success. They have come up with some great answers, and we have a good discussion. I believe the definition of real success in life is to give your very best in all that you do. You may not achieve all the goals you set out to accomplish, but in life we find out the most about ourselves in the journey, and not necessarily by accomplishing our goal. Take for instance a team in sports that loses in the end but gave their absolute best effort and preparation while sacrificing themselves for the good of the team. Are those teams considered unsuccessful? Consider the 2018 Loyola Ramblers cinderella run to the Final Four in the NCAA Men's Basketball Tournament. They were considered an underdog in the tournament as a small school from a mid-major conference and many "experts" thought they'd be lucky to maybe win one game, yet they continued to win game after game and made it all the way to the Final Four. After finally bowing out to Michigan, how could those players walk off the court of their last game thinking their season was a failure? Giving everything you have is success in itself, and even when things don't go the way you would have hoped, if you have given everything you have, you can always walk away with your head held high. I also tell my students that even if you have achieved the goals you set out to achieve, you can only maintain success by how you treat others. If you have a large mansion, beautiful cars, and endless wealth, but yet, are arrogant and unkind to others, that would be a tragedy. Material success without successful character is not real success at all, but instead a moral failing.

Happy

Many people who are asked this question will choose happy for their response. It is a good answer. We all want to be happy in life, and every good parent desires happiness for their children. The deeper question here is what will bring you lasting happiness?

In my classroom there is a poster on the top of the doorway that students see as they walk out. It reads: "If you want to be happy for an hour: watch a movie. If you want to be happy for a day: go to an amusement park. If you want to be happy for a lifetime: go out and help others." Happiness is different than pleasure. Pleasure will only last for as long as the amount of time you are involved in that pleasure inducing activity. For instance, the pleasure of eating a delicious dinner will only last for as long as you eating the dinner. The pleasure you will get from spending a day at an amusement park, a beach, or even a vacation, will only last for as long as you are there. Eventually, if we want to remain happy, we must find a different source than simply pleasure.

For as long as I have been the girls softball coach at my junior high school, I have been taking the team to a local nursing home each year where the girls visit with residents and play a softball game for them. After the event, the girls always say how much fun they had and that they really want to go back and visit. I once got an e-mail from a player's mom. The mom was carpooling a group of girls back from the nursing home and she wrote that she heard the girls talking in the back, and one of the kids said, "It just feels good that we helped them today." What happens in your heart when you volunteer your time, demonstrate an act of kindness to a stranger, or give of your time to help someone in need? Why is that when you devote your time and yourself to helping others you feel happy and content even after the event is over? Happiness is something that everyone on Earth strives to find and some search their whole life looking to find lasting happiness without ever truly finding it. My answer to finding lasting happiness lies in Prager's final option, to be good.

Good

In Lou Holtz's *Three Rules for Living a Good* Life, he writes, "One thing is certain: there will be one thing that will dominate your life. I strongly suggest it be something you can be proud of."[61] Dedicating your life to being good and to do good for others, is definitely something that at the end or lives, we will be proud of. Parents are proud of their children for many reasons. Often parents will say my son or daughter is excelling at this school or that college or my son or daughter has this or that wonderful job. There is nothing wrong with being proud of your child's success, but what parents should focus more of their thoughts on is on whether or not their children are good. In all the parent-teacher conferences I've conducted, my number one priority when communicating to parents of good children, is to tell them exactly that. To say that their child is good, or kind, or compassionate, or selfless, and that they are role-models for their peers are much more important indicators in what matters in life than their grades or test scores. Their actual grades are secondary, and there are good parents I've come across over the years that realize this. Often their first question they may ask me is, "Is my child respectful in class?" Or in other words, how does my child act in school when he or she is not home and I am not around? Good parents want to know that because they realize being good is the secret to real success and true happiness.

Another benefit of being good is that I feel it better prepares you for storms in your life. Life will undoubtedly have storms. Everything will not always go your way. If your priority is material success, when you lose that goal, there is no telling that you will rebound effectively. However, when your priority is to be good and you lose material success, you are more inclined to rebound from that because material success wasn't your number one priority in the first place and living for something greater than yourself was. What I've learned in all of life's ups and downs is that striving to do good in life is the only way we can find lasting happiness, contentment, peace, and meaning, and I can't think of a better way to live.

Finally, the Bible tells us that God is good, and if God is good, He desires us to be good and do good to others. Being good makes all the difference and as John Wooden said, "You can do more good by being good than any other way."[62] Success, intelligence, or even working towards being happy through pleasure alone, cannot save us in the end, only God can do that. So only in doing God's will by being good as he wishes will lead us to true happiness in the next life with Him. Only living in this way will lead us to fulfillment now and in the future.

27

*The Little Things
are the Big Things*

During September of 2002, my surgery date and lymph node biopsy were scheduled for the end of the month and I had a few weeks with nothing really to do but wait. I wasn't about to get a job for the little time I had before the next surgery, and besides what job could I get while on crutches?

During this time, I followed major league baseball. September is a fun time of year for baseball fans with teams fighting to make the playoffs. My White Sox were not in contention, but my second favorite team, the Seattle Mariners, were in a battle in the American League West. Seattle was my second favorite team because my favorite player and pitcher, Jamie Moyer, was on their team. Moyer was a guy that if you watched him pitch, you'd think he'd have no business in the major leagues. He threw maybe 84 miles per hour tops, which is 10-12 mph slower than the average big-league pitcher, but he had a very successful career and absolutely frustrated batters. Jamie Moyer was an artist to watch on the mound.

I had never seen him pitch live and the Mariners were not coming to Chicago for the rest of the season. As I looked at the baseball schedule,

I figured out that he would be pitching in Cleveland on a Saturday in September. With my right foot in a boot after my initial surgery, I wasn't permitted to drive so I asked my dad if he would like to drive up to Cleveland to see the Indians play the Mariners. This was the Cleveland Indians who were rivals of the White Sox and driving up to see the Indians play when they weren't playing the Sox was something my dad wasn't thrilled about, but he told me he'd think about it.

The day after I asked him, he agreed to get tickets and drive up to Cleveland for the game. I think my mom was the one who convinced him to go. This was a time of limbo for our family not knowing what the result of my future lymph node biopsy would show. So, I think my dad felt that if I somehow didn't make it through this illness, he'd regret not having spent the time to take in a ballgame with me, even if it wasn't our beloved White Sox.

We drove out on Friday night, got a hotel, and went to the game Saturday afternoon for a 12:00 P.M. start. I enjoyed the game and thought Jacobs Field was impressive. The Mariners lost the game late and Moyer ended up pitching 7 innings and getting a no decision, but I really enjoyed spending the day with my dad.

Years after I graduated from Loyola University, I started following their basketball team. I attended a handful of games here and there, but by 2015 I bought a pair of season tickets. My dad was also an alum of Loyola and he'd often go to the games with me. My dad would tell me of Loyola's great run to the Sweet Sixteen in 1985 led by great Alfredrick Hughes. The Ramblers hadn't been to the NCAA basketball tournament since then. Then 2018 happened. By this time, I have had season tickets for three years and I knew that the Loyola Ramblers were becoming a great team. Hardly anyone in Chicago had followed Loyola basketball in years past and my friends failed to see the excitement about supporting a program that failed to make it to the big stage every year. Early in the 2018 season, I told everyone I knew to watch out for Loyola this year, and my friends having heard me say that nearly every year would just laugh and brush it off.

My dad still went with me to nearly all the games. As the team kept winning, we were both getting excited about their chances to make the NCAA tournament. For the first time since having the season tickets, my dad and I decided to buy tickets to watch the Ramblers play in their conference tournament (Missouri Valley) in St. Louis. For the first time since I can remember, there was a buzz about Loyola basketball and my dad and I watched some great games, and to our amazement Loyola won the tournament, punching their ticket to the Big Dance (NCAA tournament). My dad and I were thrilled and still in disbelief that little Loyola had finally won. As their season continued, you might remember them advancing all the way to the Final Four through a series of comebacks and late game heroics. Reflecting on that time, I am so grateful to have spent that weekend with my father in St. Louis. Life goes by so very fast, and one day my dad won't be here, and I will always have and cherish that time.

* * *

One of the things I tell my students is to appreciate the little things in life. I'll ask them if their parents and the people closest to them know that you love them? If so, when was the last time you told them that? When was the last time you gave a friend or even an acquaintance a sincere compliment? Do your friends know what qualities and character traits they have that you admire? I tell them not to waste another day without telling their parents and loved ones that you love them. I also encourage them to spend time with their parents and loved ones and suggest asking their mom or dad to go out to breakfast or lunch with them or just spend quality time with them.

I think if you were to ask successful married couples the reason for their success, I think many of them would come back and say that the little things are what matters most. In our relationships with the people we care about the most, whether a spouse, a parent, or a friend, doing something elaborate or big doesn't necessarily mean the most. I think it's those consistent little things like a kind note or gesture, a compliment, a listening ear, or a smile…those little things are really the big things in life.

28

A Reminder

With years of living in remission from cancer, after a while it became easy to forget that I had gone through such a health scare in the first place. I did have some precautionary surgeries to remove moles and freckles from my body, and I always make sure to wear sunscreen and a hat if I am out in the sun for a long time. I could even go for a swim in the summer, but just not during peak sunlight in the middle of the day. Life was pretty much the same and I was living a normal life without any afterthought.

About twelve years or so after going through cancer, I started having some bad headaches. At times, they could be very difficult to go through, especially during the school day. A couple times, I'd even get vertigo and have issues with my balance. Imagine falling down in a classroom of 7th graders during a lesson! I'd sure give the kids a laugh until they realized it was serious. Luckily, I never did have a fall. After a while I did see my family doctor, and he ordered an MRI of the brain. I knew why he did. When I was initially diagnosed with cancer, as I have written earlier, I went through a series of tests, including MRI's, CT scans, bone scans, and PET scans. All of these included radiation. Furthermore, during my follow-ups with my oncologist for my first five years post remission, I had to undergo annual

CT scans to make sure another melanoma didn't emerge in my body. The scans were necessary, but still they exposed my body to further radiation. As research has been done in years past, doctors now, depending on the circumstances of each individual case, don't always prescribe yearly scans due to the fact that new cancers can develop as a result of increased exposure to radiation. Because of my exposure to radiation, my doctor ordered an MRI of the brain. He wanted to make sure that a tumor hadn't developed in my brain because of my previous exposure to radiation.

I was a bit concerned, but worry was not my overwhelming thought. The more I thought about what the tests would reveal, the more I thought about gratitude. This was 12 or 13 years after I had survived melanoma when those years may have never happened in the first place. During that time, I had got to witness the joy of seeing my brother get married and my sister get married too. I got to become an uncle, and my dream of becoming a teacher had become a reality. The years that I had as a teacher gave me so much joy and provided me with purpose and meaning like nothing else. God had been good to me and this was no time to have anger or pity.

I've read *Tuesdays with Morrie*, a book by Mitch Albom about his time visiting his dying college professor, Morrie Schwartz, who was suffering from ALS. Every Tuesday, the two had scheduled visits and had meaningful conversations about how to best live life. During one of those visits, Morrie, a man whose body was slowing failing him, had made a rule to only allow himself to feel self-pity for a maximum of five seconds a day. He reasons that feeling sorry for yourself is a real emotion, and he can't fully ignore it, but he also knows that spending your waking hours in self-pity is not going to bring contentment and happiness, but only gratitude and a positive attitude can do that.[63]

During this time in my life, I wasn't sure what a test would reveal about a possible tumor, but I decided to be grateful and happy with the blessings of my life. I didn't have the time or energy to waste on feelings of anger or self-pity.

After the MRI, I will admit the next couple of days I was a little anxious and worried about possible bad results, but not to the point that worry consumed my mind and daily life. I have really been lucky that I do not suffer from severe anxiety. This is a real health issue for many people and can be difficult to navigate through life with it. For me, after going through cancer, I look at life differently when certain risks enter my life. The way I see it, I've already been through a health scare and the worst thing that could possibly happen would be to die, so I figure anything that is not that serious should not require serious worry, especially if is out of my control.

If I were to lose my job or become ill again, those are both things that are to a great extent out of my control. As a teacher, I work very hard to give my students and my school community all that I have to offer, and if I was to ever lose my job, it wouldn't be because I wasn't giving my best at it. As teachers know, school administrators can come and go, and I can't control whether or not my boss gives me a poor evaluation, but I can only control my effort and energy.

If I were to fall seriously ill again, I can't worry about that unless it actually happens. I try to live a healthy lifestyle by eating right and exercising, but in the end God will decide when my time on earth is done. If an illness is to take over my body, however, there is a certain peace in trusting God's will. He is in control of my life and as long as I have God, I have everything, even if I lose my life on this Earth, because for me as a Catholic, I am hopeful to live in everlasting happiness with God in the next life.

As it turned out the MRI was negative! There was no brain tumor found and I had much relief. The scan did reveal a benign cyst however, that may have had an effect on the headaches. After seeing a neurologist, I was diagnosed with migraine headaches. The neurologist I saw was a wonderful man who treated my case with much confidence. Today, I live with the migraines, but now I know what I have to do to lessen the severity and duration of the symptoms.

Everyone in life has something they are fighting. Some have to battle anxiety, some struggle with depression, some live with diabetes, some have learning disabilities they work to overcome, some have physical limitations, and still, some are fighting things far worse. I live my life monitoring sun exposure and struggle from time to time with some migraine headaches and intermittent back issues as well. Compared to what others must live with or even have died from, I'd say I'm pretty lucky. I'll happily take my share of life's burdens and move on. Going through these headaches only gave me a greater sense of appreciation for life and gratitude for God's blessings.

29

Giving Back

After I returned from my pilgrimages to Lourdes as well as my trip to Nevers, France, I had a more urgent realization to do some good in the world. I had a deep sense of gratitude and with that came a desire to express a thanksgiving to God by giving back in small ways. I wanted to make good use of the time I still have left on Earth, so over the years I have devoted some of my time and energy to what I consider worthwhile causes. My time given to certain organizations and volunteer causes has been fulfilling and a blessing. The following are some volunteer endeavors that I have been involved with.

The Mother Teresa of Chicago

I was never really a reader until later in life, but as a teacher with more free time during the summers, I started using some of that time reading more books. Now I read much more often and have realized that reading is one of life's greatest joys. One of the books I read was Walter Payton's autobiography, *Never Die Easy*. I knew Payton had this great reputation as someone uniquely genuine with a giving spirit. One of the stories in the book that captivated me was how Payton began his Christmas toy drive. He ended up getting the idea to begin the toy drive after hosting a Thanksgiving Day event for underprivileged children. With hundreds of kids there, Payton's charitable organization had Santa Claus, Mrs. Claus, Frosty the Snowman, and the Easter Bunny all present for the children. That day, one little boy came up to Walter Payton crying. When Walter asked what was wrong, the boy said, "I can't believe it, I can't believe that Santa Claus is here and that Santa would come all the way from the North Pole just to see me."[64] After that Walter Payton wanted to create a program that would provide kids like these with gifts from Santa Claus.

Payton put so much effort into the program and made sure toys and gifts went to those most in need, and much of the gifts are delivered to children that are in the custody of the Department of Child and Family Services and other local group homes within the Chicago area. The book tells the story that one year in running the toy drive there was a fifteen year-old girl who was accidently given a gift bag for a five-year old. After realizing the mistake, the group home called the Payton Foundation wanting to exchange the gifts for ones more appropriate, but in the end, the girl decided to keep the toys because she had never had a toy before.[65] The kids that receive these toys are the ones that need it the most, and this was really who Walter was to the core, being someone who always had a knack for finding those most overlooked in life.

After I read the book, I wanted to see about getting involved with the charity, which after Walter's passing had changed to The Walter and Connie Payton Foundation. I looked up the foundation and sent an e-mail to them asking if I could help in any way. Later during the football season, I was able to help the Foundation collect toys and donations from Bears fans during one of their home games. Volunteering that day, I met Walter Payton's wife, Connie, and their children, Jarret and Brittney. It was wonderful helping collect donations, but what struck me the most was the sincerity and down-to-earth demeanor of Connie, Jarret, and Brittany. They were all so warm and friendly and treated me like they had known me for years. The Payton's are basically the first family of the Chicago Bears, and here they were so real with everyone they met. I knew that this wasn't at all an act, and that this was just the way they were on a daily basis. It's nice to know that when meeting someone in the public eye that you are not disappointed, and Connie and her family are an example of this. I remember after my first day volunteering, I told my Bear fan friends that Connie Payton gave me a hug! One home game a year, the foundation collects toys and donations at Soldier Field, where the Bears play, and afterwards, the Payton family treats all the volunteers to lunch while we watch the game on TV. One year as I said goodbye to Connie, I ended up spilling a glass of soda on her lap! Connie, in all her grace, said that it was her fault (it wasn't!) and not to worry one bit. I really don't think there would be many celebrities out there who would have reacted like that, but she is the real deal.

For over ten years now, I have also supervised a toy drive for the Walter and Connie Payton Foundation at my Junior High School. Students and staff alike have donated in total about two large boxes of toys to the foundation each year. We are very happy to be able to contribute to the Foundation and I have become more and more impressed with the Payton Family and their commitment to helping others.

I once told Connie Payton that I think she is the Mother Teresa of Chicago, and naturally she laughed it off, but she truly is a special woman, filled with warmth, compassion, and a selfless love for others. The following story will speak to her genuine kindness. In a span of two years, we had a young junior student, who had donated her own birthday gifts to the toy drive for both her 7th and 8th grade years. We also had another young girl who had really went above and beyond promoting the toy drive. I reached out to the Payton Foundation and told them about these two kind-hearted girls who had given so much. Connie was so touched that she made a special trip to our school and spent over an hour visiting and talking with these girls. I bought some tea and scones for the occasion, and the kids were asking Connie for all kinds of life advice, and Connie was just amazing with them. She answered all their questions and gave them some beautiful advice and wisdom that they probably would never had gotten in a classroom. Of course, when Connie's visit was over, she gave the kids big hugs. There's just a warmth about her that can't be denied and everyone I have ever met who's also met her says the same thing.

Connie also devotes much of the Foundation's resources to providing shelter and care for homeless veterans. Her heart just continues to give, and it's been inspiring and a blessing to volunteer with her organization. Her spirit, much like Mother Teresa, is contagious to all who cross her path, and I wish we had more people like her in the world.

The God Squad

If you have ever visited downtown Chicago during the Christmas season, you may have seen the life size nativity scene displayed every year in the public square at Daly Plaza. Terry, a family friend, has been one of the people who has been involved with organizing and planning its setup every year since my childhood. Terry and Jim, a friend of Terry's, have taken the responsibility to organize the Nativity's Scene's setup for many years, but recently they have both retired and have since looked to pass on the torch to someone a bit younger and keep the tradition of maintaining the nativity scene at Daly Plaza. Years ago, Terry asked my good friend Gabe, who is also a family friend of Terry's, and myself to take over the responsibilities of ensuring the Nativity Scene will continue.

There is an interesting history behind the Chicago Nativity Scene and there have been great sacrifices made over the years to ensure that it is kept up. The story begins when the American Jewish Congress sued the city for having a nativity scene inside the lobby of City Hall. They lost their first case, but later a U.S. Circuit Court of Appeals overturned the ruling and the nativity scene was removed without a fight from Chicago's legal department. Once this occurred, some Christian Chicagoans led by William Grutzmacher and Reverend Hiram Crawford decided to put up a nativity scene in Daly Plaza, a public square where free speech and political demonstrations have long taken place. A permit was obtained from the Public Building Commission, but after pressure to remove it, the Public Building Commission reversed itself and ordered government employees to demolish the Nativity Scene, figures and all. When employees started to demolish the nativity, nativity volunteers attempted to defend it from being destroyed and the TV camera crews caught the episode on tape with footage of the destruction and volunteers struggling with government employees. A lawsuit ensued in the U.S. District Court of Northern Illinois, Grutzmacher Vs. Public Building Commission, and despite pressure from the American Jewish Congress, the ACLU, and the American Atheists, Judge James B. Parsons ruled in 1989 that the Public Building Commission was discriminating against all forms of religious expression and thus ordered the Nativity Scene to be erected. Today the Nativity Scene and figures are life-sized and have become a Chicago tradition for many years.[66]

Gabe and I, and well as another volunteer, Ed, agreed to take over the reins, and we all felt that is was privilege to do so. When we said yes, however, we may not have fully realized how much planning, preparation, and work are needed to ensure that this all comes together each Christmas season. We have to ensure we have enough able volunteers to assemble the Nativity. This crew, who call themselves the "God Squad," include everyone from carpenters, electricians, and other volunteer tradesman and they all make sure to set aside time during the Christmas season to ensure the Nativity tradition continues in Chicago. We also have to secure a permit, insurance, and help transport the Nativity Scene and its contents back and forth. All this can be quite expensive and we each also send out donation letters to potential donors because without them, the entire project would be financially impossible.

Gabe and I at the Nativity Scene Dedication in 2018

In the end, all the hard work comes together and it's well worth it to see the beautiful Nativity Scene during the Christmas season and help people remember the real meaning behind Christmas. On the Saturday after Thanksgiving, we have a little ceremony commemorating our Nativity. My good friend Tom and several choir members from his local parish sing Christmas carols after blessings are given from a Catholic Priest and the Pastor of Israel Methodist Church, the same church the Reverend Hiram Crawford, who was instrumental in the fight to keep the Nativity Scene years ago, once presided over. Catholic parishioners and Church members from Israel Methodist as well as family, friends, and Christians from all over Chicago come together that day to celebrate the coming birth of Our Lord. For my family, we have made this a Christmas tradition that we look forward to. Over the years, I've met some truly wonderful people in helping put up the Nativity Scene, and it's nice to be involved with something that brings many people together.

The Most Important Game

When I became the girls' softball coach at my school, I had this idea that I wanted to take the team to play a game for fun at a local nursing home. Not really knowing where to begin, I went to a nursing home not too far from our school community and spoke to someone at the front desk, but whoever I spoke to was a bit taken back. They told me they'd get back to me, but after a week of not hearing from them, I decided to look elsewhere. I tried another nursing home and met Nancy who was their Activity Coordinator for this home. Nancy was full of energy and after I told her about what I wanted to do, she said we could play in the nearby field and asked if we could even come on the next Saturday. After being given the run around from the other home, I was shocked at Nancy's flexibility and eagerness to help!

We ended up playing a 16-inch softball game (a Chicago tradition) as residents of the nursing home came out of the home in their wheelchairs and watched the girls play a game for fun. Later we set up batting tees where residents were able to take swings with a whiffle bat and ball. The girls were great with the residents, and they all gave player introductions to the residents announcing their position on the team, their favorite athlete, and their personal baseball allegiance of Chicago, the White Sox or Cubs.

We've taken our softball team to the same nursing home each year for ten years and counting (minus 2020), and I still haven't figured out who gets more out of the visit, the residents or the girls. After the visit, many of the girls keep saying that they want to go back and visit their favorite residents, and over the years many of the kids have. During my second year coaching softball our team made it to the Illinois State Tournament, and when we did, one of the nursing home residents sent us a good luck card wishing us well with a check for $50 to take the girls out for pizza. The team wanted to say thank you and each of the girls autographed a softball for that thoughtful resident. After that, I have the girls sign a couple of softballs each year and we give them to some of the residents.

Some years it's too hot on our scheduled visit to play a softball game outside, so we have had to improvise. We still are able to let residents bat a whiffle ball in the activity room, but we have also made time for the kids to interact with residents. A couple years we gave about ten residents a softball and I had the girls sit down at tables while each resident would take their turn getting players to sign the ball one at a time. This allowed the kids and the residents a chance to visit and talk for a minute.

Just recently, we had a memorable visit. Again, the weather was too hot to play a game outside and the team and a number of residents were all in the Activity Room inside the home. One the female residents, in a not so friendly voice, asked us, "Why are you here?" The girls were a little surprised with the question, but they all found it humorous. After our visit and while the residents were returning to their rooms, the girls came up with the idea of making greeting cards for the residents and they wanted to deliver them to their rooms and they especially wanted to see that crabby lady. When the team arrived to her room, she was just so appreciative and told the girls the she was just having a bad day, but you could tell that little trip delivering a card to her room made all the difference and really brightened her day.

I've joked over the years with the girls and have advised them not to date until they get married, which many don't quite get the joke. However, one thing I do tell them is that when they do start dating well into the future, any guy that would not be willing to volunteer at a nursing home or the like is not worth their time. I've been lucky to have coached both some talented players and some even kinder girls over the years, and being their coach is something I treasure. The compassion they have towards perfect strangers in need of a pick-me-up is a sign of good character, and service at a nursing home helps put their character into action. While wining has its place and importance, the greatest result of the season is not whether we win a championship, but whether kids grow up living lives of character with a generous spirit for doing some good in the world.

Angels from Heaven

Again, around the time I returned from my trip to Lourdes, I noticed there was a local Special Recreation Agency located close by one the school buildings within my school district. I don't know why I never noticed it before, but there it was. One day I decided to inquire about volunteering there and walked into the office. I met with someone there about getting involved with the organization, and after a background check, I was able to begin volunteer work.

The agency oversees and organizes recreation activities and events for those with special needs. There are programs like swim lessons, arts and crafts sessions, but also special events like going to a dance, having dinner, or taking in a movie. The agency also has their own Special Olympic Teams that compete with other agencies in the area.

On my first day, I went to a minor league baseball game with a group of participants and had a great time. I enjoyed talking with participants and the agency even paid for my hot dog and soda! What a deal! My first year there, I made some special events, was a regular aid during their bowling season, and helped coach Special Olympic Softball. I enjoyed my time very much and I've learned a lot about what is important in life from witnessing the happy demeanor (well most of the time!) of the participants I worked with. These were mostly adults who had real physical and or mental struggles in their lives, yet they seemed like they were always happy, and they were grateful for the time you spent with them. I'm convinced that some of them are angels from heaven that God has sent to us to show us His love and what is really important in life.

After volunteering for a year, I realized I could get paid for my time, so I inquired about being made a part-time employee, and I have been working for the agency for many years now, coaching mostly Special Olympic Softball and helping to supervise special events like dances, theme park visits, movies, and the like. My time there has been incredibly rewarding and fulfilling working with those with special needs and I feel that once you have an experience with those with disabilities of any kind, your outlook on life will change for the better. We are filled with deeper gratitude for our blessings, but also a great respect to those working through life with special challenges.

30

If I Were Ever Prosecuted...

As I wrote in a previous chapter, the character talk I give to students at my school about the *Seven Things to Do*, can be said that it has Christian undertones. John Wooden was a devout Christian, and the card that his father gave him advises to read the Bible and pray. As I noted, since I teach in the public school and can't teach or encourage one religion over another, I have to edit those parts of the card I give the students. However, every public school, and nearly every teacher models their student environment on the motto of the "golden rule," to treat others as you want to be treated. The golden rule is derived from Christianity as Christ explained that we should "love your neighbor as yourself" (Mark 12:31). However, in a public-school setting, good teachers and administrators realize that universal truths are worth modeling to students, regardless of where they come from and they are wise to encourage students to live by the golden rule.

Another one of my favorite John Wooden quotes reads that "if I were ever prosecuted for my religion, I truly hope there would be enough evidence to convict me."[67] Some of my students know that I am Catholic because several of them see me teaching religious education classes at one of the local community parishes, and some of the kids in CCD are actually my former 7th grade math students in school. However, that is only a fraction of my students. I hope, more importantly, that my students and anyone who comes in contact with me knows that I am Christian by the way I live my life and by the way I treat others. A good question for us Christians to ask ourselves would be: How do people know that I am a Christian? We hope it would be by how we live instead of seeing us in church once in a while.

I know that I am a work in progress. I have done plenty of things in my life that I am not proud of and I am by no means perfect, but then again no one is. For each time in my life that I have been an example of following Christ, there's probably another example of how I was not. The beautiful thing about being a Christian, about being a Catholic, is that what matters most is your decision to work towards improvement, to work towards being a better person, and if you keep making that commitment, to get up when you fall, Christ will walk with you, and slowly you will start making strides and grow into a better person, the person He intends you to be.

* * *

It's not easy being a kid these days. I don't envy my students who are growing up in today's climate. There are far too many distractions and temptations, and far too few role-models and good influences. Sadly, in my career in education, I've seen kids who in their early teens are depressed and searching desperately to find their way during the uncertainty of adolescence. Kids are searching for meaning, for love, and for truth, and our secular world can limit and hide the answers to their search. I've had the good fortune to work with some wonderful school counselors and social workers during my career. They have a tough job, and while they can never divulge confidential conversations they have with students, they have told me from time to time that this student or that student identifies me as someone that they feel they can trust and talk to. Over the years, students have sought me out for help. In middle school, it can often be the trivialities of being an early teen, but sometimes it's more serious.

There are sometimes very difficult things that kids have to face during these years like the loss of a loved one or coping with the divorce of their parents. I've also had students suffer from depression, and unfortunately sometimes to the point of suicidal thoughts. Obviously, students going through grave circumstances are working with our support staff, but when they also confide in me, their teacher, I have to be authentic with them. Most of the time, I just try and reassure them that they will get through this, that they should take things one step at a time, and that I am always there for them whenever they need me.

Whatever the case may be, when a student approaches me with a serious situation, I will ask students if I could pray for them, and all the students I've asked have always been more than alright with it. Sometimes, I've asked kids if they are Christian, and if they are, I give them more encouragement, and advice for them to trust in God. For kids that were Catholic or Christian, with parental permission, I've even given families holy water from Lourdes for loved ones suffering from illness, or in other cases I have given a student a little prayer card. Every time I've encouraged my students in ways like these, they appreciate that I was willing to open up to them, and I've had several parents write letters of thanks to me for simply giving their children some encouragement and sharing little acts of faith.

While I'm not an expert in counseling, one thing I have found to be true is that when we are feeling down and depressed, we always feel better if we are able to volunteer our time to help others. It's the very act of service to those in need that helps us look beyond ourselves and realize that most of our problems are small compared to the circumstances of others. When I've worked with kids battling depression, at times I've encouraged them to volunteer in some way. Some students take me up on being a peer tutor during their lunch break in my classroom. For others, I have worked with parents and counselors on setting up volunteer opportunities at a local agency that works with those with special needs, and I've seen some wonderful changes in their outlook towards life. It is amazing how our view of life can change when we spend time in service to others.

* * *

For years now in Illinois if you can believe it, our state allows for schools to have a moment of silence each day after saying the pledge of allegiance. This is there for kids who would like to pray silently for a half-minute to have the opportunity to do so. I advise my students to respect those who say a prayer to begin their day and mention to them that this is something I do as well. Every morning after the pledge of allegiance, I make my sign of the cross, say a prayer to myself, and end also with the sign of the cross. Kids seeing me do this is the only outward indicator to them that I am Christian, but to some it may be the only time they witness someone praying. This act isn't a big deal to kids, but it is a sign that as a Christian, I am called to live my life and treat others in a certain way, and it's a reminder to me that I must live up to this calling to be a good example of a practicing Christian for those that cross my life path, especially my students.

I am not one to hide who I am as a Christian, but I am also not preachy. I am in no position to judge anyone, and I feel that acting in that way is one sure way to repel someone from Christianity instead of attracting them to it. I don't go off spouting my opinions and beliefs, but if asked or challenged, I won't shy away. I want to be someone who despises the sin, but still empathizes with and loves the sinner. Over the years, the teaching staff at my school have come to know me as "religious." I take this as a compliment. I try to live my life as a practicing Catholic, and I don't know how that would be possible if I didn't place a value on religion. There is a negative connotation with the word religion today, and many people consider those who are religious to be "fanatical." I attend Mass, go to Confession, and pray the rosary, so if that makes me a fanatic, then so be it, but I'm also a regular guy not afraid to attend a ballgame and have a couple of beers every now and again.

A few years ago, I was scheduled to be in a meeting concerning a student's future. There is a reason that no one says, "I wish I was in junior high school all over again." It's a difficult time for students as they try to fit in and find their way during adolescence. As a man, who was once a boy, I can attest that there are many short circuits that I went through in my early teen years and navigating through it all wasn't an exact science. Many boys during these years are navigating through maturity, responsibility, and acceptance in school, and this school meeting like many of the hundreds of meetings I've had for male students, had a lot of those familiar middle school boy issues. In the meeting was one of the school's social workers, who was actually a former student of mine from my first-year teaching. He was always a good student when I taught him years before, but I had gotten to know him on a different level as a co-worker and we've now become friends. I was pleased to find out that he also was very faithful to his Christian Faith. The staff and administration were a little concerned about how the meeting would go. We were all invested in the young student finding success at school and have had mixed results along the way. Besides the boy's parents, I was the last person to arrive at the meeting, and while I was on my way, unbeknownst to me, our social worker had asked the staff if we could say a prayer before the parents arrived, and oh yeah, he wanted me to lead the prayer. I walked in, sat down, and then was promptly asked, with the agreement of all the 7 or 8 staff members in the room, if I would lead them in prayer. I was confused, and I thought that maybe they were joking. I asked if this would be ok, to pray before a meeting with teachers and staff at a public school? Would I get in trouble? They all said no, and they were adamant that they wanted me to lead a prayer. It took me a few seconds to realize that they were indeed serious. I then did what they asked. We prayed and I asked the Holy Spirit to provide us with the wisdom and guidance to what was best for the child and asked this in the name of Jesus. The meeting went unbelievably well, and in fact, it couldn't have gone better. What surprised me the most however, was what the boy's mother did at the end of the meeting when she said, "maybe I should start taking my son to church."

That meeting taught me something. For one, how can you expect God to come into a situation if you never ask Him to? I knew that I had to pray for his guidance and assistance more often. I also realized that although I had never had conversations about my faith with nearly all of those staff members in the meeting, they knew that my faith was an important part of my life, and they trusted and encouraged me to pray.

All of us wonder from time to time, what it will be like when we die, and for those that are Christian, we wonder what Christ will ask or say to us after our death? I imagine that He might ask us how did we love in our life? How did we give? Were we embarrassed of Him in front of others, or did we embrace Him? I'm not sure exactly what will happen or if any questions will be asked at all, but one thing I do hope for me when I die would be that I hope that Christ recognizes me. I hope I have lived in a way in that He wouldn't consider me a stranger. I hope that in the end, I would have served Him in serving others, and I hope I would have prayed in a way confident of His help, and grateful for His love and mercy.

31

No One is Beneath You

Can you think of the worst date that you have ever been on? Everyone has a story of their worst date and I have mine. I had lunch with a girl in downtown Chicago on a first date, and throughout the meal all she talked about was how everyone she worked with in her office was "worthless" or a "waste of time." She kept going on about how her coworkers were unintelligent and incompetent while giving me the impression that she was somehow above them. I have to admit that after a few minutes of this I started to tune her out and actually ordered another beer to get through the meal.

As I was walking back through downtown Chicago, I couldn't help but feel pity for this girl. She had no idea what she sounded like and I didn't have the heart to tell her. A person may have some noble pursuits and donate time or money to some very worthwhile charitable causes, but to me a better judge of character is how someone treats people in their daily life. That is who the person is day in and day out. On my walk back to my car, a homeless man came up to me and said, "I'm hungry, can you help me?" In Chicago, like many other major cities, there is a homeless population. Many people don't bother with them and just keep walking, and I will admit that some of the people who claim to be homeless are actually not. However, just because some are not truthful does not mean that all are trying to mislead you. I could tell that the man who came up to me that afternoon was genuine, so I said, "sure." I saw a food court type place across the street, and I told the man that I'd buy him something to eat. I bought him a sandwich and something to drink. I also bought a soda for myself and we sat down and talked for a while. During those few minutes he told me of his situation, his children, but he also remained upbeat and hopeful to find a job soon and I even remember him cracking a few jokes. I realized quickly that I had enjoyed my time with this homeless man much more than I had on my date.

We live in a fast-paced world and often those that are in most need of affirmation of their humanity are usually the ones most overlooked. Even if I don't have anything to spare or any time to give, the least I can do is acknowledge and smile at someone less fortunate. Nowadays, I always keep $5 gift cards to local restaurants in my car, and when I see someone in need, I can at least ask them if they'd like one. It's not much, but it's a little something to let someone know that they aren't alone.

As a teacher, my job is affected by the economy and the population of our community, and I fully realize that my current employment is not guaranteed from year to year. If I were to lose my job, it would only be a matter of time before my situation would dramatically change and who knows, I could be homeless or in dire need.

I've always felt that one of the greatest judges of someone's character is to watch how they treat those in lesser thought of jobs or circumstances. How does someone treat workers like waiters and waitresses, fast-food staff, retail staff, or custodians? Do they say please and thank you no matter what the situation? Will they clean up after themselves or will they say something like, "that's not my job?" Being a teacher now for over 17 years, I have always made it a point to befriend our custodial and maintenance staff and our bus drivers. I have gotten to know them well, enjoy speaking with them, and have taken an interest in their lives. Every Christmas, I make sure to give our school's custodial and maintenance staff a small gift of some kind, which is usually a gift card with a thank you note. It's easy to overlook them at school. Everyday students and teachers enter a school that is clean and beautiful and each day we leave school, and it is dirty until the night crew goes from one classroom to another vacuuming and wiping down walls, desks, and sometimes removing gum. We arrive the next morning without much of a second thought. After I started giving small gifts to custodial and maintenance staff for Christmas, the reaction I get from them is like I just gave them a thousand dollars, even though it may be just a $10 gift card for coffee. It's not about the gift at all, it's just that someone cared enough to notice and say thank you.

Just like the parable about Lazarus and the rich man in Luke's gospel (Luke 16: 19-31), those that may have wealth and esteem in this life, may not be so lucky in the next life. While having security is by no means wrong, we must be careful not to look down upon those who are in need or seem forgotten in the eyes of the world. St. Paul further writes that "God chose the lowly and despised of the world, those who count for nothing, to reduce to nothing those who are something" (1 Cor 1:28). C.S. Lewis also reminds us that, "a proud man is always looking down on things and people; and, of course, as long as you are looking down, you cannot see something that is above you."[68] If God is above us in Heaven, then we won't be able to see Him while we're looking down on others.

32

Do the Next Right thing

How do we create character? How do you create good citizens, good spouses, good parents, and good employees? Every community wants a good citizen. Every spouse wants a committed marriage. Every child wants reliable parents. Every employer wants honest and trustworthy employees. There is one constant ingredient in becoming all of these, and that simply stated is character.

In thinking about how to be at your best in life, I think it is relevant to analyze those who are at their life's worst. Consider those suffering from addiction. Let's take alcoholics for example. Many in our world today suffer from alcoholism, and some have lost the ability to control their addiction so much that it ends up costing them their spouse, or their family, or their job, or in some cases, all three. Those who have hit rock bottom eventually come to the realization that the only way to regain happiness and peace in their lives is through sobriety. Like anyone in situations like these, those who want to get their life back must make better decisions. They undoubtedly will know that in the future they will be faced with temptations to have a drink, so after committing to sobriety, they must decide to do the next right thing over and over again. When walking past a bar, they must decide not to enter. When a friend offers them a drink, they must say no. If they are invited to a party that they know they can't handle the temptations to drink, they must decline. When that next temptation comes, they must do the next right thing. Eventually winning these little battles minute to minute, hour to hour, day to day, week to week, month to month, and year to year, they can overcome their addition and they can win the war. They can get their life back together one piece at a time.

The same logic applies in building character from an early age. Doing the next right thing time and time again creates good character, and this begins in childhood. Good parents tell their children at an early age to listen to their conscience, the "little voice inside your head." When that little voice is loud in our head, it shows that we have a healthy conscience. It should bother us until we make the right decision, or acknowledge and rectify a mistake made. On the contrary, the more we ignore that "little voice," the softer that voice will be and eventually it will completely go away. When you see stories on the news of horrendous crimes being committed, I imagine those crimes aren't committed by those with "loud consciences." I imagine that those who commit heinous crimes stopped hearing even a soft voice in their head long ago. To build a good conscience, requires building good character, and building good character requires making the next right decision.

If children are taught at an early age the value and reward of having character, they will work to build it. When faced with a challenging decision, they will want to make the right choice that elevates their character, not the choice that will destroy it. Temptations and trials will come to all with and without good character, but those who understand the value of character will be more likely to overcome the wrong decision, such as getting behind a wheel after drinking too much or choosing to try drugs just to see how it feels. Just think of those people with successful marriages and successful careers. Yes, this requires hard work and commitment, but to have lasting success, good decision-making cannot be discounted. It's paramount to success. To be successful in marriage, spouses must make the right decisions every day. Husbands and wives must choose to listen, choose to raise their children together, choose to make sacrifices for each other, choose to stay faithful, and choose to love each other. In the same way, consistent good decisions must be made in the workplace. To be successful in any career, you must choose hard work even when difficult, choose to be honest even when it may seem easy not to, choose to learn from criticism even if it may be hard to hear, and sometimes choose to adapt to circumstances even if you are set in your ways.

Doing the next right thing consistently also prepares us for the really big decisions in life. When we are especially young, we are faced with the peer pressures of drugs, alcohol, sex, and what types of people we let into our lives. These are choices that could drastically affect our future. In adulthood, we are faced with more decisions such as the choice of a spouse, the choice of a career, and how to best raise our children. These are all life-changing decisions that force us to listen to our conscience and prayerfully consider where God may be leading you. If we have that habit of doing the next right thing for the little decisions, when it comes time to make a life-altering decision, more times than not, we will be on the right side of those choices.

Doing the next right will not always be easy, but if you make it an everyday commitment, in the end you can reflect on your life with more integrity than most people achieve today.

33

Highs and Lows

Life is filled with peaks and valleys for sure. Everyone will have their ups and downs, and often they stem from what people say about you. As a teacher and coach, I've had my fair share of praise and criticism as you might imagine. What I've learned over the years is that whether getting compliments or insults, it's best to remain balanced in your self-perception.

When we're getting lots of praise, we have to take a step back in order to avoid praise going to your head. It's nice to get compliments, and we should give them to others, but we have to be careful when on the receiving end. If not careful, arrogance and conceit can creep in and change the person that you are for the worse. If you think about it, arrogance is just about the worst personality trait that one could have. I for one, can't imagine having a very close friend that is filled with arrogance.

Another one of John Wooden's poems that rings true is:

> *Talent is God-given: be humble.*
>
> *Fame is man-given: be thankful.*
>
> *Conceit is self-given: be careful.*[69]

Compliments are a blessing to receive, but they don't represent our entire self. We are never as perfect as someone can make us out to be. There will always be a character flaw that each of us needs to work on, and there will always be changes we need to make in order to be the best person we can become.

On the flip side, a slew of insults and cut downs can really take its toll on our soul as well. While we're never as good as people can make us out to be, we're also never as bad as people may say as well. As a teacher, and more so as a coach, I've had my fair share of negative comments from parents about a game decision I may have made or playing time for a son or daughter on a team. For any coach, this comes with the territory, and for the most part, it is unavoidable. I take pride in being a coach that gives each of my players a fair shot at playing time, but when these kind of complaints happen, I have to remind myself that I'm doing my best to be fair to all my players while putting a team together I feel puts my players in the best possible position to succeed. It's also good to not take things like this personal. If verbally attacked, I also have to remind myself that someone could be just having a bad day and may have got caught up in emotions. When emotions run high, people can say things that they don't really mean, and sometimes, but not always, they will apologize later for their words or actions.

Nowadays, social media has taken verbal attacks to a new level, which for our young adults, can become detrimental to their mental and emotional health. This is also true for adults. It's easier to insult and verbally attack a person behind a screen than it is to do so to someone's face. Over the years, I've prayed for and worked towards having a calm demeanor willing to listen to opinions and thoughts of others, while still having strong opinions of my own. However, increasingly in the days of social media, people are less and less willing to listen to the thoughts of others, and even more quick to verbally abuse. For me personally, the abuse I received on social media for sharing my opinions was more than my soul could bear, and I have since deactivated my Facebook account. After I decided to do so, I found great relief and more happiness with more time to focus on self-improvement.

Social media does indeed have avenues for positivity, but for teenagers navigating through junior high and high school, it can be disastrous for their health and well-being. Kids at this age especially are emotionally vulnerable, and attacks from peers on social media can be devastating. As a teacher in a public school, I am well aware that the vast majority of kids have some kind of social media account. While there are always exceptions, I do advise my middle school students they don't need to have a social media account and life will go on without them just fine, but if they do choose to have an account (with parent permission of course), I remind them to use it for positive outcomes only. As my mom repeatedly told me time and time again growing up, "If you can't say something nice, don't say it all." That motto still applies in the online world. Still, it's inevitable that insults and nasty things will be said online, and I make it a point to tell my students not to use social media to measure their self-worth, and that each and every one of them are worth more than all the stars in the sky, and definitely more that a few likes on Facebook.

Success and failure in life also bring highs and lows. It's perfectly natural when success comes our way, we can feel indestructible. Likewise, when we are overcome with failure, it's easy to feel there is no way out. It's good to remember that success and failure are never permanent. Whether going through periods of success or strings of failures, there is much wisdom in John A. Simone's advice, "If you're in a bad situation, don't worry, it'll change. If you're in a good situation, don't worry it'll change."[70]

Having balance in life makes all the difference. Not getting too high with compliments and refraining from getting too low with insults gives stability in your life. This life balance leads us away from one the most troublesome character flaws, arrogance, while leading to one of the most admirable character traits, humility.

34

Take Courage

Courage is often thought of as the most important of all virtues, meaning that without it, no other virtue is possible. One of my favorite quotes is one from Maya Angelou when she said, "You can be kind and true and fair and generous and just, and even merciful, occasionally. But to be that thing time after time, you have to really have courage."[71]

If you really think about that quote, it makes a lot of sense, so let's take a moment to analyze it. If you want to be kind, you must have the courage to do so even when it is difficult to be kind to someone that is difficult or unkind themselves. To be true to yourself, you must have the courage to follow your convictions and faith, even when no one is looking or if you have to stand alone. If you want to be fair, you have to practice that in all situations and to all people, even when being fair means saying no to a friend. To be generous, it takes courage to be generous and loving in such a way as giving your own lunch away to someone who needs it more or giving to a charity or to a collection basket, even though doing may require making some sacrifices to make it through the week. When we are just, we must have the courage to work for justice for everyone, and not just the people in our life's circle or community. And if we are to be merciful, we must have the courage to forgive no matter how difficult doing so might be.

Courage is one of the most difficult virtues to live out, yet it is vital for us to embrace if we want to grow in personal character. In today's society, I think it would be safe to say that our world is in desperate need of men and women who are willing to have the courage to do the right thing. The deficiency in courage is evident with many public figures. I can think of several celebrity types or those in the public eye who will easily lie about some scandal they've been involved in until the very end, only finally admitting to their lie when the truth is apparent. Sadly, some of these figures are actors or athletes that kids look up to, but what message are they giving our youth? It seems there are few men and women, either public or private, that live lives of courageous character and we as a society are in dire need of them.

As a teacher, there have been a couple times in my life where I had to have some courage. One year there was a group of Christian students at my public school that organized an event where they would meet before school at our flagpole and pray together. I loved the idea, and wanted to join them, but when I learned of this scheduled day, I did hesitate a little. I wondered that if I participated and joined them in prayer, would I be fired or disciplined at my job? I could have easily avoided the situation all together and arrived at school through a different entrance, but I knew I couldn't do that. I was a Christian too, and I had to acknowledge them, even if doing so meant that I may lose my job. The 1st Amendment of the Constitution protects freedom of religion and freedom to assemble, and although I knew my rights as an American, I am also aware that in today's day in age, some municipalities are unwilling to recognize it. Praying at a flagpole before school began is a far cry from leading students in prayer or Bible study during the school day, and I was confident my school district would see that, but still there is always a chance. I couldn't help but think of what Jesus said when he told the apostles, "whoever acknowledges me before men, I also will acknowledge before my Father who is in heaven, but whoever denies me before men, I also will deny before my Father who is in heaven" (Matthew 10: 32-33). My answer was clear. The next morning, I did join the students at the flagpole. I prayed the *Our Father* with them, and I told the kids that I was really proud of them for their courage.

If we see a problem within our society and we don't have the courage to act, how can we expect anything to change. I am pro-life, and I feel that the judgement of a society can be determined by how they treat their most vulnerable. The unborn are society's voiceless and defenseless, and I can't think of anyone more vulnerable than an unborn child. As a Catholic however, I do want to point out that I also believe in God's infinite and limitless mercy, and for those who have experienced the pain of an abortion, God's forgiveness and love are really the only thing that will provide lasting peace. I hope to never be one to judge those who have made mistakes and are trying to find healing, because when it comes down to it, we are all broken in one way or another.

Standing up for the unborn is something that I've always been passionate about! I just can't understand how some people advocate for abortion when adoption is such a loving option. Every child is unique and beautiful, and the arguments that abortion is women's healthcare do not ring true, as an unborn child has separate DNA from their mother while having their own independent heartbeat as early as 16 days after conception.[72] Sadly, I feel that many women feel forced into an abortion from a boyfriend, husband, or family pressure, and my heart goes out to them.

A few years ago, there was pro-life rally around the neighborhood of my school community. I have attended several pro-life rallies, but this one was different being in my school community. At first, I wasn't sure if I would attend, but then again, I remembered the words of Christ when he warned about our choice to either acknowledge or deny Him, so I knew I had no excuse to stay home. I did go, and it turned out that I did run into a student of mine riding his bike. He stopped to say hello, and asked what I was doing, so I told him. I said that I was pro-life, and that I thought the lives of all unborn children are precious. I think it was a good example for him to see that some things are worth fighting for.

The desire to be liked, which is a desire we each have, is one that can be an obstacle to courage. Whether speaking your mind in person, in a group, or on some social media outlet, it is increasingly challenging to take a stand for what you believe because you may lose friends, may receive public ridicule, or in drastic cases lose your career or livelihood. All those things, even the most severe, are worth the risk if it means you are being faithful to God and to yourself. My relationship and friendship with Christ is what matters most, because that relationship is meant to last beyond our earthy lives. While I don't look so much to those in the public eye for courage, those that I do look up to are those that are willing to speak their mind in order to be true to themselves. I may not even agree with everything that they have to say, but when someone acts courageously in a world that lacks it, it is distinguished, inspiring, and refreshing to see. In my own life, because of having differing opinions, I've lost some longtime friends while other friendships and relationships have become strained. Still other friends, although having differing opinions, still love and respect me for being myself, and I feel the same about them. These are friendships and relationships that will stand the test of time and I cherish them. Just one friendship of this magnitude is worth more than any number of superficial friendships.

Courage Today

I wrote most of this book during the difficult spring and summer months of 2020, but as I finish writing this current chapter near the end of 2021, our society has become increasingly more challenging. As I have mentioned, I am an Illinois public school teacher in the southwest Chicago suburbs. In the matter of a few months, laws have been passed in Illinois that will soon require students in grades 6 through high school to receive sex-education instruction that includes teaching kids that abortion is an option to terminate a pregnancy. Additional coursework is also to be provided on "gender identity." Besides the sex education legislation, Illinois lawmakers have also passed a bill that teaches "Equity Standards," in which I believe will lead children to undermine the teachings of Dr. Martin Luther King, Jr. Instead of following Dr. King's dream of judging not by the color of our skin, but by the content of our character, I feel that students will learn to define others primarily by their skin color, which will in turn lead to hate and not love.

These laws will go into effect starting in the year 2023 and I have made preparations to leave my job and even work outside of Illinois, if I must. Although, my school district may not require me to teach these topics, and they may even not teach them all together in their schools, I still wrestle with staying in my position when my current state endorses ideas I believe to be evil. If I am to stay in my position, I may be able to help kids think independently and make their own decisions. I know I am not perfect, but as a Christian, we all try to live a life of Christian example in how we treat others and spend our daily life. I try my best to be that type of example for my students, and if I leave my current job, I feel in some ways that example may be lost to kids. However, what I struggle with is the realization that I teach in a state that promotes indoctrination of ideas, and even though I could never, and will never teach these topics, there may become a time where I have no choice but to leave. As I have mentioned, I have made preparations to relocate. I have sold my home and secured a teaching certificate in another State. I ask the Holy Spirit to guide me to where He wants me to be, and I know God will place me where He desires.

If you were to ask me maybe 5 years ago if I ever thought a day would come where I felt I had to leave behind my beloved Summit Hill Junior High School, I would not have believed you. I have loved being a teacher and a coach at Summit Hill. I have poured my heart and soul into my school, students, athletes, and community, but at the end of the day I feel I need to protect my soul. I will never teach that abortion is ok, or that gender is a feeling, or that skin color defines a person. I know that my

Catholic faith teaches us that the lives of all unborn children are sacred to God, that there are only two genders, and that God does not judge us by our skin color, but by how we live our lives. I realize that my school district may accommodate me and that I may not be forced to participate in the teaching of these untruths, but still this weighs on my heart. I don't want to participate in a system that helps to lead students into moral relativism and confusion. Even though it pains me to consider leaving, I trust that God will place me where I am supposed to be at this point in my life.

If courage was easy, then we wouldn't have second thoughts about living it, but it is difficult to live sometimes. Sometimes there will be consequences for standing up for what we believe in. We could lose friends, we could be arrested, or we could even lose our job, but in the end, when we stand up for *truth* and our *faith*, we can never lose for no matter what the situation, for if we have God, we have everything!

35

The Rule of Five

To this day, I have been very fortunate to have many friends. For the most part, I've always had the ability to get along with others, and I make an effort to try to have a positive outlook on life. This has allowed me to make friends easily, however, as time passes, I have realized that there is a big difference between a casual friend and a friend who genuinely cares for you, who wants the best for you, and who is someone whom you can always count on in times of need. Those kind of friends, real friends, are so rare in life that you will be lucky if you can say you have five true friends.

This is what some call the rule of five. If you were to ask a student in middle school, high school, and even college, they may say that they a lot of friends without thinking much about it. But by the time you reach your mid-twenties or afterwards, you might have a different answer. It's those friends that are left after your college years have long passed that are usually the ones that are in it for the long haul. As I look at my own life, the number of close friends who have my best interest at heart, that I can truly count on, I could probably count them on 1 to 2 hands.

These are people that sincerely have your best interests in mind for you, and you should also have their best interests at heart too. As you may have seen especially in teenage years, kids will be friends with one person for different reasons. It could be that they simply want to fit in with the "in crowd," or this person can do something for them, or they may have something that I want. These friendships are obviously very superficial and will not stand the test of time. Real friends are giving of their time and of themselves, so if you are the one that is constantly giving or doing something kind for a friend, and that person does not take the time or energy to be kind back to you, then you probably are wasting your time with this person, and should focus your time and energy on those who do genuinely care for you.

What is a real friendship? Think of it this way, how many of the friends you have now would answer a call from you at 3 A.M., get out of bed, and rush over to be there for you in a time of need? If you're as old as me, you've probably seen the movie, *It's a Wonderful Life*, starring Jimmy Stewart and Donna Reed. Every Christmas season, even today, you can find it being played on several television stations throughout the holidays. My favorite seen is the very end of the movie. George Baily, Jimmy Stewart's character, has sacrificed everything in his life for others. He sacrificed going to college and pursuing his own dreams to run the Building and Loan Company that was left to his family after his father's passing. This was not the life he wanted at all, but for the sake of his family, his wife and children, and his friends in the community, he devotes his whole life to helping others have their chance at the American Dream. In the end, through an unfortunate mistake, he is about to lose the Building and Loan, maybe his family, and even in a moment of desperation, George tries ending his own life, only to be saved by an wingless Angel who shows him what life would be like had he never been born. In the end however, his wife alerts all his friends, family, and those who love him to come to his aide, and the movie ends with hundreds of people gathered at his home donating large sums of money to save his company, his family, and his life. The movie ends with a quote from Mark Twain as it reads, "No man is a failure who has friends."[73] I have watched the movie coutless times, but even to this day when I watch that scene, I can't help but get a little emotional. But the question remains, how many of our friends would be there for us during our greatest hour of need?

Another quality about a true friendship, is that a friend is not simply being a people pleaser, someone that will just tell you what you want to hear. Friends like this will never help you grow as a person, and they definitely won't provide the necessary challenge to become a better person. I have been lucky enough in life to have friends that have been bold enough and honest enough to tell me when I was wrong and point out that I needed to make an adjustment and decide a different course of action. In some ways, friends and parents are similar in that they both challenge us to be better. If you had wise parents like I have had, you might recall times in your life where you were somewhere that you shouldn't have been, or did something that you shouldn't have done. Parents must have these super-powers sometimes since they always find out where you were, or what you did before you realize it, and a simple question like "where were you?" or "what did you do last night?" have strategic implications. Parents that ask these questions to their children ask them full well knowing the truth, but they are testing your honesty and your character. Good friends might never question you in the same way your parents did, but a good friend still is someone pushing you to be your best. As I have gotten older, I have also gotten to a point that I recognize my parents as not only my parents, but also friends, and with time it's interesting that they seem to have become smarter and smarter even though they haven't changed.

I have friends that I enjoy going to a sporting event with, taking in a ballgame on television, or just meeting up for a beer. It's good to have friends that have the same interests and enjoy the same things, but what I have learned in my life is that the deepest friendships are with those who share the same core values, and for me that includes my Christian faith. My closest of friends and I share a common faith in Christ, and we are never afraid to ask for prayers, to share the Bible, and to encourage each other with reminders of hope and trust in God. These are the friends I would trust with my life. These are the friends who would drop everything and be there for each other in a second. As we get older, get married, have children, and take on responsibilities, we don't often get to spend as much time together as we used to, but when we do have time together, no matter how long it may have been since the last time, we pick up like it was yesterday. Real friendship will always keep strong bonds, and there is no greater bond than a common faith in each other and more importantly, God.

36

The Road Less Traveled

One of the many certainties in life is that eventually our lives will come to an end. The time we have on Earth has a limit and we must choose to spend it as wisely as we can. As I have mentioned before, you'll never see a Uhaul truck behind a hearse, which means there is more to life than simply accumulating material possessions.

While this is not the greatest example of making drastically life-altering decision, I do remember having to decide on whether to coach our school's boys basketball team or supervise and coach our chess club. When I was hired back at Summit Hill, I told my principal, Beth Lind, that I was willing to coach anything that she needed me to. I had begun coaching softball and continued to coach track. I also supervised the 7th grade math team during my lunch break part of the year. Beth told me that there was a need for a chess coach and a boys' basketball coach, both of which had seasons that overlapped. In addition to softball, track, and Math team, I coached both basketball and chess for two years, and while I enjoyed both, supervising five sports/clubs in addition to my regular teaching duties definitely took its toll on me both physically and mentally. George Bernard Shaw once said, "Use your health, even to the point of wearing it out. That is what it is for. Spend all you have before you die; do not outlive yourself."[74] For sure there is much truth to what he said, but I realized that I couldn't coach both basketball and chess another year longer. If I did, it would begin to take a toll on my energy every day in the classroom and affect my teaching and moreover affect my students. Also, it wasn't fair to my basketball and chess players. They deserved someone who was completely committed to them.

I had to make a decision. The basketball coach position paid more than double the chess stipend, but it did require more time with either a practice or a game every day after school and we also practiced during Christmas break, during a time when my mind and body were begging for a rest. On the basketball team, I could have as many as 15 players on the team, but chess however wasn't limited to the number of kids that could join, and both 7th and 8th graders, boys and girls, could join the club. During my second year running the club we had over 30 kids. The basketball money would be nice for sure, as my teaching salary wasn't affording me a life of luxury, but money isn't everything as we know. The funny thing about money is that no matter how much we have, there is always a desire in our human nature for more, even if we realize that it won't solve all our problems or provide lasting happiness. An extra few thousand dollars would be great, but what would I be giving up?

As I thought more and more about my choice, I realized that with chess, I'd have more free time as we would meet 2-3 times on most weeks, but more importantly there wasn't a limit to how many kids I could have in the club. I also thought, and certainly there are exceptions, that most kids that make a junior high or high school basketball team are kids that are in a good place emotionally as teenagers. Athletes in middle school and high school are usually well-liked by their peers and are rarely lacking in self-esteem. Again, there are exceptions, but chess kids on the other hand are kids that often get overlooked, but they are kids that are just as talented as anyone in school and chess gives them that opportunity to shine. They need chess much more than the average basketball player needs basketball, and I wanted to choose the option that would make the bigger difference for kids and devote my time accordingly.

As of today, I have been our school's chess coach for thirteen years and I am so happy that I made that choice. Over the years, it has become the norm that we will have fifty or more kids in our club. We have boys and girls. We have honors students and students with special educational plans. We have athletes and book worms. We have popular kids and kids under the radar. I love the dynamic of kids we have in the club. Just like in any sport I've coached, I still have expectations of sportsmanship and that all my players respect each other. It's nice to see kids from all walks of life form friendships through a common bond of playing chess.

I learned to play chess from my dad when I was young and coaching our chess team got me hooked once again. Once you start playing chess, it's easy to get addicted. As I've played more and more, I've become a better player and have learned more and more as I go. My students all want a chance to beat me, and usually during the first half of the year, I beat them with some ease, but as they continue to improve, a handful of players are able to get the best of me here and there and are ecstatic when they do so. I never let them win either. If I did that, they would know it, and winning a game knowing full well your opponent is letting you win just doesn't have the same meaning. When you win in that way, you can't help but feel insulted that your opponent isn't giving their best. I don't want to do that to my students, and I want them to continue to improve and improve enough so that if they beat me, it means something. I'm not one who believes in participation trophies and after coaching adolescents for 15 years, I know that kids feel the same way too.

As you can imagine, running a club with fifty plus kids can be a challenge. After my first few years coaching, Steve, a father of one of my best players, asked if he could come to our chess club meetings. Needing all the help I could get, of course I said yes! Steve started coming more and more often and after a while his attendance became anticipated by the kids and myself. Steve became another much needed coach to help me run such a large group. Like me, he plays any kid that wants a challenge, and win or lose, Steve and I use each game as teaching moments for players to show kids different game strategies while discussing moves or mistakes made during the game. His son, Dominic, who played on the team for his 7th and 8th grade years, is now a college student long gone from junior high school. His daughter played chess as well in our club, and she too has moved on to high school, but Steve continues to volunteer his time and attends our club meetings on a regular basis. The kids still look forward to his attendance and a chance to beat one of the "pros."

Steve and I are basically the same level player. We have probably played each other about 100 times over the last 8 years, and most likely we'd each have 40 wins, 40 losses, and 20 draws. Although Steve is a good chess player, that wasn't a prerequisite for him to volunteer. He is a wonderful father to his children, and his generous nature and giving heart provides our students with a role-model and caring adult to look up to. He has a wonderful rapport with the kids, and I've been very fortunate to come across his path. Every February is our Illinois State Chess Tournament held in central Illinois. We take 14 of our best 7th and 8th grade players. When Steve's son Dominic was in middle school, he was one of our top players who played in the tournament, but even after Dominic graduated years ago, Steve still makes the trip downstate and buys our team dinner and lunch the next day. Thanks to him, our chess kids, who often go unnoticed in school, are treated like royalty for a weekend.

One of the things I am proud about, thanks in large part to Steve's help, is that our chess team has been very successful. In the eleven years that Illinois has had a state tournament, we have been one of the top schools in the Chicagoland area, and out of roughly 50 schools that complete in the state tournament, our chess team has finished in the top ten at the state tournament in nine of those years. Chess has given these kids, who are often mild-mannered and under-the-radar, something to be proud of. It has given them an avenue to build confidence in a time in their life when they need it the most.

Over the years, I've had old students come back and visit the chess club and play a few more games. Some are high school students that come periodically during the school year while others are in college and take time to visit during their winter break. Chess has allowed me to continue to have a relationship with students after they leave junior high and I am blessed for that opportunity. As I look back on the decision I had to make years ago, I'm sure if I had chosen basketball, things would be just fine. However, I just can't imagine that my experiences would have been nearly as gratifying as I've had in chess. Choosing to go where you are most needed is something I think that those who do will find a more profound meaning in their time spent on this Earth, and for me at least, I have found that to be true and I'm incredibly grateful for it.

37

Setbacks

If you have ever had a conversation with a teacher about the behavior of their students, then maybe you've heard a teacher answer with something like, "All my students are great, but there's always one." Every teacher knows that in some classes, there is always at least one student who can be challenging to manage in the classroom. I know that in my 15 years in education, I found this to be true, but knowing this going into each year, now as a veteran teacher, I'm prepared for anything.

There have been kids over the years which drove me crazy and have tested my patience to the limits. There have been some years due to sheer exhaustion, that I am relieved to see certain students move on to the next grade so I can get a chance to catch my breath. Even with that said, I believe all good teachers refuse to give up on even the most troublesome students and try and find the good in every child that enters their classroom. Author and speaker, Josh Shipp, has famously said that "every kid is one caring adult away from being a success story."[75] As a teacher and coach, I've found his words ring true. Often the kids who are the most disruptive are acting out as a cry for help. There is something deeper under the surface that they are fighting and struggling with, and many times when a teacher takes time to let the child know they care about them, the child starts to make some positive strides. I've had many conversations with kids that are acting out and one of the main points that I try to convey upon them is I am not going to give up on them. The idea of not giving up goes far beyond a teacher-student relationship and also applies to everyone who has a family member or friend that has fallen away from our lives. Whatever their circumstances, providing some glimmer of hope to them may not seem like a lot, but to an individual, it could mean everything. I can't imagine living life without hope, so providing a sense of hope to those in need may make all the difference. Disruptive students, even the most difficult ones, actually want their teacher to tell them to make changes in their behavior. When teachers don't do this, they are sending a more debilitating message, a message that says they have given up on the student, that they have lost all hope.

Just being there for a troubled child, however, is not always enough. Sometimes the issues a child is going through will require more than what a teacher or caring adult can offer. There have been a few kids over the years that even after I have tried every possible intervention and every act of kindness or encouragement, my efforts alone were not enough. When these things happen, my human nature can't help but think I have failed the child and it does hurt my soul knowing that after a year in my classroom, the child hasn't made any significant improvements.

Deep down I know that this isn't my fault. I have come to the realization that I have to only focus on what I can control, and at the end of the day, if I feel I have given everything I have to help a child, I can at least walk away knowing I did all that I could. Christ Himself during his time on Earth did not bring conversion to everyone he encountered. The decision to change is a decision that one must make for themself. We can't expect to be everything to everyone that comes our way. We can only give each one on our path all that we have. I pray for my students and I know I need to do more of it, but for those children in my class whom I sense are hurting and calling out, I pray for them maybe a little harder. For those kids that I have been unable to reach during their time in my class, I still do try to keep them in my prayers. As a child, when the subject of a difficult person came up, I remember my dad telling me we just have to pray for that person. We all have difficult people in our life, and although there are definitely exceptions, raising your voice and angrily calling them out for their actions or their attitude more often than not will not help the problem and sometimes can make it worse. This approach can be useful in life and especially in dealing with adolescents, although as a teacher there are times when raising your voice in discipline must be done as kids are looking to learn that there are indeed boundaries in life. Kindness and an attempt at understanding may be of help, but our actions alone will not change a person. Only God can completely do that, so prayer is really the most powerful remedy.

There have been times as a teacher, when troubled kids after leaving my class will come back a year or so later looking like and acting like a completely different person. It's wonderful to see them doing so well and sometimes they will even apologize for causing problems when they were in my class. There are kids however who leave my classroom and I never really know what becomes of them, and as they move on in their own lives I can only hope and pray that they find peace. For people to truly change, it's not enough to just to tell them the right thing. Often when we do that, we wonder why people still are not making a change. What are the odds that a person will be in the right emotional place and ready to listen to advice at the exact moment that we try to give it? Change is ultimately up to each individual and you can only choose to make changes in your life if you choose to.

Every good teacher, like every good intentioned person, believes that one life can make a difference in the lives of others. Everyone we come across in life is another soul created by God and we need to treat them as such no matter how difficult it may be. Most of the time, in our encounters with difficult people, we may not see a significant change in that person soon or at all, but we still must try and be the best person we can be and make an effort to be a positive light to that person. We can only hope that after time, a person may change, and in the end, we will never know the lives we may have had an impact on. These are things that we can only hope to know when they are revealed to us by God when our life is complete. We will all look back on our time on Earth at some point, and when we do, it would be a shame to know that we had a chance to help someone that came across our path and we chose not to reach out and offer help.

38

The Danger of Screens

It's safe to say the answers to life's biggest questions will not be found during time spent looking at a screen. Watching television or movies, roaming through social media sites, and playing video games are likely not going to give us meaningful wisdom and purpose. Today however, this is exactly how many of us, especially young adults, are spending our time. In a study done by the Kaiser Family Foundation in 2008, the results found were striking. The Kaiser study, which took data from American pre-teens and teenagers, found that by the age of 21, this generation will have played more than 10,000 hours of video games, sent and received 250,000 e-mails and text messages, spent 10,000 hours on their phones, watched more than 20,000 hours of TV, and seen 500,000 commercials.[76] What is even more alarming about the research is that it was done during a time when smart-phones and tablets were not yet relevant. In addition, with the increase of screen time, our attention spans have declined. In 2000, Microsoft Canada reported that the average human attention span was twelve seconds, but in 2013 that number fell to only eight seconds. Also, according to Microsoft Canada, the average attention span of a goldfish is nine seconds.[77] The increased consumption of technology is indeed troubling!

How we spend our time has the greatest impact on what will become of our lives and what we value as important. I have received great wisdom in my life from my parents, family, friends, but I have also found wisdom in prayer and from reading good books, including the Bible. Most importantly, I have found the greatest wisdom from God, and the best wisdom my parents and closest friends have given me over the years have come from their faith. In the 1940's, a London newspaper ran a series of letters written by C.S. Lewis. The Letters, which were later put into the book, *The Screwtape Letters*, describe a senior devil, Screwtape, "mentoring" a young apprentice devil, Wormwood. In one of the letters, Screwtape advises Wormwood that "we will make the whole world a noise in the end."[78] Looking at today's world filled with personal smartphones, digital videos, countless social media websites, television, movies, and music, the world really has turned into great noise. Most of us, if we are honest, will admit that we become awkward in the midst of silence, hence the phrase "uncomfortable silence." Yet, it is in those moments of silence and prayer that God will speak to our hearts. C.S. Lewis was right that if we are to surround our every waking hour with noise of some kind, we won't be able to hear the voice of God.

The more we surround ourselves with technology, we are finding that it is affecting our humanity in increasingly harmful ways. One of those harmful effects is the rise of addiction to screens. A Common Sense Media survey done in 2016 found that one out of every two teens feels addicted to his or her device, while 59% of parents felt that their teen child is addicted to their device.[79] Dr. Peter Whybrow, Director of Neuroscience at UCLA, even goes as far to call computers "electronic cocaine."[80] Research on video games and their addictive nature is even more startling. A 2011 Indiana University School of Medicine brain imaging study anchored by lead researcher Dr. Yang Wang found that video game playing alters the brain in the same way that drug addiction does.[81] The addictive nature of technology is frightening, and I really don't believe that we can become the best version of ourself, the person God wants us to become, if we are addicted to screens.

Study after study also links the increased use of technology to depression and anxiety. In 2014, a study done by the journal, *Comprehensive Psychiatry*, looked at 2,293 seventh graders and found that Internet addiction exacerbated depression, hostility, and social anxiety.[82] Social media sites for certain are giving rise to depression among teens in that many are using it as a way to compare themselves to others. A 2010 study performed by Case Western University School of Medicine found that "hypernetworking teens," teens that spent more than three hours a day on social networking sites, were linked to higher rates of depression, substance abuse, poor sleep, stress, poor academics, and suicide.[83] These are just a couple of studies, but there are several more, one after the other, that confirm similar findings.

Many kids today use social media and the like as primary means of communication, and there are great dangers to this, one of which is a vulnerability to depression as studies show. I think that if teens and young adults spent more time offline, happiness and fulfillment in life would become a reality. The late physician, Paul Dudley White, had said years ago that "a vigorous five-mile walk will do more good for an unhappy but otherwise healthy adult than all the medicine in the world."[84] In breaking the cycle of tying self-worth to social media likes, a five-mile walk seems it would be a productive step towards healing and seeing the reality that the world is a lot bigger than a computer screen and our lives are infinitely more valuable that what others think of us online.

Thomas Kersting, author of *Disconnected: How to Reconnect our Digitally Distracted Kids*, writes: "A child who spends all his time socializing through a headset and screen, and no time engaging in face-to-face interaction, will not develop the necessary communication skills that are required to succeed in the real world. Just the thought of face-to-face communication for kids like these can cause serious distress. It goes back to the science of neuroplasticity – if you don't use it, you lose it."[85] Face-to face interaction is where lasting relationships begin, and when we consume ourselves with connecting our lives primarily through media, we are less likely to find real relationships and lasting friendships, because those connections are usually the ones which begin with face-to-face communication.

One of the treasures in life is genuine friendship, and real friends do not spend time comparing themselves to one another. Authentic friends take the time to have meaningful conversations about what is most important in life while having each other's best interest in mind. If true friends do have a disagreement on any issue, only a true friendship can move past something like that because only a genuine love and value for the relationship can overcome differences. If we use our time on social media as a means to value our self-worth and our friendships, then after looking at current research and reflecting on our own feelings, it may be wise to look elsewhere beyond social media for self-value and authentic connections. Our lives are all designed for meaningful relationship, much more so than connections developed only through screens. Meaningful relationship was the means by which Christ established His Church. He did this by being present to others in meaningful ways and was willing to have a relationship with all who desired one with Him. His apostles took this lesson to heart and helped expand Christianity and its message of mercy and salvation throughout the world from person to person.

All the studies on the effects of increased technology are not to say that all technology is bad. For certain in the modern world, technology will not be going away, but our lives do not have to revolve around it and we definitely should not be seeking out our life's purpose consumed in screens. Like anything in life, moderation, balance, and perspective need to be considered when entering into the world of technology, and if done thoughtfully, a happy medium can be achieved. We must be careful however as the realities of addiction, depression, and anxiety can be consequences of overusing technology.

In the end, our lives are meant to be bigger than a screen. Similarly, our lives on Earth are not meant to last forever, and each one of us is called to a bigger and eternal purpose in the next life with God in Heaven. If we are to reach the eternity of perfect happiness with a perfect God, we may have to take a step back and analyze how we spend our time. The lures of screens can be strong, but if in the end if we are spending more time with screens than time with our God and other souls whom He has created, then we probably need to re-evaluate how we are living our life.

39

Choose to be Happy

In the United States for instance, we are living in a time in which the standard of living is at an all-time high. In the 1980s, the only people who had a cellular phone were maybe the President, higher up officials, and the incredibly wealthy. Now, nearly everyone has a personal cell phone that acts as a miniature computer that can provide us with nearly anything we desire at the touch of a button. Don't get me wrong, there is still great poverty in our country and much needs to be done about it, but as a whole, our average living standards have become luxurious compared to only decades ago. With that said however, we are also living in a time where studies have shown that depression and self-harm are at record highs.

How can this be? How can so many, especially kids, be unhappy today? There are many possible explanations and I don't have all the answers, but there are a few trends that could provide some clarity. Today there are more people who do not identify with any religion, so less and less people look to God for guidance and meaning in life. On the contrary, people are looking to the world for answers to questions only the Creator of the universe can give. Advances in technology and intelligence have increased while at the same time an appreciation and desire for wisdom has become an afterthought.

Maybe this is the case because of what makes news these days, but it seems that we are seeing more and more stories about crime and how people are taking advantage of each other while there are less examples of others giving of themselves. Maybe you have noticed this just interacting with strangers in public. Of course there are exceptions and wonderful people all throughout the country, and I haven't been keeping statistics, but compared to maybe ten years ago, while out in public I've noticed less smiles, less people saying "please" and "thank you," few that are willing to apologize, and in general, people just seem less friendly. Many people seem to be in a rush to get what they want and to get it immediately, no matter what the cost. Again, I know there are great people all over and I've witnessed this too, but I have just noticed a difference in how people treat each other, and it is concerning to me.

How do we attain happiness? One thing is for certain, you cannot be happy without gratitude. Radio host and founder of PragerU, Dennis Prager, has always voiced his belief that one cannot be happy unless they have gratitude. This makes perfect sense as you will never meet anyone in life that is happy yet ungrateful at the same time. It's an impossibility. Today however, especially with the advent of social media, people often compare their happiness or lack thereof to what others have. There is a social comparison component in today's society that is detrimental to happiness and contentment. As I have stated before, there will always be someone in life who may be better off than you, and there will always be someone in life who has a tougher lot, so be grateful for the blessings in your life that you do have.

Besides gratitude, to be happy and at peace in our own lives, we must strive to be just as happy for others when good fortune arises for them as we would have been if it happened to us. This is a state of mind that gets us to think more of others and less of ourself. Simply put, thinking of others makes us happy. Consider for example going grocery shopping. If you were behind a family in the checkout line whom you felt was struggling to provide food for their family, and you decided to pay for their bill, a deep feeling of happiness and joy would overcome not only you, but the family in need. You would feel it because you did something good while the family would feel joy because someone cared enough to help during a time of need. Hope in the world, even if for only that moment, would be restored. There is a reason why we have those feelings, that we feel "good about ourselves" when we give of ourselves in noble ways. Helping others less fortunate gives us a natural feeling of happiness and goodness. Those feelings are inherent in all of us, but it is up to us to decide to give. No one can force you to give of yourself. Only you can choose to deny yourself in order to put someone else before you.

The mindset of Bertrand Russel rings especially true when he said that "to be without some of the things you want is an indispensable part of happiness."[86] Imagine a world in which we could get anything we want whenever we wanted it. It may seem like an amazing concept, but if we had everything that only the world has to offer, eventually our happiness would end, and we'd find that something is missing. I'd imagine we find that happiness without meaning is fruitless and would be no way to live. If we are looking to only the world for complete and total happiness, sadly we will be disappointed. Only perfect happiness and perfect love can be found from a perfect God! Our desires for perfection are completely natural and they only confirm that we are not meant to spend eternity here on Earth. With that said, we still have the choice to have a relationship with God. God loves us with all He has and desires authentic love back from us. In the same way romantically speaking, maybe there was a time in your life that you felt that if you could just be with this person or that person, then you'd be happy. But if the person that you love does not love you back and doesn't want to be with you, then that isn't a love that is free and authentic. Our relationship with God works in the same way. It must be a two-way street. God loves us completely and he only desires complete love in return.

Being happy and acting happy isn't always easy. Even if we are grateful and have found meaning in our lives by giving to others and having a relationship with God, we are still human beings living within our human nature. There will be days when circumstances will make it difficult to be happy. On those days, as Dennis Prager has said frequently on his radio show, we have a moral obligation to be happy. If we choose not to be happy, then we are putting an unnecessary burden on those around us, and in that way, we are taking away from their happiness. My advice here is to try and be someone that is easy to be around. Think of someone in your life that is difficult. Do you enjoy or look forward to being around them? Be easy. Don't be someone that causes others to walk on eggshells around you. A life like that is exhausting for everyone involved.

A lot can be learned from Aristotle's belief that "Happiness depends upon ourselves."[87] In the grand scheme of things, to be happy is a choice that we can decide upon every day. Only we can choose to be grateful. Only we can choose to help others. Only we can only choose to have a relationship with God. And only we can choose to be happy!

40

Say Yes to Life in Spite of Everything

Happiness is a choice much like anything in life. Making the right choice can often be difficult, but when we do so, happiness and peace are our rewards. We must choose to forgive even when hard, choose to say we're sorry even when we don't want to, and choose to love even when it seems impossible. Additionally, choosing to live, no matter how hopeless a situation may seem, is also a choice, and one with the greatest consequence of all.

Psychiatrist Viktor Frankl was one such man that understood how great a gift life is even as his life was filled with great tragedy. He realized that there is meaning in every human life on Earth and that each one of us has our own unique purpose to be discovered. Frankl, a Jewish Psychiatrist from Vienna during the time of Nazi occupation, survived four different concentration camps including the horrifying Auschwitz death camp. Others dear to him were not as fortunate. His mother, father, brother, and his newly pregnant wife all died in Nazi concentration camps. I don't think I have ever read about someone who has gone through more pain in one lifetime than Viktor Frankl, yet he found reason to keep moving forward with the faith that life itself is worth living. His life story is incredibly inspiring.

Frankl authored several books, but his most famous book chronicled his survival in the concentration camp and his perseverance in life afterward. The book is entitled, *Man's Search for Meaning*, but its original title was supposed to be "Say Yes to Life in Spite of Everything."[88] In fact, just recently a book with exactly that title has been written long after Frankl's death that includes a series of lectures he gave shortly after regaining his freedom from the death camps. *Man's Search for Meaning* is a book that I wish would be required reading for all high school students and I believe that everyone that reads it would surely have a greater appreciation for life.

Under Nazi rule of four different concentration camps, Viktor Frankl had only two choices. He could choose to give in to impending death or he could choose to fight for his life. He chose the latter. Frankl was well aware that he could not control his fate and circumstance, but he could control how he responded. Amidst the worst of conditions, Frankl willed to remain hopeful of his survival. He chose to be positive in the most difficult of times which included physical, mental, and emotional torture and the constant thought that each day could be his last. His outlook was contagious, and he found that those of his fellow inmates who shared his emotional strength and hope had much better odds to survive.

After Frankl survived the concentration camps, he got back to his work as a psychiatrist in Vienna not even a full year later. He began seeing patients and amazingly he maintained a positive outlook on life and faith in humanity. For his positivity, he took criticism from some members of the Jewish community, but Frankl in his heart believed "there are two races of men in this world, but only these two—the race of the decent man and the race of the indecent man."[89] Incredibly, he had a willingness to forgive and devote his life to helping rehabilitate his patients, no matter how dire their circumstance.

Other than his incredible survival, Frankl may be most well-known for his development of "logotherapy," which he presented as healing through meaning. In his estimation, meaning in life can be found in three ways: through our action, through our love, and through our suffering.[90] First, we can find meaning through action, working and dedicating your time and energy to something noble and worthwhile, something of which is bigger than ourselves. In today's generation, we often see people looking forward to consuming and attaining things that only give us short-lived happiness, while service to others gives us a meaning far more substantial than possessions or status.

The second aspect of logotherapy that can provide us with meaning is that we find meaning when encountering something true and beautiful, or in loving others. It's common and even natural, especially for teens and young adults, to search for their identity trying to be members of this group or that group. What young people are really looking for though is meaning, a greater purpose, for love. Instead of searching endlessly trying to fit in to a certain group, many of life's most meaningful answers can be found in spending maybe an hour alone in a chapel or outdoors in solitude with only nature and God.

The third and final component of logotherapy represents finding meaning during times of great struggle and darkness, something that Frankl knew more than anyone. In our darkest days of life, sometimes meaning and purpose are simply found in the will to live and persevere though hardship. Frankl believed that everyone of us, because of our own uniqueness and differences, are irreplaceable, and because of that fact only in our own distinctive life can we alone make a uniquely valuable contribution to the world.

Unfortunately, many of those who decide to take their own life are teens and those in their young adult years. Sadly, many suicides occur during high school years. If young kids that are living through the difficulties of their teenage years could just get through high school and see that the world is much bigger than their surrounding town, they would find their meaning in life is much bigger than their high school halls. Like the expression, "this too shall pass," high school will soon be over and for those struggling, brighter days will lie ahead! No life is free from trials and difficulty, but if for those who have found their meaning and purpose, God's design for our life, they will find the strength to persevere through life's adversities.

Viktor Frankl's work and life was a gift to humanity. No matter our state in life, there is something that we can all take by his outlook and approach to living. I'm sure Frankl would indeed have agreed with Archbishop Fulton Sheen's view of life as can be ascertained from the title of his once popular television series, *Life is Worth Living*, or Saint John Paul the Great when he said that "every human being is unique and unrepeatable."[91] In Frankl's logotherapy, he showed us all that each life has a unique meaning and one that can be found by action, love, or even by our approach to life in times of great suffering. No matter how dark some days may be, we must remember to "say yes to life in spite of everything."

ACKNOWLEDGEMENTS

I would like to thank my parents, Steve and Linda, for the guidance and example they have shown me throughout my life, and not to mention the countless prayers they have prayed on my behalf. In your lives, you have showed me the meaning of sacrifice. To my siblings, Jenny, John, and Kevin. Because of you, I know family can make the best of friends too. Thank you also to my grandparents. Your wisdom and example has made my life rich.

I am eternally grateful to the late, great Jerry Shepherd, who showed me what it means to be a friend. Many thanks to Father Peter Armenio, my spiritual director, who has shown me a wonderful example of what it means to live as a humble servant of God by always putting others first. Thank you also to all my close friends, of whom I consider to be my brothers and sisters.

Much gratitude to all my colleagues at Summit Hill Junior Hgh School, especially Scott Chromcak, Fred Pufahl, Amber Ostrowski, and so many others. Your friendship, professionalism, and dedication to children is amazing. Special thanks to Julie Sajewich, a friend and former colleague, who spent many hours editing the final copy of this book. Julie, thanks for helping a math teacher fix so many grammarical mistakes. I couldn't have done it without you!

I also would like to say thank you to my three wise men, Dr. Micheal Byrnes, Dr. James Schlenker, and Dr. Suby Rao. Your care has saved my life, and I owe to you all to make the most of mine.

There are countless people that have come in to my life that I need to thank. Friends, teachers, coaches, professors, co-workers, and students; I don't believe in coincidences, and I want to thank you for making an impact on my life.

NOTES

Preface

1. Lewis, C. S. (1971). *THE GREAT DIVORCE* (Later Printing ed.). MACMILLAN.

1 – The Waiting Room

2. *Success Stories.* (n.d.). Midtown Educational Foundation. Retrieved July 16, 2020, from https://www.midtown-metro.org/success-stories

2 – Faith During Uncertainty

3. *Melanoma - Statistics.* (n.d.). Cancer.Net. Retrieved July 16, 2020, from https://www.cancer.net/cancer-types/melanoma/statistics

4. *Positron emission tomography scan - Mayo Clinic.* (n.d.). Mayo Clinic. Retrieved July 16, 2020, from https://www.mayoclinic.org/tests-procedures/pet-scan/about/pac-20385078

5. *Positron emission tomography (PET) scan - Canadian Cancer Society.* (n.d.). Www.Cancer.Ca. Retrieved July 16, 2020, from https://www.cancer.ca/en/cancer-information/diagnosis-and-treatment/tests-and-procedures/positron-emission-tomography-pet-scan/?region=on

4 – Thanksgiving

6. *The message of Lourdes.* (n.d.). Bienvenue Au Sanctuaire Notre-Dame de Lourdes. https://www.lourdes-france.org/en/message-lourdes/

7. Ibid.

8. Ewing, J. (n.d.). *Do You Know About these 10 Amazing Miracles of Lourdes?* The Writings of Cora Evans. Retrieved July 16, 2020, from https://www.coraevans.com/blog/article/do-you-know-about-these-10-amazing-miracles-of-lourdes

10 – Finding Bernadette

9. *Going to the Baths.* (n.d.). Bienvenue Au Sanctuaire Notre-Dame de Lourdes. https://www.lourdes-france.org/en/going-baths/

10. *Bernadette of Lourdes Facts.* (n.d.). Your Dictionary. Retrieved July 16, 2020, from https://biography.yourdictionary.com/bernadette-of-lourdes

11. Trochu, F. (1985). *Saint Bernadette Soubirous: 1844-1879.* (Rev. ed.) Rockford, IL: Tan Books and Publishers.

12. Martens, Fr. Carlos (Producer and Director). (2015). *Sacred Relics of the Saints: Treasures of the Church* [Documentary; DVD release]. United States: Treasures of the Church.

13. Ibid.

13 – Unlucky in Love

14. *Oral Contraceptives (Birth Control Pills) and Cancer Risk.* (2018, February 22). National Cancer Institute. https://www.cancer.gov/about-cancer/causes-prevention/risk/hormones/oral-contraceptives-fact-sheet

15. *Hormonal Birth Control Products and the Risk of Blood Clots.* (2020, April 24). Pandia Health. https://www.pandiahealth.com/ resources/birth-control-blood-clots/

16. Williams, P. (2011, Pg. 59). *Coach Wooden: The 7 Principles That Shaped His Life and Will Change Yours* (Reprint ed.). Revell.

17. Korson, G., & Pepino, J. (2008). *The Wonders of Lourdes: 150 Miraculous Stories of the Power of Prayer to Celebrate; the 150th Anniversary of Our Lady's Apparitions* (First ed.). Magnificat.

14 – Fatima

18. Santos, Lucia. (1976, Pg. 162). *Fatima in Lucia's Own Words: Sister Lucia's Memoirs.* Edited by Fr. Louis Kondor, SVD. Translated by Dominican Nuns of Perpetual Rosary. Fatima: Postulation Centre.

19. Ibid.

20. Apostoli, A. (2012, Pg. 73). *Fatima for Today: The Urgent Marian Message of Hope* (First ed.). Ignatius Press.

21. Carollo, D. (2017, May 23). *Call for consecration of Russia to the Immaculate Heart is hopeful sign of the times.* Our Lady's Blue Army - World Apostolate of Fatima U.S.A. https://www.bluearmy.com/call-for-consecration-of-russia-to-the-immaculate-heart-is-hopeful-sign-of-the-times/

22. Caldwell, Z. (2018, January 2). *Russia's Orthodox Church has opened 30,000 places of worship in last 30 years.* Aleteia — Catholic Spirituality, Lifestyle, World News, and Culture. https://aleteia. org/2018/01/02/russias-orthodox-church-has-opened-30000-places-of-worship-in-last-30-years/

23. Santos, Lucia. (1976, Pg. 162). *Fatima in Lucia's Own Words: Sister Lucia's Memoirs.* Edited by Fr. Louis Kondor, SVD. Translated by Dominican Nuns of Perpetual Rosary. Fatima: Postulation Centre.

24. *The Message of Fatima.* (n.d.). Congregation of the Doctrine of Faith. Retrieved July 16, 2020, from https://www.vatican.va/roman_curia/congregations/cfaith/documents/rc_con_cfaith_doc_20000626_message-fatima_en.html

25. Kengor, P. (2017, Pg. 343). *A Pope and a President: John Paul II, Ronald Reagan, and the Extraordinary Untold Story of the 20th Century* (1st ed.). Intercollegiate Studies Institute.

26. Gillen, G. (2017, September 27). *"One Hand Pulled the Trigger, Another Guided the Bullet."* St. John Paul II Society. https://www.stjohnpaul.org/one-hand-pulled-the-trigger-another-guided-the-bullet/

27. Kosloski, P. (2017, June 30). *Are there more martyrs now than in the early Church?* Aleteia — Catholic Spirituality, Lifestyle, World News, and Culture. https://aleteia.org/2017/06/30/are-there-more-martyrs-now-than-in-the-early-church/

28. Apostoli, A. (2012, Pp. 129-134). *Fatima for Today: The Urgent Marian Message of Hope* (First ed.). Ignatius Press.

29. Santos, Lucia. (1976, Pg. 161). *Fatima in Lucia's Own Words: Sister Lucia's Memoirs.* Edited by Fr. Louis Kondor, SVD. Translated by Dominican Nuns of Perpetual Rosary. Fatima: Postulation Centre.

30. *Fatima Miracle - Shielded from Death.* (n.d.). America Needs Fatima. Retrieved July 16, 2020, from https://www.americaneeds-fatima.org/Miracles/fatima-miracle-shielded-from-death.html

31. *The Five First Saturdays Devotion | Our Blessed Mother | ANF Articles.* (n.d.). America Needs Fatima. Retrieved July 16, 2020,

from https://www.americaneedsfatima.org/Our-Blessed-Mother/
the-five-first-saturdays-devotion.html

15 – The Good Shepherd

32. Wooden, J., & Jamison, S. (1997, Pg. 13). *Wooden: A Lifetime
of Observations and Reflections On and Off the Court* (1st ed.).
Contemporary Books.

17 – Seven Things To Do

33. Ibid, Pg. 9.

18 – The Parent Lottery

34. Ju, A. (2008, May 24). *Courage is the most important virtue,
says writer and civil rights activist Maya Angelou at Convocation.*
Cornell Chronicle. https://news.cornell.edu/stories/2008/05/
courage-most-important-virtue-maya-angelou-tells-seniors

20 – Planting Seeds

35. *Faith in Flux.* (2009, April 27). Pew Research Center's Religion
& Public Life Project. https://www.pewforum.org/2009/04/27/
faith-in-flux/

36. Smith, G. A. (2019, August 5). *Just one-third of U.S. Catholics
agree with their church that Eucharist is body, blood of Christ.* Pew
Research Center. https://www.pewresearch.org/fact-tank/2019/08/05/
transubstantiation-eucharist-u-s-catholics/

37. Cruz, J. C. (1991, Pg 6). *Eucharistic Miracles: And Eucharistic
Phenomena in the Lives of the Saints.* Adfo Books.

38. Carrozza, F. (2018, June 4). *Eucharistic miracle of Buenos
Aires –.* Rev. Andrew P. Carrozza. https://fathercarrozza.com/tag/
eucharistic-miracle-of-buenos-aires/

39. Ibid.

40. Ibid.

41. *Saint Maksymilian Maria Kolbe | Biography, Facts, & Death*. (n.d.). Encyclopedia Britannica. Retrieved July 17, 2020, from https://www. britannica.com/biography/Saint-Maksymilian-Maria-Kolbe

42. von Huben, E. (2014, August 14). *9 Things to Know about St. Maximilian Kolbe*. Word on Fire. https://www.wordonfire.org/ resources/blog/9-things-to-know-about-st-maximilian-kolbe/4426/

43. Martens, Fr. Carlos (Producer and Director). (2015). *Sacred Relics of the Saints: Treasures of the Church* [Documentary; DVD release]. United States: Treasures of the Church.

44. Ibid.

45. Ibid.

46. *St. Maria Goretti - Saints & Angels*. (n.d.). Catholic Online. Retrieved July 17, 2020, from https://www.catholic.org/saints/saint. php?saint_id=78

21 - I'd Rather Tie Shoes

47. Wooden, J., & Jamison, S. (1997, Pg. 73). *Wooden: A Lifetime of Observations and Reflections On and Off the Court* (1st ed.). Contemporary Books.

48. Meeter, B. (2018, January 22). *How can coaches and athletes be a positive influence after a heartbreaking loss?* Trusted Coaches. https://www.trustedcoaches.org/ can-coaches-athletes-positive-influence-heartbreaking-loss/

22 – Beat Your Time

49. Hillenbrand, L. (2010). *Unbroken: A World War II Story of Survival, Resilience, and Redemption.* Random House Trade.

50. Williams, P., Walton, B., & Wimbish, D. (2006, Pp. 74-75). *How to Be Like Coach Wooden.* Health Communications, Incorporated.

51. Douglas, S. (2017, October 31). *Our Ranking of Meb's 5 Greatest Marathon Performances.* Runner's World. https://www.runnersworld.com/news/g20863006/ our-ranking-of-mebs-5-greatest-marathon-performances/

52. Hallongren, B. and Arnold, M. (Producers), Arnold, M. (Director). (2008). *The Long Green Line.* [Documentary; DVD release]. United States: LGL Productions, LLC.

53. *The Mother Teresa Connection - Dr. Kent M. Keith.* (n.d.). Kent M. Keith: Finding Personal Meaning in A Crazy World. Retrieved July 17, 2020, from http://www.kentmkeith.com/mother_teresa.html

24 – Find the One

54. *Keep Calm and Carry on: Good Advice for Hard Times* (First ed.). (2009). Ebury Press.

55. Payton, W., & Yaeger, D. (2001, Pg. 171). *Never Die Easy: The Autobiography of Walter Payton* (Reprint ed.). Random House Trade Paperbacks.

56. Ibid, Pg. 172.

25 – Be a Role-Model

57. Williams, P., Sielski, M., & Selig, A. (2004, Pg. 19). *How to Be Like Jackie Robinson.* Health Communications, Incorporated.

58. *Quotes - The Official Licensing Website of.* (n.d.). Jackie Robinson. Retrieved July 17, 2020, from https://www.jackierobinson.com/quotes/

26 – Smart, Successful, Happy, or Good

59. James, A. (2019, May 21). *More than 75 colleges host blacks-only graduation ceremonies.* Washington Examiner. https://www.washingtonexaminer.com/red-alert-politics/more-than-75-colleges-host-blacks-only-graduation-ceremonies

60. Wooden, J., & Jamison, S. (1997, Pg. 198). *Wooden: A Lifetime of Observations and Reflections On and Off the Court* (1st ed.). Contemporary Books.

61. Holtz, L. (2019, Pg. 76). *Three Rules for Living a Good Life.* Amsterdam University Press.

62. Wooden, J., & Jamison, S. (1997, Pg. 201). *Wooden: A Lifetime of Observations and Reflections On and Off the Court* (1st ed.). Contemporary Books.

28 – A Reminder

63. Albom, M. (2002). *Tuesdays with Morrie: An Old Man, a Young Man, and Life's Greatest Lesson, 20th Anniversary Edition* (Anniversary, Reprint ed.). Broadway Books.

29 – Giving Back

64. Payton, W., & Yaeger, D. (2001, Pg. 181). *Never Die Easy: The Autobiography of Walter Payton* (Reprint ed.). Random House Trade Paperbacks.

65. Ibid, Pp. 182-183.

66. Hodges, T. (n.d.). *History of the Chicago Nativity Scene*. Chicago Nativity Scene. Retrieved July 17, 2020, from http://www.chicagonativityscene.com/history.html

30 – If I Were Ever Prosecuted…

67. Wooden, J., & Jamison, S. (1997, Pg. 199). *Wooden: A Lifetime of Observations and Reflections On and Off the Court* (1st ed.). Contemporary Books.

31 – No One is Beneath You

68. Lewis, C. S., & Norris, K. (2001, Pg. 124). *Mere Christianity* (Revised and Amplified Edition). HarperCollins.

33 – Highs and Lows

69. Wooden, J., & Jamison, S. (1997, Pg. 151). *Wooden: A Lifetime of Observations and Reflections On and Off the Court* (1st ed.). Contemporary Books.

70. *Keep Calm and Carry on: Good Advice for Hard Times* (First ed.). (2009). Ebury Press.

34 – Take Courage

71. Ju, A. (2008, May 24). *Courage is the most important virtue, says writer and civil rights activist Maya Angelou at Convocation*. Cornell Chronicle. https://news.cornell.edu/stories/2008/05/ courage-most-important-virtue-maya-angelou-tells-seniors

72. Bilger, M. (2016, October 11). *Amazing New Research Shows Unborn Baby's Heart Begins to Beat at 16 Days*. LifeNews.Com. https://www.lifenews.com/2016/10/11/amazing-new-research-shows-unborn-babys-hard-begins-to-beat-at-16-days/

35 – The Rule of Five

73. Capra, F. (Producer and Director). (1947). *It's a Wonderful Life*. [Motion Picture]. United States: Melange Pictures, LLC.

36 - The Road Less Traveled

74. *Keep Calm and Carry on: Good Advice for Hard Times* (First ed.). (2009). Ebury Press.

37 – Setbacks

75. Shipp, J. (n.d.). *The Power of One Caring Adult in the Life of a Child*. Teen Expert Josh Shipp. Retrieved July 17, 2020, from https://joshshipp.com/one-caring-adult/

38 – The Danger of Screens

76. Kersting, T. (2016, Pp. 17-18). *Disconnected: How to Reconnect our Digitally Disconnected Kids*. Van Haren Publishing.

77. Alter, A. (2018, Pg. 28). *Irresistible: The Rise of Addictive Technology and the Business of Keeping Us Hooked* (Reprint ed.). Penguin Books.

78. Lewis, C. S. (2001, Pg. 120). *The Screwtape Letters* (1st ed.). HarperOne.

79. Kersting, T. (2016, Pg. 58). *Disconnected: How to Reconnect our Digitally Disconnected Kids*. Van Haren Publishing.

80. Kardaras, N. (2017, Pg. 21). *Glow Kids* (Reprint ed.). Griffin.

81. Ibid, Pp. 67-68.

82. Ibid, Pg. 127.

83. Ibid, Pg. 90.

84. *Keep Calm and Carry on: Good Advice for Hard Times* (First ed.). (2009). Ebury Press.

85. Kersting, T. (2016, Pg. 49). *Disconnected: How to Reconnect our Digitally Disconnected Kids*. Van Haren Publishing.

39 – Choose to be Happy

86. *Keep Calm and Carry on: Good Advice for Hard Times* (First ed.). (2009). Ebury Press.

87. Ibid.

40 – Say Yes to Life in Spite of Everything

88. *Back from the dead | Nicholas Kardaras | TEDxUrsulineCollege.* (2014, November 12). [Video]. YouTube. https://www.youtube.com/watch?v=Vy2dRxc4Sm4

89. Frankl, V. E., Kushner, H., & Winslade, W. (2006, Pg. 86). *Man's Search for Meaning*. Beacon Press.

90. Frankl, V. E., & Goleman, D. (2020, Pg. 10). *Yes To Life In Spite of Everything*. Van Haren Publishing.

91. Kengor, P. (2017). *A Pope and a President: John Paul II, Ronald Reagan, and the Extraordinary Untold Story of the 20th Century* (1st ed.). Intercollegiate Studies Institute.